HUNGRY START-UP STRATEGY

HUNGRY START-UP STRATEGY

CREATING NEW VENTURES WITH LIMITED RESOURCES AND UNLIMITED VISION

PETER S. COHAN

BK

Berrett–Koehler Publishers, Inc.
San Francisco
a BK Business book

Berrett-Koehler Publishers, Inc.
235 Montgomery Street, Suite 650
San Francisco, CA 94104-2916
Tel: (415) 288-0260   Fax: (415) 362-2512   www.bkconnection.com

Ordering Information

Quantity sales. Special discounts are available on quantity purchases by corporations, associations, and others. For details, contact the "Special Sales Department" at the Berrett-Koehler address above.

Individual sales. Berrett-Koehler publications are available through most bookstores. They can also be ordered directly from Berrett-Koehler: Tel: (800) 929-2929; Fax: (802) 864-7626; www.bkconnection.com

Orders for college textbook/course adoption use. Please contact Berrett-Koehler: Tel: (800) 929-2929; Fax: (802) 864-7626.

Orders by U.S. trade bookstores and wholesalers. Please contact Ingram Publisher Services, Tel: (800) 509-4887; Fax: (800) 838-1149; E-mail: customer.service@ingram publisherservices.com; or visit www.ingrampublisherservices.com/Ordering for details about electronic ordering.

Berrett-Koehler and the BK logo are registered trademarks of Berrett-Koehler Publishers, Inc.

Printed in the United States of America

Berrett-Koehler books are printed on long-lasting acid-free paper. When it is available, we choose paper that has been manufactured by environmentally responsible processes. These may include using trees grown in sustainable forests, incorporating recycled paper, minimizing chlorine in bleaching, or recycling the energy produced at the paper mill.

Production Management: Michael Bass Associates

Cover Design: Irene Morris Design
Cover Photos: (c) Ocean Photography/Veer
Author Photo: Brad Norman

Library of Congress Cataloging-in-Publication Data

Cohan, Peter S., 1957–
Hungry start-up strategy : creating new ventures with limited resourcesand unlimited vision / Peter S. Cohan.
    p.   cm.
Includes bibliographical references and index.
ISBN 978-1-60994-528-2 (pbk.)
1. New business enterprises. 2. Strategic planning. 3. Venture capital. 4. Entrepreneurship. I. Title.
HD62.5.C6353 2012
658.1'1—dc23
                                        2012032895

First Edition

17   16   15   14   13   12   10   9   8   7   6   5   4   3   2   1

To Robin, Sarah,
and Adam

CONTENTS

PREFACE

THIS BOOK IS AN EFFORT to sate my own hunger.

Let me tell you where my hunger comes from. I've spent most of my career—about thirty years—in the field of business strategy. For most of that time, the work of Michael E. Porter, a business strategy guru whose work I will discuss more fully in Chapter 1, has dominated the field.

Then, in 2005, I began teaching undergraduate and MBA students at America's leading school of entrepreneurship, Babson College. Its curriculum, probably like most around the world, pounds Porter's ideas about strategy into students' heads.

I discovered that when I asked students about the usefulness of Porter's ideas for their own business, they replied with frustrated stares that signal a desire to change the subject.

This frustration came to a head during a faculty meeting I attended in August 2010. There, one of my colleagues reported that executives were tired of hearing about Porter. When I heard this comment, my thought was: *Bashing Porter is fun, but does my colleague have any better ideas?*

More specifically, I wondered whether there were better ideas to help start-ups make strategic decisions. Why do start-ups matter to me? I've invested in six of them: Three were sold for a total of $2 billion and three went out of business. I also started my own business in 1994 to provide strategy consulting to business and governments, and venture capital (VC) to start-ups.

My interest in start-ups may have something to do with my family background. My great-grandfather was an entrepreneur who owned, among other businesses, a chain of gasoline stations in Massachusetts. One grandfather started and ran a clothing retailer in Missouri. The other started and ran one of central Massachusetts's largest accounting firms. And, with his MIT roommate, Amar Bose, my uncle co-founded Bose, the sound-system company.

Before I started my own business, I never anticipated great success working as someone else's employee. But I sensed implicitly that there was no way I could start a company unless I knew how to do something socially useful. When I entered college, I had no idea what that might be.

By 1994, I had left graduate school, tried IT and strategy consulting, and worked in insurance. I took a shot at starting my own strategy consulting firm—focusing on helping high-tech companies identify, evaluate, and profit from growth opportunities created by changing technology.

And in so doing, I had a chance to realize another goal—to invest in start-ups. I was lucky that I had published a book, *Net Profit: How to Invest and Compete in the Real World of Internet Business*, just as the wave of Internet start-ups was gathering momentum.

When the book came out in 1998, audiences around the world paid me to present my roadmap on which specific sectors of the Internet would make the best investment opportunities for business and individual profits—and which ones to avoid.

Internet start-ups found value in my relationships with print and TV media. As a result, many companies gave me the opportunity to invest in them and, in some cases, to help them develop growth strategies.

A few lessons have emerged from my start-up investment experience. The most important of these is that it's pretty simple to tell which start-ups will succeed and which will fail. The ones that have a growing customer base are going to survive and the ones that spend all their money refining their product before getting users will not. For the purposes of this book, we'll call the first type of start-up "hungry start-ups."[1]

Two examples come to mind. One software company raised capital with a video of the founder discussing how its customers were using the product to evaluate the effectiveness of their Web sites. The other sought capital using a team of well-educated people to describe a general approach to a new kind of software (not specified) that would support partnerships.

I invested in both companies. The first one was sold for $440 million after filing for an initial public offering. The second one never figured out a product and never took on a customer; not surprisingly, it shut down after burning through its cash.

In general, I have seen two kinds of capital-raising pitches from entrepreneurs. The first, and by far the most common, uses an abstract calculation of a huge potential market for the company's product but lacks detailed insights into the customers who will make up that market. The second tries to persuade me that the start-up wants to solve a real problem facing real people, by explaining the results of individual conversations with real customers.

Why do you suppose it is so rare for an entrepreneur to present the second kind of business plan (when that is the one with greater odds of foreshadowing start-up success)? I think it's because the entrepreneur:

- Lacks a deep passion for the business and is mostly interested in building the venture to make a quick buck.
- Prefers working behind a compuer screen or sitting in a research laboratory than talking to real people.
- Thinks that there is no point in talking to customers before the product is ready to sell.

To paraphrase the late Peter Drucker, the purpose of a business is to get and keep customers. So start-up CEOs need good answers, which they can apply to their own start-ups, to the following questions:

- How do we pick the right goals?
- How can we get customers before too much time and money have been spent?
- How do we decide which customers to target, and how do they win over enough of these customers to keep going?
- How do we raise capital?
- How do we decide who to hire?
- How do we adapt to unpleasant surprises and unexpected opportunities?

This brings me to the hunger that prompted me to write this book: The need for better answers to the questions start-up CEOS are facing.

For readers who are not familiar with Porter, he offers concepts to help managers deal with two fundamental questions of strategy.

- *Where should a company compete?* Porter argues that managers should compete in industries with relatively high return on investment based on the relative strength of five forces that shape their future profitability: (1) the threat of new entrants, (2) the bargaining power of buyers, (3) the level of rivalry among existing competitors, (4) the bargaining power of suppliers, and (5) the threat of substitute products.[2]
- *How can a company win in its selected industry?* Porter suggests that earning superior returns in an industry comes from its choice of *generic strategy—low-cost producer* (selling a product at the industry's lowest price and setting costs below that price) or *differentiation* (selling at a high price by offering a better product that costs more to make and deliver).

These two questions are important ones facing start-up CEOs, but I've found that Porter's answers are more effective for big companies and that start-up CEOs need answers to some questions that Porter does not address.

In 162 interviews, I have learned that start-up CEOs are hungry in two ways, one that appeals to their right brains, and the other to their left brains. On the right—the one that pertains to emotions—entrepreneurs hunger to create a working world in which they want to live. And on the left—the analytical side—they need to make choices in six dimensions (reflected in the questions on the previous page), so they can turn their emotional hunger into a thriving enterprise whether or not they start with sufficient money and staff.

Sometimes, entrepreneurs' hunger for meaning exceeds their urge for wealth. Consider Jeff Hammerbacher, a 2005 Harvard College graduate who worked at Bear Stearns and Facebook before starting the data-analysis firm Cloudera, in 2008. A Facebook colleague described Hammerbacher as "scary smart, a maverick, individualistic, dynamic, a sponge when it comes to new ideas, and his interests evolve quickly."

When Hammerbacher started Cloudera he walked away from a fortune in Facebook stock—a move he dubbed an egregious act of wealth destruction. But trying to realize Cloudera's mission—to apply the computing power he had built at Facebook to solve more important problems—satisfied Hammerbacher's hunger more than those extra Facebook millions ever could.

Instead of helping to answer what a group of friends "like" the most on Facebook, Cloudera customers would be able to answer questions such as, "Which gene do all these cancer patients share?"[3]

At Harvard, Hammerbacher took a core course on moral reasoning which required him to read philosopher John Rawls's concept of *The Veil of Ignorance*. As Hammerbacher described it, Rawls's idea was that if the moment before you were born, you could decide which part of the world you would be born into, how would you design that world so you would have a fair shot at life?[4]

Hammerbacher's vision is to build Cloudera to last. He said, "The vision is to build an exceptional, standalone enterprise software company respected for its technical depth and expertise. We'd like to help commoditize the infrastructure for analyzing all kinds of data at arbitrary scales, so that companies can derive more business value from the data they generate. DEC, Tandem Computers, and Sun are companies that, in their prime, had cultures similar to the one we're trying to build."[5]

Hammerbacher is not the only hungry start-up CEO. The MBA students I've been teaching since fall 2011 have demonstrated a big appetite for them. I have created and taught two courses on hungry start-up strategy, and they have both been oversubscribed, I think for the following reasons:

- *Failure of big organizations.* The 2007 financial crisis has collapsed the assumption of people in college that they would be able to get a job in a Wall Street bank, a big company, or government. With unemployment rates around the world at very high levels—nearly 25 percent in Spain by July 2012 and above 8 percent in the United States, for example—the job market for college students is very difficult. And tales of the frustrations of working in large organizations have persuaded many young people that if they want to have a meaningful career, they will have to start their own companies.
- *New start-up environment.* The environment for start-ups in 2012 is different in important ways from the one in 1998 about which I wrote in *Net Profit.* Back then, successful IPOs created high returns for VC firms. These firms are partnerships that sell limited partner interests to foundations, endowments, and wealthy individuals, and their general partners typically earn management fees of 2 percent of the assets under management and 20 percent of the profits they generate during the decade-long life of their funds. VC returns spiked at 83.4 percent for the decade ending June 1999, and huge checks were written to plow those returns back into new start-ups. Much of that money went into splashy parties and marketing. Since the dot-com crash of 2000, VC returns have turned negative—plunging to –5.1 percent for the ten years ending June 2010—and most start-ups can't get those big checks, nor can they borrow money against their houses as they did until 2008. In response to this lack of capital, start-ups have reengineered their approach to strategy around the concept of hunger.[6]

This book is not just for entrepreneurs. My conversations with large, established organizations suggest they are also hungry—for more growth and innovation. Sure, many of them have succeeded in lowering their costs by outsourcing and achieving growth by exporting to developing markets.

But plenty of big companies are not growing as fast as they wish, and disappointing growth is cutting into their stock prices. They are looking for strategies that can produce more rapid growth, and start-ups provide an attractive option for achieving that.

Now that I've written the book, my hunger is still not satisfied. That won't happen until I see whether the ideas in the *Hungry Start-Up Strategy* actually take hold.

Ultimately, start-up CEOs are not satisfied with merely achieving a competitive advantage; they want to change the world. It's my hope that *Hungry Start-Up Strategy* will help satisfy their appetite to do just that.

Peter Cohan
Marlborough, Mass.
July 2012

INTRODUCTION

THERE ARE PLENTY of reasons not to start a company. Here are just four:

- *Odds are good that you will fail.* As an investor in private companies, I have repeatedly been told that a venture capitalist is thought to have a successful track record with one big success out of ten bets. I was considered unusually successful because only half of the ones in which I invested went out of business.
- *If you, friends, family, or others invest money in the start-up, chances are that the money will be lost.* A corollary of the high odds of start-up failure is that any money invested in the start-up is likely to be spent without generating a return for investors. Unless you do a good job of preparing investors for this, you may damage important relationships when your start-up goes down.
- *You may not have what it takes to be an entrepreneur.* Considerable research has been conducted on the traits of a successful entrepreneur. But as a very small-scale entrepreneur myself, and one who has interviewed hundreds of others over the years—either for my research or to decide whether to invest—I have noticed that successful entrepreneurs seem to share several common characteristics (Chapter 9, Resources, offers more about that).
- *Your reason to start the company may not be good enough.* Based on my investing experience, I have noticed that people sometimes can't say why they are starting a company. In at least one case, a start-up failed because the CEO realized that he was not really very interested in the product the company was trying to build. As a result, the company floundered until it ran out of money. Given the long hours and low pay required to get a start-up off the ground, be sure to have a well-thought-out and deeply felt reason for starting your company.

What are some concrete reasons to start a company? Most commonly, people start companies to capture what they perceive as an irresistible opportunity or to solve a vexing problem; the entrepreneur often assumes that if he can come up with a workable product, then enough other people will buy it to make the company grow.

1

Once you figure out a good reason to start the company, you need to make six key choices to turn your vision into a viable business. To illustrate these choices, let's look at the case of BrewDog.

James Watt and Martin Dickie, a pair of Fraserburgh, Scotland, twenty-somethings, liked to brew beer. There must be hundreds if not thousands of home beer brewers around the world. But Watt and Dickie were different. They thought it would be fun to try to turn their hobby into a real business.

By May 2012, BrewDog was a successful public company that provided a world in which the co-founders wanted to work, while also feeding customers, employees, suppliers, partners, and shareholders with custom-cooked meals that satisfied their distinctive cravings.

My interview with co-founder and captain, James Watt, reveals how.

Why did you and your co-founder start BrewDog?

BrewDog's co-founders started the company because they were bored with their conventional jobs, disliked conventional beer and the conventional corporate cultures they represented, and wanted to do something they loved.

As Watt said, "The idea to start our own brewery certainly wasn't something we consciously set out to do.[7]

"I guess like any good idea it just had this natural flow about it that . . . kept rolling and has never really stopped. BrewDog officially began in April 2007 but it was some months before that, when [Martin and I] were having a beer that BrewDog was 'born.' The subject of monotony and the fact that all supermarket or big brand beers taste the same was the topic of conversation.[8]

"[With Martin] having just finished a degree in brewing, beer often took precedence in our conversations, but this time words became actions and we decided to try and create our own beer as a means of remedying the stuffy ales and fizzy yellow lagers that had come to dominate the UK drinks market.[9]

"That evening we set up a makeshift and pretty sketchy looking brewery in Martin's garage and created the first batch of what has now become known the world over as Punk IPA."[10]

Their next move was to see if anyone in the world would like what they had brewed. Watt continued, "From here we took our pilot beer to a series of open tastings and—by chance—were discovered by the late beer guru Michael Jackson at an event in Glasgow. Upon tasting our beer, Michael told us to quit our jobs and go into brewing fulltime. This is exactly what we did."[11]

Their next challenge, with very little money and difficult access to more, was to build a brewery big enough to meet that demand. As Watt explained, "Both only 24 years old, we leased a building, got some scary bank loans, and poured our heart, soul, and life savings into a fledgling business we weren't even sure would take off."[12]

"BrewDog started with only $48,000 [bank loan] so the first year involved living, eating, and sleeping at the brewery—a drafty warehouse on Fraserburgh's coastline. Exposed to the elements and running short on funds, Martin and I often worked twenty-hour shifts, . . . to stay afloat but also to stay warm."[13]

They were delighted to learn that through a combination of media savvy and brewing skill, they were generating a wave of popularity. Watt pointed out, "Within a year, there was already a buzz beginning to form around our beers, a media buzz that was starting to brand us as a scourge to society with our 'reckless and irresponsible' approach to brewing. The same buzz caused other people to see our beers as wildly innovative, contemporary, and making progressive changes and twists to long outmoded classic beer styles. Many people are still making their mind up over which brush to tar us with."[14]

Had you previously worked for other companies?

Both BrewDog co-founders had earned university degrees and gone to work at conventional firms. But for different reasons, they did not feel that they fit.

Dickie seems to have gotten more benefit from his education than Watt. As Watt explained, "Martin and I had both been to university in the years before BrewDog's conception and . . . studied very different subjects. I, for example, [became] bogged down in the rather tedious world of law while Martin . . . pursued brewing and consequently was working at a number of different breweries in England. After graduating [I] managed to get a place at a law firm but within two weeks [I] walked out."[15]

If so, what did you like about working there? What frustrated you about it?

Watt's revulsion with law was visceral and he quit his job quickly. He said, "Law—in a word—is dull and there was a big part of me that totally pan-icked thinking 'f*ck is this it?' The last thing I wanted to do with the next forty years of my life was to sit behind a desk, sorting out paperwork and other people's problems, constrained by a nine-to-five and a smart casual wardrobe. When I quit I didn't know what I would do, but literally a week later Martin and I started experimenting with beer, so I wasn't stuck watching daytime TV for long."[16]

What were the factors that led you to decide to turn your hobby—home brewing beer—into a business?

Watt and Dickie founded BrewDog because they were passionate about it and they thought the consequences of failure were minimal.

Watt said, "The opportunity to do something both Martin and I were genuinely passionate about was the main driving factor. Passion, drive, and determination are the key ingredients when starting any business, so it was just as well we felt that way about beer.[17]

"We also wanted to see if we could make a change. Martin and I were both in the perfect position to take that gamble—young enough and stupid enough to take big risks which—should they fail—wouldn't change our lives too dramatically."[18]

They found out in retrospect that there had been a big opportunity, but they did not have any idea it would be so significant when they decided to launch BrewDog. According to Watt, "Even now I'm surprised our business managed to stay afloat and [has] achieved some incredible things—exporting to over twenty-seven countries, being stocked in the UK's largest supermarkets, and having 1,300 shareholders invest in our brewery because they share in our vision, to name but a few."[19]

When you decided to start the company, what were the most important values you wanted to represent in your product and your relationships with others?

BrewDog is driven by a passion to create good-tasting beer in a very different way from its corporate brewer competitors.

As Watt explained, "Passion is the key value—we want people who drink our beer to get a sense that it's been produced by people who genuinely love beer. As the old BrewDog adage goes—'we're selfish because we only create beers we like.' If you aren't 100 percent interested or committed to your product then you're setting yourself up for a fall."[20]

"BrewDog is also the antithesis of corporate culture. Our staff aren't so much staff but more like family—dogs included—so it's pretty difficult to implement any kind of regulation when your employees are friends and your office is essentially a 24/7 parlor of chaos."[21]

Nevertheless, the founders needed procedures to help manage their growth. As Watt explained, "That said, it's far from a frat party in a brewery. The business is growing so quickly that we can often barely keep up in terms of the number of people we need as well as the internal procedure and infrastructure that are key to keep the whole thing from falling down around us.[22]

"The growth of BrewDog means the rest of the team and I spend a lot of time putting out fires, whether that's explaining to a loyal customer that their beer isn't ready yet or trying to get our online store fully stocked."[23]

BrewDog's beer-manufacturing approach reflects that anti-big–company ethos. According to Watt, "The problem with beer is that it's a completely organic product in that it takes time to grow and mature. If we were an automated, machine-driven multinational with millions of pounds at our disposal, then we could quite happily pump our beers full of artificial flavorings and chemicals to get them out the door as quickly as possible.[24]

"Thankfully, however, that's not the way we operate and we spend our time focusing on redefining the industry whilst beating our customers from our front door with a stick."[25]

BrewDog remains highly motivated to persuade people who buy corporate-brewed beer to switch to their crafted product. Watt said, "For us, everything comes back to one simple thing, one overarching ambition, one guiding light: to make other people as passionate about great craft beer as we are. We want to show people there is an alternative to monotone corporate beers and introduce them to a completely new approach to beer and elevate the status of beer in our culture.[26]

"Drinkers in Scotland are constrained by lack of choice. Seduced by the monolithic corporate brewers that have huge advertising budgets. Brainwashed by vindictive lies perpetrated with the veracity of pseudopropaganda. They can't help but be sucked down the rabbit hole. We are on a mission to open as many people's eyes as possible. This single goal is what gets us through pretty much anything."[27]

Its marketing approach also reflects this anti-corporate bias. As Watt explained, "Whether it is wrangling with industry regulators, pushing the boundaries in high ABV [alcohol by volume] brewing, smashing bottles of generic beer with a baseball bat, or doing a Saturday morning tasting at a local street market. This is why we work sixteen-hour days and why we only hire the most committed and passionate craft beer fans to work at BrewDog."[28]

The six hungry start-up strategy choices in Figure I.1 illustrate BrewDog's story, as follows:

1. *Set goals.* Watt and Dickie started BrewDog because they enjoyed making beer, they did not like working in corporate settings, and they wanted to create a working world for themselves and others who shared their passion for making craft beer. To make this vision a reality, they created a series of short-term goals—representing small, but ever-higher-stakes bets on BrewDog's future. If they could achieve these goals, they might be able to take the company to a higher level. Here is how they sequenced their goals:
   - *Goal 1:* Find something to do after they quit their corporate jobs.
   - *Goal 2:* After realizing that crafting beer was a good thing for them to do, create some buzz among influential beer bloggers.
   - *Goal 3:* Get a distributor in the country where they had created buzz.

FIGURE I.1 **Six Hungry Start-Up Strategy Choices.**

- *Goal 4*: Convince a bank to lend them money to build a facility that satisfies customer demand.
2. *Pick markets.* The co-founders picked the craft beer market because they liked making and drinking craft beer. They initially hoped to sell it in Scotland but ran into a brick wall. Instead of giving up, they decided to try sending samples of the product to a beer blogger in Sweden who loved the product. The blogger's influential review opened up Sweden to BrewDog's products.
3. *Raise capital.* BrewDog was able to cobble together capital in a fairly unusual way. It got a bank loan for its initial operations and then sold shares of stock to 1,300 of its customers in an innovative program called "Equity for Punks." BrewDog also raised capital by trying to delay payments to suppliers while speeding up cash collections from its distributor customers. BrewDog pays suppliers for their raw materials—such as hops, malt, and bottles—when they are ordered, but it typically has to wait sixty days to get paid by its distributors. To speed up customer payments, BrewDog offers a 3 percent discount to those who pay within ten days. But these customers are in the minority—most of them must pay before BrewDog ships its product to them. Only "rock solid" partners—such as those in Sweden and Norway (which are government-owned) do not have to pay before BrewDog delivers.

4. *Build team.* Watt makes it very clear that the values that drive Brew-Dog's efforts to gain market share—a passionate devotion to making high-quality, craft beer and an anti-corporate bias—also influence the kind of people BrewDog hires. Moreover, Watts suggests that this anti-corporate bias means that BrewDog's work environment demands very long hours and may not be as efficient as that of a large corporation.

5. *Gain share.* BrewDog's values and comparatively weak capital base led it to gain share through so-called guerrilla marketing techniques. It produces very clever and humorous videos that are inexpensive to produce and tend to attract many viewers through viral growth. Watt noted that a one-page magazine advertisement in the United Kingdom might reach a few potential customers for $8,000; however, BrewDog was able to reach 250,000 people around the world with a humorous YouTube-style video that it created for $2,400. Meanwhile, its initial market in Sweden was a result of sending a sample of its product to a prominent beer blogger there whose endorsement of the product made it much easier for Watts to sign up a big distributor in that market.

6. *Adapt to change.* BrewDog is trying to expand to more countries, and everywhere it wants to go there is plenty of competition. But Watt has a corporate North Star that helps him navigate these churning waters—his passionate belief in making a craft beer that its founders and customers crave.

BrewDog's battle for survival is typical of start-ups. Since they are born scrambling to come up with the cash to keep going, they cannot afford to wed themselves to old ways of running a business.

To that end, different questions keep start-up CEOs up at night and the answers differ from the prescriptions provided by Michael E. Porter, Bishop William Lawrence University Professor at Harvard Business School (HBS), whom I mentioned in the preface. He is a leading authority on company strategy and the competitiveness of nations and regions. And I worked at his consulting firm, Monitor Company, and directly with him on two projects.

While I have great respect for his ideas and intellect, there are important differences between his ideas and the concerns and concepts most pressing to entrepreneurs. Table I.1 summarizes these differences. The most important of these differences is that since they sprout from a hunger to create a new world with scant resources, all start-up choices are shaped by different pressures from those in large organizations.

For example, start-ups choose where to compete not based on analysis of impersonal factors but on their own skills and passions. Start-ups shape their choices as to where and how to compete based on their limited capital.

TABLE I.1   Hungry Start-Up versus Competitive Strategy

Start-Up Choice	Hungry Start-Up Strategy	Porter's Prescription(s)
Set Goals	Set three different kinds of goals: • *Mission* that communicates why founders are passionate about the venture. • *Long-term goal* that describes the ultimate outcome of the venture—such as becoming the leading publicly traded company in the market. • *Short-term goals* that spur the start-up to make a series of frugal experiments that can help them find a business model that ultimately leads them to achieve the long-term goal.	Earn above average risk-adjusted return on equity (ROE).
Pick Markets	Start-up CEOs pick markets in a very personal way—based on their own industry experience and the opportunities they believe they are uniquely qualified to capture. Company founders only attempt to estimate the size of the markets when seeking outside capital.	Focus on market segments and strategic groups with favorable and improving structural attractiveness based on the so-called five forces.
Raise capital	The availability of capital—or lack thereof—pressures founders to map out their short-term goals as a series of frugal experiments and approach capital raising differently for each.	Finance is a support activity tasked with minimizing the cost of capital. General corporate finance advice is first to choose the strategy and later to find financing.

And they use the power of their mission and long-term goals to make up for their inability to pay high salaries when recruiting their teams.

Ultimately, start-ups can gain market share—not through one of Porter's generic strategies—only through the recognition that they must offer customers a huge leap in value over competing products in order to overcome the risk to a customer of building a business relationship with a potentially ethereal supplier.

TABLE I.1 *(continued)*

Start-Up Choice	Hungry Start-Up Strategy	Porter's Prescription(s)
Build the team	With a sufficiently compelling mission, a start-up CEO can attract a top team despite a lack of cash to pay big-company salaries. The passion underlying the mission drives the values that shape start-ups' decisions of whom they'll hire, how they should act, and who gets promoted and fired.	Human resources is a support activity.
Gain share	Start-ups gain share by providing customers a Quantum Value Leap (QVL)—combining both of Porter's generic strategies with a twist. One extreme example of a QVL is a so-called freemium strategy, giving away a basic version of the product for free and, in the small number of cases where there is demand, charging customers for a more fully featured version.	Choose generic strategies: low-cost producer or differentiation and lower mobility barriers.
Adapt to change	Boundaryless company development helps start-ups to identify critical listening posts in their competitive environment and filter out the noise from the critical few signals—key threats or opportunities—to which they must respond.	Monitor rapidly evolving five forces.

WHY START-UPS MATTER TO THE ECONOMY

The typical start-up is a pretty fragile economic entity. So it might surprise you to learn that start-ups play a critical role in creating new jobs for the U.S. economy. Between 1977 and 2009 nearly all the roughly two to three million new jobs created each year were contributed by start-ups. Big companies contributed no net new jobs.

Dane Stangler, a research manager at the Kauffman Foundation, explained his views on the importance of start-ups and provided the data to back them up. According to Stangler, there are about 500,000 new businesses created annually.[29]

These new firms help maintain a total of two million start-ups—at 30 percent there are more of them than any other type of company. And between 48 and 50 percent of start-ups survive to their fifth year. If you net out job turnover, those start-ups create about two net new jobs every year.

Stangler points out that there are good reasons the start-ups produce most of the net new jobs. First, there are more of them. Second, the larger and older businesses tend to hire many people during economic upturns and then terminate them during periods of economic contraction and expansion.

Stangler suggests that large companies and start-ups have different attitudes toward innovation. The large companies invest in incremental technologies that have more controllable risks—and predictable returns. By contrast, start-ups invest in breakthrough innovation.

The different incentive structures for managers and investors help explain why. After all, even when a large company encourages risk-taking, there are limits to how much money a bet on innovation can lose before the person responsible for it pays a career price. By contrast, for a start-up, it is understood at the beginning that there is a one-in-ten chance of hitting it big, and if that happens, the reward will be a massive return on investment.

An interesting feature of start-ups is how they're financed. Stangler estimates that between 1 and 3 percent of the financing for start-ups comes from VC firms. And that comes later in their development. Stangler cites a 2009 study by Paul Kedrosky, *Right-Sizing the U.S. Venture Capital Industry*, which found that 16 percent of the 900 Inc. 100 companies between 1997 and 2007 took VC.[30]

During a start-up's initial stages, the funds come from friends, family, and founders. As a start-up grows, the money comes from bank loans, credit cards, and, before 2008, home equity. And only if the start-up has reached a further stage of development does it get equity investment.

Duke University researcher Vivek Wadhwa has surveyed thousands of students from China and India who returned home after getting their degrees in America. They ran into so much difficulty trying to make a go of it here that they started their companies back home instead. And China is taking steps to encourage its natives to return home to start their businesses.

Graduates of research universities such as MIT and Stanford account for a huge number of start-ups. In February 2009, MIT professor Edward B. Roberts and Charles Eesley discovered that MIT alumni started 25,800 active companies that employ about 3.3 million people and generate global sales of $2 trillion.[31] Eesley is currently conducting a similar study to estimate the economic impact of Stanford.[32]

The final reason start-ups matter is somewhat theoretical, but quite interesting. According to Stangler, for a company or a society there are diminishing returns to complexity. Initially, investment in more complexity generates an attractive return. But eventually, more complexity produces negative returns.

In Stangler's view, start-ups reset the complexity curve. Through breakthrough technological innovation, they extend the productivity frontier of companies and society. And they create new opportunities to make high-return investments in increased complexity before those diminishing returns again set in.

HOW HUNGRY START-UP STRATEGY WILL BENEFIT YOU

If you agree that start-ups are important, then Hungry Start-Up Strategy will help you. This book provides different benefits to different groups of readers, including:

- *Entrepreneurs.* Start-up CEOs and their management teams will learn how best to make six key strategic choices, how capital providers view them, and the kinds of big companies that can train them before they launch their ventures.
- *Entrepreneurship professors and students.* Business schools that teach entrepreneurship will have a new approach to strategy that complements traditional strategy frameworks. And students will benefit from advice on whether they are cut out to be entrepreneurs.
- *Capital providers.* Venture capitalists, banks, and angel investors will use the book to attract potential portfolio companies and to show them how to achieve their goals.
- *Big companies.* CEOs of large companies—particularly those that are threatened by upstart competitors and changing technologies—will learn how a handful of large companies are incorporating start-up strategies into their own organizations to create and capture growth opportunities while meeting quarterly performance targets.

Welcome to the world of the hungry start-up. If this introduction has increased your appetite to learn more, may the rest of this book sate your hunger.

PART ONE

Six Start-Up Choices

CHAPTER 1

Setting Goals

What Makes You Hungry?

START-UPS ARE BORN HUNGRY—their demand for money exceeds their supply. So start-ups need a different currency—a powerful emotional magnet that draws in talent.

Why would anyone go to work for a start-up? The hours are sure to be longer than they would be at a more established company, and the pay is likely to be lower as cash will be in short supply.

The simple answer is that some talented people are able to defer short-term economic gain in exchange for meaningful work with the possibility of a longer-term payoff.

Of course, this puts entrepreneurs in the difficult position of persuading talented people that they should stop whatever they are doing and work for them instead. And as we'll see in Chapter 3, entrepreneurs must also persuade capital providers to part with their cash to invest in their start-ups.

To recruit talented employees, entrepreneurs must mint emotional currency by way of three *hungry start-up goals*. These three goals answer the basic questions a talented potential employee might have before going to work for your start-up.

- *Why should I join your start-up?* **Mission.** The mission is the entrepreneur's most compelling case for why the start-up is going to achieve greatness. At the core of this case is a passionately held belief that what the start-up aspires to do is important. As we'll see, that passion might come from the desire to make the world a better place, the excitement that comes from being certain that the start-up could capture a great economic opportunity that nobody else has seen, or the simple desire to solve a problem that perplexes the founder.
- *How will I get a return on the stock I receive in exchange for giving up my life to your start-up over the next five years?* **Long-term goals.** Long-term

goals describe a tangible way that the entrepreneur will measure the venture's success, say, five years into the future. Long-term goals include being the leader in an important new market, becoming a big public company, being acquired by a bigger company, or remaining permanently private and independent.

- *How will you actually deliver on that promise?* **Short-term goals as a series of real options.** Short-term goals are specific milestones that the entrepreneur sets over a period of months, and the idea of real options means that each short-term goal is a frugal experiment. Setting good short-term goals reflects how effective the CEO is at getting stuff done. Many of the start-ups I interviewed tend to view these short-term goals as a sequence of go/no-go decisions. For example, the first short-term goal might be to figure out the start-up's business model, the next might be to get customers to use or pay for the product, and the third to expand success from one market to five around the world. If the entrepreneur can figure out, say, the first goal—e.g., the start-up's business model—then she continues on to the second one. Otherwise, she shutters the venture.

MISSION: RESPOND TO MARKET OPPORTUNITY, SOLVE PERSONAL PAIN, AND FOLLOW THE RESEARCH

As Figure 1.1 illustrates, entrepreneurs have different ways of picking a start-up's mission.

Entrepreneurs get the ideas to start companies from three sources:

- In many cases, it appeared clear that the founders did not consider their emotional or intellectual connection to the start-up to be a sufficiently compelling reason to devote themselves to a company. Instead, they felt a need to go beyond that personal impulse and determine whether there was a big enough market opportunity to justify the investment of time and money in starting the venture.

FIGURE 1.1 **Why Entrepreneurs Start Companies, by Percent of Interviewees.**

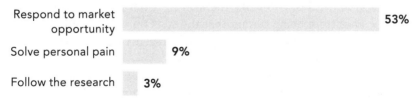

Respond to market opportunity 53%

Solve personal pain 9%

Follow the research 3%

- This is not to say that the ventures that were started purely to relieve personal pain or develop an intellectual interest did not eventually coincide with a market opportunity. Rather, these entrepreneurs were willing to defer identifying that opportunity at the time they started the company. Of the start-ups I interviewed, 24 percent sprang from a combination of personal pain *and* perceived market opportunity, and 10 percent were born of a combination of or intellectual interest *and* perceived market opportunity.

Let's take a look now at examples of each kind of mission.

Respond to Market Opportunity

Responding to market opportunity is the most common reason that entrepreneurs start companies. Their mission is to satisfy that unmet need better than the competition and build a significant enterprise in the process.

The specific nature of the market opportunity varies for each start-up and some are more studious than others when it comes to talking with customers to get external evidence to support their belief that the market opportunity is real.

Among the start-ups I interviewed were for-profits and social enterprises. And one interesting feature of these examples is that two of them— SoFi and m-Via—combine pursuit of market opportunity with a bigger social purpose. Here are some examples of the market opportunities that the for-profit start-ups perceived:

> I saw an opportunity in the $1 trillion student loan market to lower the rates that students pay on their loans while creating an attractive investment opportunity for alumni.[33]
>
> — **Mike Cagney, co-founder and CEO of SoFi**, and former vice president and head trader of Wells Fargo. SoFi raises capital from alumni at colleges to help finance loans to their students.

> ExtraHop was founded in early 2007; my co-founder and I saw an underserved market. We are targeting a large, fast-growing market. After all, Gartner estimated that the market for network and application performance monitoring products hit $3.8 billion in 2011 and is growing at an 8.5 percent annually. And we were eager to solve the problem. We spent over two years working on building a product that would work well for the customers with whom we collaborated.[34]
>
> — **Jesse Rothstein, CEO of Extrahop**, a sub-$50,000 appliance that provides IT managers with real-time system health and performance information.

I see a big opportunity in a very fast-growing industry. IDC reports that between 2001 and 2011, the market for our product—virtualization storage—grew from scratch to $11 billion. Before founding Tintri, I oversaw the development of all server virtualization technology for VMware as its VP of R&D from 1999 to 2006. I recognized the problem server virtualization created for storage early on and resolved to shift my career focus to solve this storage dilemma. To that end, I founded Tintri—it's Gaelic for "lightning." My aim was to extend the benefits of virtualization from the server side to storage—what could be a lightning bolt of efficiency if carried out.[35]

— **Kieran Harty, CEO of Tintri**, which helps companies store and retrieve information more efficiently.

While working at a mobile gaming start-up, I grew increasingly outraged as I analyzed the way the cross-border money transfer business has skillfully avoided disruption of its tactics over the last thirty years. I felt that it was unfair to exploit the weakness of people sending money home and became convinced that I could develop a service that would offer them a lower-cost, safer way to transfer money.[36]

— **Bill Barhydt, CEO of m-Via**, which helps people wire money to their families in Mexico and other countries.

From these examples, the takeaway is simple. Start-up CEOs should set their start-up's mission based on their own experience. But the mission should be bolstered by some external validation: ideally, in-depth customer research that confirms that what is important to the founder will also be important to a sizable audience.

This same principle holds for social enterprises—set up not for profit, but to make the world better. What's different about them is that they face a unique challenge in their efforts to achieve what is most commonly a very noble social purpose. It's challenging for social enterprises to make enough money to perpetuate doing social good. Here are some examples:

One of the reasons I started PoverUP was that in the summer of 2008, I volunteered in a border refugee village in Thailand. That's where I realized that a little money—I bought 50 donuts for $1—could go a long way to helping poor people start businesses that would lift them out of poverty.[37]

— **Charlie Javice, co-founder and CEO of PoverUP**, a social network for university students to get involved in social enterprises.

I developed the idea for a peer-to-peer donation service in 2005 while pursuing my master's degree in Industrial Engineering at Stanford after visiting Indonesia a few months before the December 2004 tsunami struck. Following the relief efforts, I saw stockpiles of usable medicine, large enough to overflow a football stadium, not only not being used but also costing Indonesia millions of dollars to dispose of as toxic waste. I started SIRUM to solve the supply chain problem that prevented perfectly good medicine from getting to the people who needed it.[38]

— **Adam Kircher, founder of SIRUM,** a nonprofit that gets medication that would otherwise be dumped or incinerated into the hands of poor people in California.

A mother living in a rural village outside of Bangalore, India, gives birth to a baby two months prematurely. Her family cannot afford to go to the city hospital in Bangalore, so her husband, who raises silkworms that he warms under lamps, decides to care for the baby in the same way. A few days later, their insufficiently warmed baby dies. Stopping this tragedy—20 million low-birth-weight and premature babies are born each year—is the primary mission of Embrace.[39]

— **Jane Chen, founder and CEO of Embrace, which** makes a sleeping-bag–like baby warmer that helps improve the odds of survival for premature babies born in developing countries.

Lacking the potential to attract people motivated by an opportunity to become wealthy, the missions of these social enterprises must be particularly compelling. And these examples do share the following common characteristics:

- They all spring from emotionally powerful and compelling stories about why the organization was formed.
- They attract talented people who want to help achieve that long-term goal.
- It is clear who will benefit from achieving the goal.
- The founders are likely to face a challenge as they attempt to maintain unswerving devotion to their long-term goals and generating sufficient cash flow to keep their organizations operating.

Solve Personal Pain

While the majority of start-ups I interviewed set their long-term goals based on a perceived market opportunity, some believed so strongly in the importance of addressing their personal pain that they went ahead with their companies without hard evidence of a significant market opportunity.

Here are some examples of the personal pain that spurred the creation of for-profit start-ups:

> I got the idea for AfterSteps after a grandparent died. My mother started calling me in periodic spurts with her estate plans, wishes for various personal items, and requests for how to handle her body. I decided there had to be a better way. So I started AfterSteps to bring organization, completeness, and knowledge to the end-of-life planning process.[40]
> —**Jesse Bloomgarden, founder and CEO of AfterSteps,** a service that helps people prepare their loved ones for their death.

> Before starting Huddle, I worked for a "big data" firm called Dunn-humby—it analyzed data for large retailers such as Procter & Gamble —where I led a business that grew to $60 million in revenues in three years. When the company was acquired, I left. I used some of the proceeds from the sale to finance Huddle's initial operations in 2008. I wanted to solve a problem I had at Dunnhumby—my 300-person staff could not work together on projects through a single, easy-to-use system. Huddle was started to remedy that problem.[41]
> —**Alastair Mitchell, founder and CEO of Huddle,** a service that enables big companies collaborate on projects.

> I attended an all-girls high school in India and was then admitted to one of its top engineering programs, IIT Kanpur, India. There, I was one of three girls in a class of fifty computer science majors. I was shy and studied alone while the more gregarious boys collaborated. As a result, the boys, working together, could get answers in ten minutes to questions that I spent four hours solving myself. Piazza is my way of letting the shy and the gregarious of both sexes collaborate online. I believe that Piazza works better than wikis and threaded discussion groups that are often used for student Q&A.[42]
> —**Pooja Nath Sankar, CEO of Piazza,** a service that helps students ask questions of peers and professors and get the best answers at the top.

These stories all share certain common characteristics that typify entre-preneurs seeking to solve personal pain:

- The start-up CEOs each had a compelling personal problem and wanted to develop a business dedicated to solving that problem.

- The CEOs were willing to invest their time and money in developing a solution to their problems and did not let the absence of a clear market opportunity stop them.
- The CEOs assumed that if they could solve the problem well, they would find plenty of other people who would pay them for the solution.

While the long-term success cannot yet be predicted for any of these ventures, their goals serve a useful purpose. By choosing long-term goals that relieve their pain, there is little doubt that these founders will have ample motivation to solve the problem effectively.

And in these cases, it does not take a precise market size estimate for the founders to apply some common sense and realize that their pain is widely shared—even if the precise size of the market is not of great interest to them in setting long-term goals for their companies.

Follow the Research

A few of the start-ups I interviewed were started by people with PhDs who decided to try to turn their doctoral research into a business. While this is a fairly risky business proposition, there is often a chance that their original research can be applied to an existing problem for which there is not a particularly good solution. It is also possible that their work can create a market where one has not previously existed.

Here are some examples of how following the research spurred the creation of two start-ups:

> Sifteo CEO Jeevan Kalanithi, a colleague from Stanford, and I were studying at MIT's Media Lab. He shared my interest in bringing physical objects such as dominoes back to interactive gaming. We wondered together why everything on our computers—email, files, and icons—were two-dimensional. We wanted to bring three-dimensionality to computing—to develop siftable computers that people could use their hands to manipulate—to sift and sort—like a pile of LEGOs. In the summer of 2009, we founded Sifteo to build products that would fulfill our vision for hands-on interaction.[43]
>
> — **Dave Merrill, co-founder and president, Sifteo,** which makes blocks with programmable screens that can interact wirelessly.

> I took a leave of absence from my Stanford master's degree program in computer science after earning a BS in the field—I have four classes left—to start Loki Studios. At Stanford, I met an engineer who shared

my passion for the idea of starting a gaming company that would take advantage of mobile technologies.[44]

— **Ivan Lee, CEO of Loki Studios,** a maker of mobile Pokemon-like games.

It's not very often that entrepreneurs start companies to follow the research; however, they:

- Each had a strong interest in applying new technologies to games.
- All came up with novel ways to apply existing technologies to their interest in games.
- Assumed that if they could solve the problem well, they would be able to create a market of people who would be willing to pay for their solution.

While these intellectual ventures both got started without substantial research into the market potential for the products that they were developing, it is clear from talking with the founders that they would be happy to develop their products and get them working well. If they happened to find sizable numbers of other people who shared their interest, they would be delighted.

So, if you are an entrepreneur who wants to follow the research, you should consider raising capital from investors who share your interest in the field.

Solve Personal Pain and Respond to Market Opportunity

As noted previously, about a quarter of the companies I interviewed started companies to relieve personal pain and because they believed that there would be a big market opportunity in so doing.

Here are some examples:

I left my driveway at 9 a.m. for a doctor's appointment; I signed in, waited a few hours, and finally got in to see my doctor, who prescribed medication. I get back in the car, drove to the pharmacy, waited in a line for my prescription, and paid for it. By the time I returned to the driveway, it was 2:30 in the afternoon. A fine day, wasted. I was thinking about starting a new company targeting a big market and when I was returning from the pharmacy that day, I realized that health care would fit the bill. So I decided to start WhiteGlove Health.[45]

— **Bob Fabbio, CEO of WhiteGlove Health,** which provides health care to corporate employees in their homes or offices.

I like to take photographs. In 2003, I had what I thought was a great collection that I wanted to use for a book to give 35 friends and family members. One little problem—the price tag for doing that would be a jaw-dropping $10,000. I thought that given the technology available at the time, it should not be so hard to produce that book. I set up Blurb to solve that problem. I immediately set out to research whether there would be a big enough market to make a start-up worthwhile and discovered that the opportunity was worth pursuing."[46]

— **Eileen Gittins, founder and CEO of Blurb,** a service that lets people self-publish, with an emphasis on books with digital images.

I bought some security cameras to protect my business and noticed that their quality was terrible. Having expertise in high-quality camera hardware and software, I started a company focused on building much better surveillance systems. We're targeting the $10 billion market for surveillance systems—half of which is cameras and the other half video management software. The market is growing between 5 and 15 percent a year, and we are tapping the fastest-growing upgrade segment.[47]

— **Alexander Fernandes, CEO of Avigilon,** which makes inexpensive, high-quality visual surveillance systems.

These stories share certain common characteristics that typify entrepreneurs seeking to solve personal pain and respond to market opportunity:

- The start-up CEOs each had a compelling personal problem and wanted to develop a business dedicated to solving that problem.
- They were not willing to bet their time and money on the opportunity unless they could be convinced that there would be enough other people who had the same problem and would be willing to pay to solve it.
- Their research gave them confidence that the market opportunity for solving that problem would more than offset the likely investment required to develop a solution and sell it to those potential customers.

This combination of reasons for setting a start-up's long-term goal is among the most compelling ones out there. The existence of a personal problem that the founder wants to solve is a powerful spur to invest time and money in solving it. And the ability to gather compelling evidence that the number of potential customers is big enough to justify that investment is likely to interest potential employees and investors.

Follow the Research and Respond to Market Opportunity

Some of the start-ups I interviewed combined their desire to follow the research with what I think is a sensible urge to find whether the demand for their product will justify the investment of their time and money.

Here are some examples of companies that followed the research and responded to a market opportunity:

> Company co-founder Marsha Moses and the late Judah Folkman of Boston's Children's Hospital invented a urine-based, noninvasive cancer detection technology that Predictive Biosciences has commercialized. Monitoring bladder cancer patients after their initial treatment is very expensive. Patients must submit to cystoscopy—threading a cystoscope through their urethra and into the bladder—every three months for the first two years, every six months for the next two years, and annually thereafter. Replacing this invasive test with one that detects biomarkers in the urine targets a $3 billion market for bladder cancer detection.[48]
> — **Peter Klemm, CEO of Predictive Biosciences,** which makes diagnostic tests for diseases like colon and prostate cancer.

> I started Locately in 2008 with the idea of applying location analysis to the then recently introduced Apple iPhone. To finance the company, I and fellow MIT PhD, Eric Weiss, saw success in the MIT $100K Entrepreneurship Competition. Our idea was to make use of valuable location data from mobile devices [that were] going unprocessed and unharnessed every single day. And we saw a business opportunity in packaging and analyzing that data for national brands, market researchers, and advertisers. Our goal was to provide new insights into consumers' location-relevant lifestyles while keeping individuals always in control of their data.[49]
> — **Dr. Thaddeus Fulford-Jones, CEO of Locately,** a service that helps retailers track consumers' shopping behavior as their locations change.

These stories share certain common characteristics that typify entrepreneurs seeking to pursue an intellectual interest coupled with a market opportunity:

- The start-up CEOs each had invested a significant amount of time developing the intellectual interest, and it took the form of a doctoral thesis or postdoctoral research.
- In some cases, the people who conducted the research had no interest in capitalizing on it themselves; however, they did want to license their

work to someone with a track record of successfully commercializing such intellectual property.

If the market opportunity for applying the research is sufficiently attractive, the combination of the unique, patented technology with a significant, unmet market need can set the stage for a successful venture with a clear long-term goal that galvanizes executives, capital providers, and workers.

As an investor, I find this combination of intellectual originality and market opportunity to be generally quite compelling. Potential employees would also be likely to find the goal of building such a start-up to be attractive.

There are many kinds of long-term goals that entrepreneurs can set for their start-ups. In general, hungry start-ups set these long-term goals with the idea that they will help shape the work environment that they want to create. So whether the long-term goal springs from personal pain, an intellectual interest, a market opportunity, or a combination of these, the most important thing for the company is that the founders firmly believe in their long-term goals.

Their belief in these long-term goals will motivate them to commit their time and capital, if necessary, to achieve them. That belief will also help them attract employees and capital to help achieve those goals.

THE REAL-OPTIONS APPROACH

Hungry Start-Up Approach to Short-Term Goals: A Series of Real Options

Hungry start-ups are so short on cash that what they choose to do in the short term can make the difference between surviving and running out of money. Rather than betting all their cash on one big goal, start-ups set shorter term goals—such as building a prototype of a product and getting customer feedback on it within six months.

Principles of Hungry Start-Up Approach to Short-Term Goals

Start-up CEOs think of those short-term goals as real options—inexpensive, time-limited bets. And these options will either generate a successful outcome or a failed one from which the start-up can learn and adapt. More formally, start-up CEOs think of short-term goals as a *sequence* of real options which give their holders the right, but not the obligation, to make future investments in the start-ups.[50]

Here start-ups conduct a series of frugal experiments[51] where they spend a relatively small amount of money to test a hypothesis about a potential opportunity. Through this hypothesis testing, start-ups get insight about the nature of the opportunity, which they can use to decide whether to buy another option—by making a new frugal experiment[52]—or to stop their experiment.

To set short-term goals through a real-options approach, entrepreneurs should follow three principles:

- *Use goals to limit risk and encourage learning.* The real-options approach to goal setting also forces managers to break up the very daunting challenge of building a company from scratch into more manageable bits. The art of this real-options approach is to sequence the goals so that if the first one is achieved, it will provide learning that helps to achieve the second one. The same logic applies to jumping from the second to the third goal in the sequence. Even if the company fails to achieve all the goals, if managers choose and sequence them properly, investors can limit their risk of loss.

- *Set goals that are ambitious, yet achievable.* One of the primary reasons to set goals is that they help communicate to employees why they are there—and in the case of start-ups, why they are working so many hours. Setting ambitious yet achievable goals can motivate people. With start-ups the term of those goals is measured in months, rather than years. To achieve such short-term goals demands a very high level of concentrated effort. And a larger firm with a slower cycle time may be vulnerable to the efforts of a start-up that targets the larger firm's customers.

- *Use goals to map the company's growth path.* Finally, the real-options approach to goal setting can put the company on a steep growth path. For instance, Adeptol, which offers a browser-based document reader, is owned by its founder and CEO, Prateek Kathpal. Adeptol had 2,000 customers when I talked with Kathpal after it had been in business for a mere two years.[53] And Apptio—which offers a service that helps companies' chief technology officers explain the costs and the value of their services to their corporate customers—has also exceeded ambitious short-term goals. For example, CEO Sunny Gupta set a year-two goal of 300 percent growth which Apptio surpassed by a factor of three.[54] Apptio's ability to exceed its goals highlights the motivational power of setting them and the appeal of its service to customers.

Hungry Start-Up Approach to Short-Term Goals: Defined

Goal setting—a firm's process of deciding what measurable outcomes it wants to achieve—is a critical starting point because it focuses all of its subsequent actions. Simply put, a company's strategy flows from its goals.

Start-ups' goals vary. Based on my research, if a company is largely controlled by external venture capitalists, then their goals will prevail. In general, VCs want to make an investment and sell it within a period of years at the highest price that another company or public investors are willing to pay.

Since start-up CEOs generally seek out VCs who share their goals and their industry expertise, their goals are naturally aligned. If a start-up is owned by its CEO, the CEO will determine its goal—which, in the cases I've researched, is to become a technology leader in the CEO's industry of choice.

- While each of the companies I interviewed applies this concept differently, there seems to be a common pattern they all share. As depicted in Figure 1.2, start-ups set goals according to the following sequence:

- *Real Option 1: Define the market opportunity.* While it is somewhat amazing to me, some VCs are willing to give a management team millions of dollars to take a vague idea about a particular problem facing a group of customers and let them try to figure out whether they can

FIGURE 1.2 **Hungry Start-Up Approach to Short-Term Goals.**

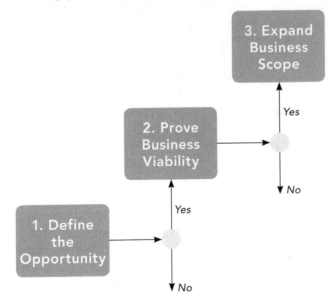

develop a version of their idea that attracts customers fast. Determining whether enough customers will use the start-up's prototype is the goal of the first real option.

- *Real Option 2: Prove business viability.* If the result of that first frugal experiment is positive, then the VC is likely to invest in another. The goal of the second investment is to try to sell the product resulting from the first experiment to enough customers to make a fact-based estimate of the likely size and potential profitability of the business. Deciding whether the business is viable is the goal of the second real option.
- *Real Option 3: Expand business scope.* If the result of that second frugal experiment is positive, then the business may have generated as much as a few million dollars in sales. This is not a big enough business to interest potential buyers and therefore it sets the stage for the final goal. The goal of the third investment is to try to scale the business to the point where the founder can sell shares to the public, to an acquirer, or to capital providers willing to pay a higher price for its privately held shares.[55] Getting the business to a size where investors can realize a return is the goal of the third real option.

Benefits of Real-Options Approach to Start-Up Goal Setting

There are three ways that start-ups benefit from the real-options approach to goal setting:

- *It bounds risk.* The real-options approach to goal setting puts a clear limit on how much risk investors will take and it makes clear what kinds of returns that risk could generate. At a minimum, real options are almost guaranteed to generate information that can be useful for decision making. If that information leads to a decision to invest again, real options can boost the odds that investors—including the CEO and top managers who own equity in the firm—will achieve an attractive return on their investment of capital and effort.
- *It focuses the company.* The real-options approach to goal setting helps to focus the efforts of a company's relatively small employee base. It forces to the top of employees' awareness that the money available to pay them will run out within a fairly short period of time. The CEO's job here is to make it clear to all employees what they need to do in order to contribute to the company's current goal. And that clear focus also boosts the odds that the company will succeed enough to persuade investors to grant it another round of capital.
- *It maps a growth path.* Finally, the real-options approach to goal setting helps the organization keep in mind the bigger picture as it becomes

focused on the start-up's day-to-day activities. Particularly during the first real option stage, the start-up can motivate people more effectively if they have a map of the longer-term trajectory of the start-up if it achieves all the goals needed to reach the ultimate outcome.

HUNGRY-START-UP GOAL-SETTING TACTICS

How can a start-up CEO turn these general guidelines into useful action? This section provides tactical advice on how to pick a compelling mission, how to choose long-term goals, and how to set short-term goals.

Effective start-up missions share the following characteristics:

- *Important to the founder.* Effective start-up missions are invariably extremely meaningful to their founder. That meaning springs most frequently from two sources, a strongly held belief that there is an untapped market opportunity and a personal passion that the founder believes he or she must pursue.
- *Relatable.* A corollary to the first characteristic is that an effective start-up mission is compelling not solely to the founder but also to other people that could help the start-up get off the ground. More specifically, missions that help a start-up hire talented people or get customers to try its product work best.
- *Spur value creation.* Finally, a mission that spurs people to create a competitively superior product for its target customers helps a start-up prevail. An example of this is BrewDog—whose focus on creating high-quality beer that its founders and employees prefer helps it take share from so-called corporate beer purveyors.

Effective long-term goals are specific, measurable, and time-linked. And such long-term goals should be measured in ways that people in the company can understand. For example, people can more easily understand goals for getting a specific number of new customers than they can more abstract market-share target. Similarly, it helps in recruiting for a start-up CEO to make it clear that he sees the company going public in some specified time period or remaining independent.

How Start-Ups Define Useful Short-Term Goals

Real Option 1: Define the Market Opportunity

How long should a start-up take to determine whether it can develop a viable business model? The answer depends on how much capital the firm has and how much capital it needs to test the business model ideas. A start-up's first real-option should make room for as many frugal experiments as it can execute given the rate at which it is burning through its scarce resources.

To know whether a venture has found a viable market opportunity, the entrepreneur must answer these four questions in the affirmative:

- Does a basic version of your product attract a small initial group of users that's passionate about your product?
- Do those initial users keep using the product after the first try?
- Do the users recommend the product to other people?
- Do initial users get more value from the product by recommending it?

Use the following approach to get yes answers to these questions:

- Listen to early adopter customers—the people who always like to be the first to try a new product—to uncover their unmet needs.
- Build and give them a simple version of the product to get feedback.
- If they like the initial version, ask them if they will recommend it to others.
- If they don't like it, find out what they don't like about it and what's missing, and try again.

Real Option 2: Prove Business Viability

If you can define the market opportunity, the next question is whether you can get people to pay for your product. If that effort is successful, then your business may be viable—particularly if the sales to those paying customers are greater than your costs.

One way to test a start-up's viability is to consider a freemium strategy. By getting a fraction of 1 percent of those customers to pay for a more fully featured version of the product, companies can use the freemium strategy to become a viable business.

Jason Lemkin is VP of Web business services at Adobe and he explained that his start-up EchoSign was acquired by the maker of Flash in July 2011. Lemkin started EchoSign in January 2006 to help people get contracts signed and filed electronically.[56]

EchoSign offered a way to integrate contract signing with customer relationship management systems and it gave its product to customers at no charge—with the idea that they would pay for a premium version. When Adobe came looking for a big player in the electronic contracting space, it knocked on EchoSign's door and bought the company.

In the four and a half months since that deal closed, Lemkin was thrilled to report that EchoSign's integration with Adobe Reader had given him more new users than he had prior to the acquisition—and it then had a total of five million people using the product.

But here's where the beauty of the freemium strategy comes in—even though a small fraction of those users were paying customers—that amounted to paying customers in the tens of thousands—including salespeople from Groupon and sales representatives from British Telecom.

By charging these more sophisticated users $100 a month for an advanced version of the product, EchoSign generated some pretty significant revenue from that small percent of users who paid—at that pay rate; EchoSign is a multimillion-dollar revenue business.

It hasn't always been smooth sailing for Lemkin's freemium strategy. Here are three lessons he's learned:

- *It takes time.* A company using a freemium strategy has to be patient and must make it extremely easy for users to sign up. In Lemkin's experience, it can take three months for a start-up company that signs up to use EchoSign extensively, and another three to five months before that user feels compelled to buy the premium version of the product. This means that it takes a long time for the business to reach $10 million in sales, less time to double to $20 million, and after that it starts growing virally.
- *Invest to make the free version very compelling.* Lemkin sees DropBox—a free service that lets users take their photos, documents, and videos anywhere and share them easily—as a compelling free utility that produces instant customer value. But if 20 percent of the users convert after, say, a month, then the service is not really freemium—it's a free trial for a short period of time.
- *Need millions of free users.* When Lemkin started EchoSign, he thought of eFax—then a $200 million service—as a good model of what his company could become. eFax had 10 million users and 10 percent of them paid. As it turned out, Lemkin was overly optimistic when he assumed that EchoSign would garner a similar 10 percent.

Nevertheless, with many of EchoSign's current customers paying, Lemkin was happy with how its freemium strategy was working once it became part of Adobe.

EchoSign's success with its freemium strategy illustrates the difference between finding a market opportunity and proving a start-up's business model. When customers used the free version of Lemkin's product, he proved to himself and his investors that he had found a market opportunity because people were using his product and recommending it to others.

However, it was not until EchoSign had gotten a critical mass of users and enough of them began to pay for the service that it began to generate sufficient revenues to become "cash-flow positive."

Real Option 3: Expand Business Scope

Once a business has proved its viability in one market, the next short-term milestone is expanding it to other markets. The new markets could be in different countries or they could be a new group of customers within the company's home market.

Here are some tests to decide whether the potential new market is likely to boost the start-up's profitability:

- Are the potential revenues and profits in the new market sufficient to offset the cost of serving it?
- Does the start-up have the products and business capabilities needed to offer customers in the new market a competitively superior value proposition?
- Are these competitive advantages enough for the start-up to gain a meaningful number of customers?

BrewDog's expansion into twenty-seven countries is a case in point. Its first customers were in Sweden because an influential blogger liked its product and let his readers know. This helped BrewDog ink a contract with a leading Swedish beer distributor. And since such distributors relieve suppliers of the cost of operating a local operation, they can generate significant profits for the supplier if the product is in high demand. Most likely, BrewDog repeated this successful pattern to add twenty-six more countries to its collection of markets.

GOALS: DO YOU HAVE THE RIGHT ONES?

The foregoing discussion of goals may be raising questions in your mind about whether your start-up has the right ones. To help think about this question, here are some more detailed questions that may help you reach a conclusion:

- Do you feel a connection between your passions or intellectual interests and your start-up's long-term goals?
- Have you considered whether pursuing those passions or intellectual interests will satisfy a widely shared human need?
- If not, are you willing to take the risk that your start-up may not be able to generate sufficient revenues?

- How confident are you that enough potential customers could benefit if your start-up achieves its long-term goal?
- Have you developed a sequence of short-term goals that build on one another?
- Do you have specific measures in mind that will help you determine objectively whether your start-up is on track to achieve the short-term goals?
- Are you prepared with a back-up plan in case your start-up does not achieve its short-term goals?

If you have solid answers to these questions, then your long- and short-term goals have been set in a way that will serve your venture well. And if not, these questions may help you rethink your long- and short-term goals until you do have solid answers.

SUMMARY

People respond to goals—particularly if they can benefit from their achievement. In order to get a venture off the ground, entrepreneurs must provide them with an initial puff of inspiration. The goal is to create a hunger for creating a new world—or at least to create a start-up with a long-term goal that attracts talented people and ultimately customers and capital for growth. Whether that long-term goal springs from responding to market opportunity, solving personal pain, following the research, or a combination, it is critical that the mission be meaningful to the founders. And while a start-up's long-term goal ought to remain constant, it is also important that entrepreneurs create a roadmap of sequential short-term goals the achievement of which will ultimately realize that long-term goal.

CHAPTER 2

Picking Markets
Feed Your Customers and They'll Feed You

WHAT IS A MARKET? Why does it matter which one you pick? A market is the place where hungry customers and suppliers set the terms at which they'll sate their mutual hunger. How participants think about markets depends on their place in the entrepreneurial ecosystem; after all, different participants have different hungers. For example:

- *Start-up product users* often hunger for a solution to a problem that no vendors provide. And if that unsolved problem is important enough to those potential customers, then there is an opportunity for the start-up to deliver the solution. However, many potential customers are reluctant to do business with a start-up because they are concerned about the costs they could incur if the start-up goes out of business. Hence, those customers will only try it if it's free. The hope is that, over time, customers will become more confident in the start-up's ability to deliver value consistently, and then be willing to pay.
- *Start-up CEOs* look at markets in different ways, depending on the source of their hunger. For example, if they're trying to solve a problem that bothers them personally, then they look at markets not in an abstract way but as a chance to satisfy one customer at a time. Alternatively, if they hunger for wealth, then they may look at markets based on the sales potential for their venture—the bigger, the better. To that end, such start-up CEOs might rank markets based on four factors: size, growth, margins, and odds of their company gaining a meaningful share. Entrepreneurs look at markets in both ways—some are more willing to talk about their interest in wealth creation than others.

- *Start-up investors* also look at markets in different ways. And those differences depend on the type of start-up investor. Friends and family may not think much about markets, and the size of the potential market may not matter; their hunger is to help out a loved one or friend with the hope that they'll "win the lottery." On the other hand, angel and VC investors are primarily investing because they think they can help build a big company. So their hunger can best be satisfied by investing in a start-up that's targeting a big, fast-growing market that—thanks to the founder's business skills—might become the dominant competitor.

Above all, entrepreneurs start companies because they are hungry to do things their own way. And that can also mean thinking about markets the way they want. Some start-up CEOs put little effort into estimating the size of the market their venture will target—as long as they think enough potential customers share the pain they want to alleviate.

But sooner or later, most start-up CEOs will be required to identify the market they are targeting and offer a compelling explanation for their choice. There are two reasons entrepreneurs ought to put a number on the size of the market they want to target:

- *Justify the investment of their time.* Since entrepreneurs theoretically have an unlimited number of possible markets that they can target, they may wish to rank those possibilities—in part—on their sales potential. In general, if the market is too small, the start-up may not generate sufficient revenues to survive. More specifically, founders should pick a market that is big enough to support the investment required to build the business.
- *Persuade capital providers to invest.* Most entrepreneurs do not spend a huge amount of time putting a number on the size of their market unless that's part of what it takes to get investors to buy shares in the start-up. This is important because start-ups need to achieve a minimum level of market share in order to provide their investors a return. For example, if an investor believes that 10 percent is the maximum market share that a company can achieve, and that the company needs to reach at least $5 million in sales to be sold, then the minimum size market required to attract capital would be $50 million. Of course, experienced investors have seen overinflated market-size estimates and they generally discount the numbers they get from entrepreneurs. Despite investor skepticism, an entrepreneur can take advantage of the opportunity to impress investors by providing a detailed explanation of the assumptions underlying the market estimates.

One critical point that entrepreneurs must recognize early on is that it is far simpler to come up with a market size and growth estimate if the start-up is going after a well-established industry with a new product or service. On the other hand, if a start-up is seeking to gain share from an industry that does not currently exist, it is much more difficult to estimate that market's size and growth rate.

In either case, however, the biggest difference between good and excellent market analysis is the degree of insight into what it will take to get customers. Interviews with customers will reveal the problems customers think need solving and which solutions they are willing to pay for.

Customer interviews can add a level of depth to an entrepreneur's understanding of the market potential. And that deeper insight can help persuade investors to write a check.

Which group of customers is most likely to be suffering from pain that a start-up can relieve? My research suggests that there are generally two ways to answer this question. The first is that the founder is starting the company for himself and he assumes that if he can solve the problem that ails him, there will be other people who share his pain and will happily buy the start-up's product. The other is to conduct customer interviews to ask them to identify painful business problems that the market is not addressing. To pick the right markets, an entrepreneur must address the following four questions (my research findings follow).

- *Are there enough such customers willing to pay for our product to keep the start-up going?* The need to develop precise estimates arises when a start-up CEO begins to develop a business plan to raise outside capital. And as we'll see, when that need arises, entrepreneurs use a variety of approaches to develop those market estimates, including conducting their own research, hiring an outside consultant, and blending internal and third-party analysis.
- *Is the market we choose growing fast, how durable are its growth trends, and who are its potential competitors?* Most entrepreneurs I spoke with have a general idea about the growth rate of their markets and how quickly their start-up is growing relative to that rate. Moreover, they often are able to cite three or four key trends driving that growth. It is important for start-up CEOs to assure themselves that the growth trends in their market will persist; this is more important than knowing the exact rate at which demand is growing. Ironically, it often helps entrepreneurs to raise capital if the market has competitors who both provide evidence that the market is significant and give the start-up a chance to position itself as a better solution for customers.

- *If we got only 5 percent of the market, would our profits be sufficient to generate a return for our investors?* As we'll see, answering this question becomes important when an entrepreneur seeks to raise capital. That's because if a venture capitalist invests, say, $20 million in a company, the partner must be confident that the start-up can reach a sufficient scale in the target market. If the start-up does not become large enough to make that $20 million share worth, say, $60 million in three years, the investor may pass. And using some basic assumptions, that means if a start-up can hope for at best a 10 percent market share, a market must be quite large—at least several hundred million dollars.

- *How much capital should we seek?* The answer to this question depends on three issues: (1) the industry (for example, medical products companies need much more capital than iPhone app developers), (2) the stage of development (the bigger a start-up's employee base, the more capital it will require), and (3) the entrepreneur's hunger for control (the greater the entrepreneur's hunger for control, the less capital he or she will want to raise from external sources). In general, entrepreneurs can get some help estimating how much capital to seek by studying the capital requirements of similar start-ups in these three areas.

PICKING MARKETS

In theory, a start-up has unlimited freedom to answer these questions any way that the founder wants.

The Experts Weigh In on How to Pick Markets

Biggest Isn't Always Best

Les Charm, an entrepreneurship teacher at Babson College, notes that most entrepreneurs pick markets that they know already. A venture does not necessarily need to target a billion-dollar market to succeed.

If an entrepreneur can raise only, say, $250,000 in capital, then he or she can build a business that generates an attractive return on that capital by targeting a smaller market or by outsourcing a critical activity—like sales. Instead of hiring a sales force, the start-up could form a distribution partnership, which would use up less capital.

And even though the start-up would get a smaller percentage of the sales, the lower cost would make the partnership more profitable.[57]

Hone Your Market

IDEO, the design firm, helps clients pick markets by trying out a series of product/market strategies and seeing which ones resonate with customers.

For example, IDEO realized that mothers had two options—traditional baby bottles and warming stations.

But neither had satisfied Yoomi's founder, Jim Sheikh. When IDEO gave mothers Sheikh's initial prototype, however, it wasn't well-received because they saw Yoomi's product as a substitute rather than a supplement for breast-feeding. In listening to mothers, IDEO learned that many mothers initially want to breast feed but in practice many end up not being able to do it.

So IDEO realized that Yoomi should not target its product to all mothers—just those who might use its product as a contingency option—namely, those mothers who intended to breast feed, for whom Yoomi's baby bottle would be there in case they couldn't.[58]

Experience Is King

Howard Stevenson, HBS Sarofim-Rock Professor of Entrepreneurship, Emeritus, believes that MBA graduates should wait a while before they start a business because their post-MBA experience will give them better insights into specific markets.

For example, he encountered one entrepreneur who learned with experience that he could succeed by going into markets where the competitors were "dumb." He felt that the customers in those markets were poorly served by rivals and that he could win those customers by doing a better job than the incumbents.

In Stevenson's view, entrepreneurs should target markets where their skill sets match the market needs. And they should hire people to supplement their weaknesses.[59]

Pick Markets with Big Price Umbrellas

William Sahlman is Dimitri V. D'Arbeloff—Class of 1955 Professor of Business Administration at HBS. He offered a unique example of a start-up that liked to pick markets in which incumbents charged very high prices for a product that few people bought.

As Sahlman explained, John Osher started a company that made a popular battery-operated lollipop. He sold the company and was looking for something else to do. He figured out another opportunity and in 1999 invested $1.5 million in the new company, which he sold to Procter & Gamble in 2001 for $475 million.

That new company made the Dr. John Spinbrush—a $5 electric toothbrush that used much of the technology he had used for the battery-operated lollipop. Osher's company only had twelve employees but it was selling to companies like Target and Wal-Mart because it found people wanted an inexpensive electric toothbrush; he was competing with $80 models. Procter

& Gamble had been trying, unsuccessfully, to do what Osher had accomplished—so it bought the company.

For Sahlman this market opportunity modeled specific characteristics that HBS students might use to pinpoint other entrepreneurial opportunities:

- It was a big market with little innovation.
- There was a large price gap between the incumbent product and the one that Osher wanted to introduce.
- People were not buying the incumbent product because it was too expensive.
- If he introduced his product, incumbents would not be able to react without cannibalizing their existing businesses.[60]

VCs Want to Invest in Start-Ups Targeting Big Markets

For one VC firm, Massachusetts-based Flybridge Capital Partners, the ultimate goal is to build a larger company that will interest either a corporate buyer or public investors through an initial public offering.

And though there is no set size that the company needs to reach in order to do that, Flybridge believes that the start-up must target a big enough market so that a 10 percent market share will yield a company that could be worth at least $1 billion.

Flybridge expects an information technology start-up to achieve sales between $20 million and $40 million within three to five years of its initial investment. In medical products, a buyer might be interested if the start-up can develop a product to the point where it's closer to market introduction than the buyer can achieve on its own—even if the start-up has no sales. Moreover, while Flybridge does not set any specific target for a start-up's market share, it believes that an ambitious but achievable goal may be around 10 percent.[61]

A VC will estimate the market size that a start-up must target based on the level of revenues required for the start-up to break even should it achieve a 10 percent share of the market. Flybridge estimates that if a reasonably sized start-up employs eighty people, costing between $15,000 and $20,000 per person-month, it will need between $20 million and $40 million in sales in order to "declare victory." To that end, the start-up should target a market that generates between $200 million and $400 million.[62]

Naturally, there are many start-up CEOs whose desire to get funding will motivate them to present an overly optimistic estimate of the market that they're addressing. It is not uncommon for start-ups to claim that they're targeting a market of over $1 trillion.

SupplierMarket.com, a business-to-business e-commerce start-up founded in 1999, claimed in the 2000 initial public offering document it filed with the Securities and Exchange Commission that its target market, direct materials used in manufacturing—for example, nuts and bolts—was worth $1.5 trillion annually, even though SupplierMarket.com sales peaked at a little over $200,000 in the quarter before it was acquired.[63]

This suggests that the addressable market for the company's services may have been much smaller than $1.5 trillion. Even if SupplierMarket's addressable market was much smaller, this large number reassured investors that it had the potential to become a sizeable company if it could gain a reasonable market share.

If a start-up is targeting a very large market and can defend its market size estimate with reasonable assumptions, then it is more likely to benefit from its ambitious forecast.

HUNGRY START-UP STRATEGY APPROACH TO PICKING MARKETS

Based on expert opinion and the companies I interviewed, a few general principles emerge for a hungry start-up strategy approach to picking markets.

Principles of Picking Start-Up Markets

The new market a start-up selects should have the following four characteristics:

- *It should ignite the founder's passion.* The odds of start-up success are low, so a founder must have the skills and work ethic to overcome those obstacles. If a start-up CEO picks a market related to her strengths, she will be more likely to have the motivation needed to leap the hurdles in her way. I invested in a start-up whose CEO lacked passion for its online business partnering service. That lack of passion contributed to the start-up's inability to focus and its ultimate failure. His next start-up, a chain of women's health clubs, flowed from a topic about which he was passionate, and it has been successful.
- *It should aid in recruiting a team.* A start-up CEO with a successful track record has likely succeeded, in part, because of the team he has built and managed in the past. If he is passionate about the new business opportunity, there is a chance that many of the team members who contributed to the earlier start-up will share his excitement about the new one. And this shared enthusiasm could help recruit a capable team.

- *It should raise the odds of market-share gains.* All these enthusiastic and talented people will not succeed unless the new market that they're targeting puts a premium on their skills. But this approach is intended to weed out ideas with a limited fit between the team's skills and the new market's key success factors. Simply put, an entrepreneur can boost the start-up's chances for market share gains by picking a market based on the founder's skills and the importance of those skills to competitive success in the new market.
- *It should boost potential returns to capital.* By adding the additional requirement of targeting a large enough market, this approach also makes it more likely that capital providers will earn an attractive return.

Hungry Start-Up Strategy Market Selection Methodology

In theory a start-up could choose to compete in any market out there. For large companies with access to huge pools of capital, that's closer to the reality of their growth opportunities. They choose where to compete, in part, based on the inherent profit potential of the industry. But a start-up is likely to pick an industry based on three simpler tests:

- Is the founder passionate about the industry?
- Do her skills enable the start-up to compete there?
- Are total industry sales high enough to support a company that can scale to sell within a few years?

While applying a systematic approach to picking markets can be useful, not all entrepreneurs approach the decision systematically. For example, co-founder Max Levchin described the evolution of PayPal, the online payment service whose 2002 initial public offering gave him the liquidity to invest in close to fifty start-ups.[64]

It is clear from that conversation that many start-up CEOs stumble their way to success. How so?

PayPal did not start off as the online auction—eBay—payment mechanism for which it is rightly famous. It was originally called Confinity and delivered security software for handheld devices, such as Palm Pilots.

But Levchin did not achieve enormous success with that business model. Levchin and his colleagues got to thinking about handheld devices and that led them to focus on wallets. They acquired funding to develop an electronic wallet, and when they delivered the product, they began to get emails from people who were using part of their service as an eBay auction currency.

Levchin thought this was a terrible idea because it was not the purpose for which they had designed the product. However, they decided to scrap their original idea after six months to focus on serving the eBay community. In 2002, after Confinity's March 2000 merger with X.com (founded by Tesla Motors CEO Elon Musk), PayPal went public, giving Levchin an easy way to turn his 2.3 percent stake into cash.

With the persistent caveat that chance plays an important role in start-up success, there are many entrepreneurs who could benefit from a systematic approach to picking markets as summarized in Figure 2.1. The five-step method can be described as follows:

- *Identify start-up's core capabilities.* The founders of the start-ups that I spoke with had at least one start-up success under their belts or directly relevant corporate experience. And they decided to base their latest start-up on an opportunity that would tap into the strengths that contributed to their prior success.
- *Decide how capabilities will shape the criteria for selecting a target market.* In general, the start-up CEOs decided to offer a new product or service in a field related to their strengths or to go back to the customers whom they had served in a previous company and solve a different problem for them. In either case, they used the strengths that helped them succeed previously to shape the criteria for picking a target market for their next start-ups.

FIGURE 2.1   **Hungry Start-Up Approach to Picking Markets.**

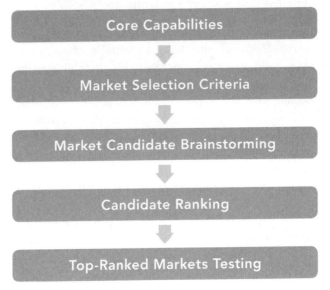

- *List potential target markets and pick ones that fit the selection criteria.* Start-ups need to come up with ideas for markets where they can use their skills. Quite frequently, these ideas emerge from a problem that they've encountered in a previous venture. For example, the founder of one start-up in which I invested had experienced tremendous frustration with the process of raising capital for his venture. So he decided to start a new company that would build a system of raising start-up capital to tap his programming skills while eliminating the frustrations he experienced in his previous venture. Unfortunately, this venture did not succeed, and a big reason was that the founder had overestimated the power of his programming skills to help the new venture gain market share in the start-up capital raising industry.
- *Rank the candidate markets by size and pick the one where the founder's strengths will yield the most market share.* This process of brainstorming ideas is necessarily creative but in order to pick their focus, start-up CEOs must shift mind-sets. Specifically, they need to rank their list of brainstormed ideas for potential markets based on specific criteria. Those criteria should include an objective assessment of how well its core strengths will help the venture gain market share and the market's total revenues and potential profits. Once they've ranked the list, it should be fairly straightforward to pick the initial focus of the start-up. But start-up CEOs should think of this initial focus as a hypothesis to test through customer feedback on prototype solutions.

Approaches to Sizing Start-Up Markets

Regardless of what sparks an entrepreneur to pick a specific market, it is critical to persuade others—including potential advisors, capital providers, employees, and partners—that the market that interests the company founders is big enough to warrant their time or money.

Some founders decline to discuss the size of their markets. Often that decision is simply due to their belief that the estimates are not particularly useful because there are too many unknowns and the numbers won't help the start-up grow. Sometimes, entrepreneurs simply do not think it's worth their time to develop a market-size estimate, choosing to defer such calculations until they are ready to charge a price for their product or service.

But most of the start-up CEOs I spoke with either outsource the market research, do it all themselves, or some of both. There is no single best answer. The advantages of outsourcing are that the provider may have better insight into the key assumptions and trends than the CEO. Doing the analysis internally forces the founder to get to know the market dynamics in much greater detail and this additional insight could help it to win in the marketplace.

Here are the different approaches I found in my research:

- *Market estimates based on independent analysis.* This approach is costly but requires the least time; it basically involves paying an independent firm, such as Forrester Research, for a report that estimates the size of the market.
- *Market estimates based on internal research.* In this approach, the entrepreneur gets research on the market size from the company's own market research or a market-size estimate from an industry association, coupled with a rough estimate of the segment of that market that the company seeks to target.
- *Market estimates based on research and assumptions.* In this approach, the entrepreneur creates a market model based on several key assumptions. These key assumptions might include the number of people in each segment that the company is trying to serve, how frequently they purchase the product or service, and how much they would pay for the product each time. When such market estimates are based on a combination of statistical data and customer interviews, it can be very compelling.

As illustrated in Figure 2.2, my interviews reveal that the most common approach is the second one.

Let's take a closer look at each.

FIGURE 2.2 How Start-Ups Estimate Market Size by Percent of Interviewees.

Market Estimates Based on Internal Research

Quantifying a market based on internal research is the most common approach. The key here is that entrepreneurs follow a four-step process:

- Decide which markets to target.
- Gather market size data from industry sources.
- Determine which segments of that market your company will target.
- Calculate the total addressable market by applying that segment's percentage of the total.

Here are some examples of how the start-ups I interviewed applied this approach to estimating the size of their markets:

Renting clothing to parents of growing children is a poorly solved problem that everybody has. After some research, I found that baby clothes represent a $24 billion market—of which 20 percent are sold at boutiques or second-hand clothing stores. Plum targets that $4 billion market segment.[65]

— **Caroline O'Connor, founder and CEO of Plum,** a service that lets parents rent clothing for their growing children.

Loki Studios hopes to persuade users to buy so-called digital goods, such as a more powerful sword to use in battles. The market for such digital goods is expected to grow from an estimated $8 billion in 2011 to $11 billion in 2015.[66]

— **Ivan Lee, CEO of Loki Studios**, a maker of mobile Pokemon-like games.

We got started in 2005 by a tax accountant and his MIT-grad client who were frustrated by the need to handle so many different tax-related documents. Our market is the $20 billion paid each year to individuals who prepare tax returns. We wanted to eliminate the annoying process of manual data entry from tax receipts and forms.[67]

— **Ed Jennings, CEO of Copanion,** which helps taxpayers to coordinate all the supporting documents for a tax return.

Estimating market size based on internal research reflects an entrepreneur's hunger to get the maximum amount of useful insight for the executive team and investors with the minimal investment. The benefit of this approach is that it gets that job done quickly and with limited expense. The negative is that it does not necessarily capture the insights that might result from getting the help of an experienced industry analyst whose extensive industry contacts might provide deeper insight.

This hungry attitude toward market research is well expressed by Pablo Fuentes, CEO of Proven.com, a service that connects blue-collar workers to potential employers. Fuentes did not provide details on the market size but he did say that he spent eight hours estimating Proven.com's market size—four hours on bottoms-up analysis (based on a customer-by-customer analysis of potential purchases) and four hours on top down (thinking about broader economic and market trends that would affect the size and growth of the market).[68]

Fuentes does not think that spending six months putting together a perfect quantitative analysis is worthwhile but he does think that product-market fit is important. This reflects Fuentes's belief that Proven's success depends far more on its ability to take market share by providing competitively superior value to customers.

While making a detailed estimate of the size of its potential market could help attract outside capital, Proven's ability to win new customers is better helped by understanding their specific unmet needs and how Proven can satisfy them.[69]

Nevertheless, Fuentes's views on this, while common, do not reflect the only—or even the best—way to estimate the size of the market. As a potential investor, I have listened to many presentations on market size and have often found that estimates based on internal research are a bit superficial.

This approach generally results in big market-size numbers intended to give investors comfort. However, if an entrepreneur is giving a presentation and cannot answer detailed investor questions about the market estimates, her request for capital may be turned down. That's why some start-ups apply a different approach to estimating the size of their market.

Market Estimates Based on Research and Assumptions

Quantifying a market based on internal research and assumptions about key variables driving the market size is the next most common approach. The benefit of this method is that it combines the best available top-down market-size estimates with very specific assumptions based on each company's evaluation of its market.

Developing market estimates based on research and assumptions is a four-step process:

- Decide which market segments to target.
- Gather market-size data from industry sources, focusing on the number of potential consumers in the market.

- Identify key assumptions such as purchase frequency and price.
- Calculate the total market size by multiplying the number of potential customers by the purchase frequency and price.

Although there are many variations of this basic approach, the general difference from the previous one is that entrepreneurs develop their market size estimates using a more detailed understanding of how customers actually purchase the product. This contrasts with the previous approach which is simpler, quicker, but possibly less accurate.

Here are three examples of how the start-ups I interviewed quantify a market based on internal research and assumptions.

T2 Biosystems

T2 makes diagnostic kits to help identify and stop deadly hospital infections. To turn this general concept into a viable business, T2 decided to focus on the problem of septic shock. This is a condition that occurs when patients get infections that rapidly shut down their immune systems. One such infection, Candida, is a fungus that occurs in 90,000 hospital patients a year and has a 40 percent mortality rate.

T2 used a logical approach for estimating the size of its potential market. It identified the number of people who present symptoms of Candida and multiplied that by the price per test that would be reimbursed by health insurers. T2 then went a step further; it estimated the benefit of its test in terms of cost savings for hospitals as a way to persuade them to buy its product.

As T2's CEO, Joe McDonough, explained, "We did make this estimate, and the U.S. market opportunity for our Candida panel is approximately $1.5 billion. This is based on 9 million patients that present with signs and symptoms that need to be tested and the reimbursement rate which is already in place at $150 per test based on the configuration of our test."[70]

T2 has also evaluated the costs that its test could save hospitals if widely adopted. Thanks to ongoing pressure on hospitals to control costs, such calculations are critical to persuading hospitals to invest in T2's product. According to McDonough, "The incidence of Candida is approximately 1 percent in the U.S., of the 9 million people who would be tested, or 90,000 people, and the cost savings associated with rapid detection of Candida is approximately $50,000 per patient. If we were to test and detect early for all of the 90,000 patients in the U.S., we could save the U.S. healthcare system approximately $4.5 billion (90,000 patients x $50,000 in savings per patient)."[71]

The general lesson from T2's approach to estimating its market opportunity is that a start-up must know the priorities of the people who pay for its product. And McDonough recognizes that cost savings are more important than saving lives when it comes to hospitals' decisions about whether to use T2's product. As McDonough explained, "While we have a Candida panel that can reduce the mortality rate for the 90,000 Candida patients from 40 percent to below 11 percent, market adoption will also require us to prove the economic benefits associated with the test. This has always been true but there is heightened need and awareness now in these interesting economic times."[72]

T2's approach to sizing its market reflects the priorities of its CEO, who wants T2 to deliver value to its stakeholders, including investors, customers, and patients. He is convinced that T2 could become a significant company and earn investors an attractive return if it can take a large enough share of the market for Candida testing. And in the process of doing that, T2 could save many lives while cutting billions in costs from the healthcare system.

Putting numbers on these benefits helps T2 gain market share and grow in value.

Trade Show Internet

Trade Show Internet (TSI) provides relatively inexpensive Internet connections for people attending trades shows. One of its founders was an actuary, hence he is skilled in quantitative forecasts. However, he does not believe that there is any value in taking the trouble to make these forecasts unless they will help TSI achieve its goals.

And TSI's goals have evolved. Initially, its co-founders were not concerned about estimating the potential size of the market. Since they had both experienced the pain of paying too much to access the Internet at trade shows and they had attended many such shows over the years, they knew from their own personal experience that there were many people who needed Internet access at trade shows.

So it was only when they decided that it was time to raise capital to finance the company's growth that they tried to estimate TSI's revenue potential. According to CEO Seth Burstein, "When we initially estimated the size of the industry, we did it by *feel*. When we were considering raising money, however, we did a back of the envelope calculation and calculated the size of the market to be $100 million."[73]

To get to that estimate, Burstein started with the number of trade shows, made an estimate of the number of exhibitors, and made an educated guess (there are no public data on this industry) about the portion of those exhibitors that would need Internet connectivity.

Here is how Burstein described the process of estimating the market size for TSI. He explained that the $100 million estimate "was based on the fact that there were 5,400 large shows annually in the U.S. (over 5,000 square feet). We figured each show would have an average of 100 exhibitors, 10 percent of which would need Internet connectivity. Then, from talking with others in the industry, we learned that the show organizer needs to yield about the same amount of money as the exhibitor needs, which brings the estimate to just over $100 million. Again, this is just a quick calculation, as the main player in the industry is a private company and there [are] limited data to base our estimates on."[74]

TSI's approach to estimating the market size is typical of companies competing in new industries. If there are no trade associations or industry consultants who have done market-size estimates, then entrepreneurs must make estimates based on the best available data.

In so doing, TSI applied a basic principle of hungry start-up strategy—develop a good-enough answer using a minimum of cash and time. For TSI, this approach has worked effectively to give investors the information they need and to reinforce the start-up's belief that it is targeting a market that's big enough for its ambitions.

Oyster

Oyster sends investigators out to hotels around the world to evaluate and rate them so travelers can make informed decisions about where to stay. To estimate the size of the market opportunity for investors, Oyster had the benefit of going after a market that already had publicly traded companies such as Priceline and Expedia. To give investors an idea of the potential value of Oyster—and hence their likely return on investment—the company simply added up the market capitalization of those companies and calculated Oyster's value if it could get a small share.

Ariel Charytan, Oyster COO, told me that he and his co-founder estimated the market capitalization of the publicly traded companies in the online travel industry and arrived at $50 billion. They reasoned that if they could get 2 percent of that market, their company would have a market capitalization of $1 billion which would give investors who gave them $20 million a very attractive return.[75]

They picked the market because they had a passion for the industry, and based on a previous start-up realized that they wanted to start a company that would resolve personal pain that others shared. They also wanted to make sure the potential market was big enough to justify a significant investment. Also, since Bain Capital was their investor, they got access to Bain & Co. consultants who conducted much more detailed market research.[76]

Oyster picked an investor whose decision to participate was based on Oyster's co-founders' successful track record and what the investor perceived as a sizable market opportunity based on the market capitalization of rivals.

Fortunately, for Oyster, its investor had access to the analysts of a leading consulting firm that provided much more detailed market analysis. Oyster did not have to pay extra for that. The lesson of this case is that if you pick an investor that cares about precision in market-size estimates, it helps if that investor has a world-class team of consultants to do the estimating.

The general lesson from all these examples is that a hungry start-up needs to be willing to take the risk of making an estimate of the market size that ultimately proves to be too big or too small. Entrepreneurs—particularly those who are targeting markets that have never been tapped by competitors—must be willing to make estimates using reasonable assumptions and explain those estimates clearly to potential investors.

Moreover, some entrepreneurs care about this because it helps convince them that their effort will pay off. Others do so only because investors require it. But a hungry start-up will find a way to do it well and with minimal expense and time.

Market Estimates Not Important

According to my interviews, CEOs who do not consider market-size estimates important constitute the third largest group when it comes to estimating market potential.

In general, there were two reasons that start-ups did not provide the market size estimates:

- The start-ups questioned the value of the estimates, particularly early in their development when it was not clear whether customers would pay for their product.
- They thought that the process for estimating market size and the reason for doing so were far more significant than the actual numbers that they derived.

Here are three examples of start-ups that did not consider it important to develop quantitative estimates of the size of their markets.

Apture

Apture is a service that lets Internet content consumers get more information about a typed phrase by moving their cursor over it. Apture did develop market-size estimates using a combination of research and assumptions. But its CEO, Tristan Harris, did not disclose the figure it developed largely because it had quickly become irrelevant.

His discussion reveals that he was guilty of a common error: Entrepreneurs think they need to develop detailed market size estimates before they meet with investors, whereas it is more important to discover which services customers are willing to pay for.

Harris believes that Apture did a good job of estimating the size of its market, but when its business focus changed, that effort proved to have been wasted. As Harris explained, "We did estimate the market size. I don't remember all the exact calculations we used, but we looked at Internet market statistics tracker comScore, reports for the top publishing sites on the Web, their aggregate unique visitors and page views, estimated the conversion rate from total page views to average links per page, to total number of Apture impressions to get a sense for our ability to impact a massive audience. Of course in all these calculations we were way off. . . . We had to first build a product all these publishers would actually want and it took us arguably one and a half tries before we got to that point."[77]

New entrepreneurs can frequently get sucked into believing that they need to devote weeks or months to developing very detailed market estimates. In Harris's view, it is important to think about whether the consumers of those estimates really need that level of analysis. As he said, "I think entrepreneurs commonly make the mistake of trying to do big projections of the market potential and impact of what they're doing, and don't spend nearly enough time verifying their underlying assumptions about why people would adopt their product, how quickly their customers will adopt it, and what kind of work it will require to get people to adopt it if they haven't already."[78]

When asked why Apture bothered to make projections in the first place, Harris replied, "That's a fun story. We pitched many angel investors, and one of them wanted us to—get this—create seven-year revenue projections. It was an absurd exercise when we hadn't baked the product yet (we'd only had a prototype), but in the end, it was more about getting ourselves to empathize with whether we really believe in our assumptions, and to think about a seven-year haul . . . beyond that, to pitch our angel investors on the $500K we raised, we also needed to show them a believable revenue model, even though we ultimately changed directions midway through."[79]

An important lesson from Apture's experience is that the hungry approach to estimating markets can pay off for start-ups. If Apture had sounded out the consumers of its market analysis—what I believe to be a very useful input to making many start-up decisions—it might have been able to give them the information they needed with less time and cost.

Cloudera

Cloudera's chief operating officer, Kirk Dunn, told me that it is very common for start-ups to pick a target market based on their revenue projections. Thus Dunn does not put much faith in market-size estimates. Instead, he advises start-ups selling to companies to find out how much those potential customers are spending to solve the problem the start-up is trying to address and to figure out whether that amount is trending higher.

Cloudera figures it's targeting a multisegment market worth "tens of billions of dollars of market opportunity." As Dunn said, "Most start-ups do their revenue projections and then look for a market that is big enough to justify the projections assuming a reasonable ramp up in market share to, say, 10 percent."[80]

But Dunn does not think this macro approach to the market provides much insight. Instead, he tries to talk to potential customers about how new and existing workloads are not being served by today's solutions, how big a budget they have allocated to solving the problem of extracting insight from large quantities of data, and how that allocation has been changing and is likely to evolve.[81]

The Cloudera example illustrates an important insight: Most investors and company executives look at revenue projections as a necessary piece of homework that is generally fraught with assumptions intended to yield a desired outcome. And that outcome is convincing investors to write a check.

But to get at the truth of a company's revenue potential, a more in-depth customer interview process yields better insight for decision-makers.

Yoomi

As we mentioned previously, IDEO worked with Yoomi, to develop its product and help with its business plan.

IDEO did not disclose its market-size statistics; however, more helpfully, it did reveal its approach to developing estimates. IDEO worked with Yoomi to develop market-size estimates in two ways: top-down, estimating the company's addressable market based on the total market size; and bottom-up, quantifying the market by multiplying how much each potential customer might spend by the number of potential customers.

As IDEO's Tom Hulme explained, "We did do initial sketches for market size in two ways, simply as a sanity check, top down and bottom up. In order to size the market top-down we looked at existing baby bottle and bottle warmer sales (the product slotted between the two), particularly the premium end of both markets. In order to size the market bottom up we estimated usage by each individual and then made assumptions around adoption rates based on our channel strategy. Finally, in order to take a view on potential adoption cycles/rates, we looked at new product launches in this market, particularly of luxury/innovative baby products."[82]

Hulme suggests that the primary customer for this market research was the founder and the team developing Yoomi's product, and they wanted confirmation that the business was worth building. As Hulme explained, "The thought exercise was simply to sanity check that the market was big enough to justify tooling etc., if we were going to launch solely in the UK initially, we didn't use the market sizing at all beyond that."[83]

Just because a company does not provide market-size estimates, it does not mean there is not a market for its products. These examples suggest that many start-ups find value in making detailed estimates of the market size in order to convince themselves and potential investors that there is a big enough opportunity to warrant investment of time and money.

The various approaches discussed in these examples offer useful methods that start-up CEOs can apply to their own companies.

Market Estimates Based on Independent Research

Quantifying a market based on independent research is the least common approach. This approach can be quite inexpensive and fast, because often the entrepreneurs can quickly search for a research report on their industry by a leading analyst and cite that research in their business plans.

Here's an example of how Adeptol, a start-up that I interviewed a few months before it was acquired—in October 2011 by Accusoft Pegasus[84]—applied this approach:

> The market opportunity for Adeptol is Enterprise Web 2.0, which is expected to be [worth] $4.6 billion by 2013 (estimated by Forrester). Enterprise 2.0 is cloud and Web 2.0 without social networking. I think it is not about market size; it is about how big an opportunity there is and how big . . . a share of that pie [you see you can take]. It is a validation that you are creating a product for a segment for which there is a demand and you can sell to a percent of that easily. Market size also defines how much work you need to do on marketing and for selling your product. A larger market size means easier selling, as people already know the issue and are ready to spend to get it taken care of.[85]
> **— Sid Joshi, marketing vice president of Adeptol**

Using independent research to size markets is quick and generally inexpensive—unless the start-up actually hires a research firm to develop a customized report. In that sense, it is a hungry approach because it does not cost much to find a report on the Web and apply it to your market. The question is whether the research answers the questions of concern to start-up founders and investors. If so, that research can be very cost-effective. If not, other approaches—along the lines outlined earlier in the chapter—should be used.

HUNGRY-START-UP MARKET-PICKING TACTICS

An entrepreneur is highly likely to choose a market based on his or her knowledge, experience, and skills.

These factors are all interrelated. For example, entrepreneurs tend to choose their first work experience based to some extent on what they're good at doing. That's because companies have plenty of potential hires from whom to choose and they try to hire the best.

While the specific company and position that hires the future entrepreneur may appear somewhat random at the time, the simple fact of being hired can be seen as the market's way of telling you what you're good at. Similarly, the companies that reject that future entrepreneur's job application provide information about where that person's weaknesses may reside.

If 10 is the ideal number of years for an entrepreneur to work for someone else before going off on his own, then he will likely have three or more work experiences before taking the first plunge in those bracing start-up waters.

Those work experiences will shape the start-up CEO's thoughts about his strengths and weaknesses relative to competitors. They may also help the CEO see opportunities or experience "pain" that he believes will be something he can alleviate through his work running the start-up.

It's difficult to put a precise number on the size of the potential market opportunity that an entrepreneur might want to attack, particularly when the start-up faces no competitors and is thus creating a market out of thin air.

The need to estimate the size and growth of a start-up market opportunity may not be very high for the entrepreneur.[86] However, it is almost certain that an investor—particularly a VC firm—will demand a well-thought-out market-size estimate before writing a check to the start-up.

Entrepreneurs often believe that such a process is a waste of time. Instead they make a guess about which market they believe will need their product or service, build the product, and if the supposed customers do not appear, they change their focus until they find customers who do.

For example, Steve Rothschild, an entrepreneur in Worcester, Massachusetts, mentioned two start-ups he ran that changed their initial focus. Bulbs.com sells light bulbs online and Rothschild expected that consumers would be its primary customers; however, by early 2012, 82 percent of Bulbs. com's customers were businesses. The reason is that while both groups of customers "loved the service, businesses used lots more bulbs—placing large orders and doing so more frequently."[87]

Rothschild also runs a lighting fixtures retailer, Access Fixtures, which he expected would generate most of its revenues from "end user businesses who were investigating lighting solutions." However, electrical contractors turned out to be its "bread and butter."

So why should start-ups bother to engage in a structured process for picking markets? The short answer is that this structure can save time and money for the entrepreneur. Instead of spending money to build a product and try to sell it to someone who doesn't want it, a structured process can help the entrepreneur find those dead ends before spending time and money. And this process also can help the venture get started on a customer with a real need.

Here's how entrepreneurs can apply the hungry start-up strategy approach to picking markets.

Identify Start-Up's Core Capabilities

The market values core capabilities—skills that a CEO has demonstrated through prior experience. Examples of such core capabilities include designing new products, selling to new customers, and managing a talented staff.

But when it comes to picking markets, it's not enough for the CEO to be good at such a skill. The entrepreneur must also be better at the skill than the CEOs who run their current competitors.

The reason competitive superiority is so important should be obvious: If the start-up is not better than the competition in important skills that the market values, then it's probably going to be harder for the start-up to gain market share.

So what should start-up CEOs do to determine whether their ventures have such core capabilities? Here are four steps you might follow, possibly with help from an objective outsider:[88]

- *Identify potential competitors.* This step could be accomplished by talking with potential customers for your venture and asking them who they would consider buying from besides your company and why.
- *Evaluate the skills of competitors' key executives.* Although few start-up CEOs believe this is worth doing (perceiving that focusing on competitors will not help customers), the opposite could well be true. That's because if competitors are more capable of meeting customers' needs,

you could have a much harder time gaining market share.[89] Entrepreneurs who believe that evaluating competitors' executives is important should take the following steps:

- Identify the key executives in the competing venture.
- Evaluate your competitors' strengths in key skill areas based on their stated experience and interviews with their former colleagues.
- Rank their skills based on each one's importance to helping the venture compete.
- Score each executive's skills relative to the potential competitors.

- *Conduct an objective assessment of your venture's skills.* Next, follow the same steps and apply them to your own start-up.
- *Decide whether your venture's capabilities exceed those of your competitors.* Finally, the CEO should compare the start-up's executive skills to competitors' and reach a conclusion about whether the start-up has what it takes to win in the targeted market.

Decide How Capabilities Will Shape the Criteria for Selecting a Target Market

If the results of the previous step identify a set of core capabilities, the next step is to identify the tests you can use to determine the criteria to use that will help you select from among a long list of potential markets. Here are some potential criteria you might use to select target markets:

- Large number of potential customers.
- Upward trends in prices.
- Meaningful trends supporting rapid market growth.
- Established competitors who will have difficulty copying your product.
- Customers who are looking for a solution to an important unmet need.
- The start-up has the capabilities that could provide customers a solution that competitors would have trouble replicating.
- Potential to win a significant share of the market.

List Potential Target Markets and Pick Ones That Fit the Selection Criteria

The next step—brainstorming about potential markets—is hard to structure effectively. Unless he or she is very uncomfortable with the process or believes that being involved would stifle creativity, the start-up CEO should lead this brainstorming process.

Here's a general approach that can help surface a wider range of ideas:

- Assemble a team with different backgrounds and experience—including potential customers.
- Encourage all participants to do their own research—consider the markets that current or potential competitors are targeting, read articles about the start-up's technology, talk to industry experts—before meeting.
- Start the meeting by discussing the purpose and the underlying values for the brainstorming session, emphasizing a desire to get as many ideas as possible, to encourage questions and creative problem solving by all participants, and to shun efforts to shut down idea generation.
- Finish the meeting by developing a list of all the ideas generated and ask participants to give each idea a grade (e.g., A, B or C), and a reason for each grade.

Rank the Candidate Markets by Size and Pick the One That Will Yield the Most Market Share

The final step is to apply an analytical approach to ranking all the ideas generated in the brainstorming session. To do this, the CEO should take the following steps:

- Rank the market evaluation criteria developed previously.
- Gather research with the help of the brainstorming team to evaluate each of the potential target markets.
- Develop a spreadsheet for force-ranking each of the potential target markets on each of the evaluation criteria.
- Ask team members to review the research and develop their own preliminary ranking of the potential market segments.
- Moderate a team discussion of the preliminary findings of each of the brainstorming group members.
- Synthesize the results of this discussion and develop a preliminary ranking of the potential market segments.
- If there is consensus around the top five segments, focus on the first several segments. If not, conduct further research to explore whether disagreements over the market rankings can be resolved.

Such market discovery is wonderful, when it works. However, the process described here is intended to use research to screen out the most unlikely market targets so the venture can make the most effective use of its time and money.

MARKETS: DID YOU PICK THE RIGHT ONES?

The foregoing discussion of picking and sizing markets may be raising questions in your mind about whether your start-up has the taken the right approach. To help you reach a conclusion, here are some more detailed questions:

- Do you know who will use your market potential estimates?
- Do you understand why the market potential estimates are important to them?
- Can you describe what specific information they need to make up their minds?
- Have you provided the information required using credible sources and reasonable assumptions?
- Did you develop the market estimates in the quickest and lowest-cost manner possible while still satisfying the needs of people using your market potential estimates?

If you have solid answers to these questions then your choice and rationale for your target markets will serve your venture well. And if not, these questions may help you rethink those choices until you do have solid answers to them.

SUMMARY

Picking the right markets for a venture is a crucial decision. However, early in a venture's development, it may be difficult to know which market will place the highest value on its product. Because of that uncertainty and hungry entrepreneurs' urge not to spend time and money on initiatives with limited payoff, they may defer precise market-size estimates. Yet many start-up CEOs want to spend just enough time to assure themselves that their product development efforts are likely to yield a meaningful return for the company founders. Moreover, investors are likely to be interested in market-size estimates, and this chapter has provided several effective approaches for developing compelling estimates without spending too much time or money.

The key to this frugal and fast approach to developing market estimates is to find people with expertise in the market you are targeting. Entrepreneurs should search for the following kinds of people:

- Scholars who specialize in that industry

- Successful entrepreneurs who are now investing in the industry
- Consultants who focus on estimating the size and key trends driving industry growth

Entrepreneurs should approach these people and ask them to share their thoughts on the industry and to propose introductions to others who might have an interesting perspective—as well as people who might need the company's product. In this way, within a matter of weeks, the entrepreneur can obtain significant insight into the market size, growth rate, and key trends.

CHAPTER 3

Raising Capital
Maintain Your Fighting Weight

WHEN IT COMES TO hungry start-up strategy, there is often no more compelling trade-off than the one between the hunger to control the start-up's destiny and the need to pay its bills. Most entrepreneurs postpone as long as possible taking money from outside investors.

And the reason is fairly simple: Taking an investor's capital means ceding some control of the venture. And since controlling the way they spend their time is often the most important reason that founders start their companies, it can be painful to raise capital. Of course, with capital comes the pleasure of being able to meet a start-up's financial obligations and to pay for its growth initiatives. But that hunger for control means that capital's silver lining also has a cloud.

This raises a series of burning issues that start-up CEOs struggle to resolve. There are many answers to these questions and we will explore them through the lens of the companies and experts I interviewed for this book. Here are the key questions and my summary of the key findings from these interviews below:

- *How can an entrepreneur finance the start-up without selling an equity stake?* The best way to do this—there are not too many examples of people I spoke with who do this—is to operate the business in such a way that its customers finance its growth. The reason this is so rare, is that in most industries, there is sufficient competition that a business with low capital costs and attractive operating margins will draw in competition that will narrow the gap between prices and costs. But a few businesses have pulled off that trick. As we saw with BrewDog, it's also possible to get suppliers to finance your business by letting you delay payment. If that does not work, all is not lost, if you happen to have a large pile of cash, you can finance a start-up's losses out of your own pocket. Many ventures keep going by borrowing against credit cards and—before the financial crisis of 2008—their home equity. Needless to say all these options have the benefit of allowing the company to maintain control of its destiny; but customer and supplier financing does so without draining the founder's pockets while the other ones are riskier.

- *If selling stock is the only option, who should the entrepreneur approach to raise the venture's initial capital rounds?* Quite often, entrepreneurs who decide they must sell a piece of their company try to raise small amounts of capital from a variety of classes of investors. These include so-called "angel investors"—wealthy individuals who typically make five- or six-figure investments in start-ups—as well as friends and family. The angels, generally with prior business experience that helped them generate their nest egg, can be the best option for start-ups at the earliest stages because they can apply their expertise to boost the venture's growth rate. But some angels can get too aggressive about imposing their views on start-up founders. Because of this risk—and because angels are less likely to finance a first-time entrepreneur—friends and family can be the best or only option for raising seed capital. Unfortunately, it can be particularly difficult to tell your father and mother that you just burned through the $100,000 they gave your company and that you are going to shut it down.

- *Whom should an equity-selling start-up CEO target for later capital rounds?* As it happens, many of the companies I interviewed faced this question. And they concluded that it makes sense to sell shares to a VC firm or corporate investor.[90] Each of these kinds of investors has specific strengths and weaknesses from the start-up's perspective. VC firms—if well-selected—can bring prestige, access to customers and partners, and skills that help the start-up's manage its growth. However, VCs may also decide to replace the founder and to shut down the start-up if it does not meet its performance goals. Corporate investors generally do not bring the same level of prestige or company-growing experience; however, start-ups that depend, for example, on big telecommunications companies to deliver their services often find it useful to invite these corporate customers to invest as a way to align more closely the interests of the start-up with those of the corporate partner.

- *How can start-up CEOs pick investors who boost the chances that the benefits of raising outside capital will exceed its costs?* Start-up CEOs should choose the specific individuals from the investment firm who will be working with their venture. To find the right individuals, start-up CEOs should talk to other CEOs who have worked with the specific individuals to figure out how they deal with the inevitable turmoil of a venture during board meetings and under what circumstances they have fired CEOs of their portfolio companies. More specifically, start-up CEOs should work with partners or executives from their capital providers who pass the following three tests:

- *Chemistry.* The partner or corporate executive who will take a board seat and the start-up CEO get along well.
- *Shared vision.* The VC firm or corporation and the start-up agree on what the company ought to look like in the future (e.g., they share a vision for the company).
- *Value-added.* The VC firm or corporate investor can "add value," e.g., it can help the start-up grow by offering practical help beyond writing a check, including introducing the company to customers or partners and helping to hire engineers.[91]

RAISING START-UP CAPITAL

The most important insight for start-up CEOs is to reject the conventional wisdom—develop a business plan and use it to snare a check from big VC firms—about how to raise capital. As we hinted earlier, there are some significant problems with this approach, particularly for a freshly minted venture. These problems include:

- Loss of control to the VC firm
- Wasting time trying to raise capital from VCs who will not pay attention to your business because you were not introduced by a mutual acquaintance, target a business that is outside the VC's area of expertise, or lack a track record of entrepreneurial success
- Inability to negotiate favorable terms because of a failure to demonstrate the viability of the venture's business model

The Experts Weigh In on Ways to Raise Start-Up Capital

Perhaps, then, it comes as no surprise that very few start-ups raise VC. Dane Stangler, a Kauffman Foundation researcher, estimates that between 1 and 3 percent of the financing for start-ups comes from VC firms. And that comes later in their development. He pointed out that a 2009 study written by Paul Kedrosky, *Right-Sizing the U.S. Venture Capital Industry*, found that only 16 percent of the 900 Inc. 100 companies between 1997 and 2007 took VC.[92]

During a start-up's initial stages, the funds come from friends, family, and founders. As a start-up grows, the money comes from bank loans, credit cards, and, before 2008, home equity. And only if the start-up has reached a further stage of development does it get equity investment.

But this is not the only start-up financing path. Different methods work for different ventures, depending on many factors, including a venture's stage of development, its industry, and its business model. Consider the advice of Stevenson.

Get Customers to Fund Your Start-Up

Rather than urging entrepreneurs to go out and raise VC, Stevenson argues that the best source of capital is customers, the second is suppliers, and the third is funds from angel investors or VC firms.[93]

And regardless of where you get the capital, Stevenson believes that entrepreneurs should sip gently from the capital cup, rather than slurp from it. To that end, Stevenson argues that start-ups should not spend money on expensive furniture and other frills that will siphon off capital that could be used to create value for customers.

While the idea of raising capital from customers may seem intuitive, it can take two forms. The most basic one is that customers buy your product and after you've covered the costs of producing the product and your fixed costs, you have money left over.

Another way customers can finance a start-up is to buy an equity stake. This approach can be quite helpful because when customers make such an investment, they signal that they are getting enormous value from the start-up's product and are willing to bet money that other customers will come to the same conclusion. In general, capital investment from customers also signals confidence in the start-up's management team.

This can be a dangerous approach because it puts the start-up at the mercy of the customer and amounts to an acquisition at a very low price. As Proven's Fuentes said, "If a large customer buys a stake, they have you by the balls . . . you have to listen to everything they want whether or not it makes sense for the company, and they can potentially scare other customers and/or acquirers."[94]

Fuentes rejected such an opportunity to avoid these risks. "I personally turned down a *very* large potential customer who wanted to do exactly that . . . because we would have essentially turned into that company's R&D arm at a shit valuation . . . I would rather die as a baby elephant than live as a full-grown mouse."

Get Suppliers to Fund Your Start-Up

To understand how this would work, it helps to step back and examine Stevenson's definition of entrepreneurship: the pursuit of opportunity beyond resources currently controlled.

This definition suggests two important principles for entrepreneurs:

- They should be able to identify good opportunities.
- Currently controlled resources should not constrain their ability to imagine those opportunities.

These principles have important implications for small and large companies. Start-ups with few resources should assume that if they can find the right opportunities, they will be able to persuade others to give them the resources required to capture those opportunities. And as we'll see in Chapter 8, established companies ought to find a way both to preserve the best of their existing resources while creating new business initiatives to capture new opportunities.

To explain these implications, Sahlman offered the example of Barnes & Noble vs. Amazon. He praised Barnes & Noble for seeing an opportunity in locking up the best retail locations and filling them with 125,000 books. When Amazon decided to get into the bookstore business, Sahlman noted, it decided not to try to compete for locations but used real estate in a different way—to store millions of books in warehouses that it would ship to customers after they ordered online.[95]

Unlike Barnes & Noble, Amazon had no retail locations or other assets to protect. Amazon redefined the opportunity and captured it with a very different financial model in which its suppliers helped finance its business.

Sahlman, who started teaching entrepreneurial finance at HBS in the early 1980s, emphasized that Amazon was operating a $34 billion business with *negative* $3 billion in so-called operating capital (inventory minus accounts payable plus net plant and equipment). By contrast, Barnes & Noble used $1.3 billion in *positive* operating capital.

Simply put, negative operating capital is a measure of how much capital suppliers provide a company. Sahlman's analysis of its operating capital reveals that Amazon was able to get its suppliers to delay paying $1.3 billion more money that it owed them than the value of Amazon's inventory, plant, and equipment.

This does not work for all start-ups, but Amazon's negative operating capital hints that suppliers can be a source of start-up capital (even though Amazon has not been a start-up for well over a decade).

The Launchpad Approach

Since there is no one-size-fits-all approach to raising start-up capital, it helps to have a mind-set that encourages frugal experimentation and learning. For that, it's worth considering an approach developed by Stanford University's Design School—called Launchpad.

Developed by Michael Dearing, a former eBay executive, and Perry Klebahn, a former COO at clothing retailer Patagonia, Launchpad teaches an approach to start-up development that can be applied to all the key choices that entrepreneurs make, including raising start-up capital.[96]

In a nutshell, Launchpad's so-called "design thinking" approach consists of four steps (illustrated by Pulse, a news-reading app builder started by a pair of Launchpad grads):

- *Observation.* A Launchpad team might observe that the technology for consuming online news could be much easier to use. For example, Pulse noticed that a typical online news site forces users to navigate to the bottom of a hierarchy of stories to read the one they want and then click their way back to the top to get to the next story. This raised a basic question: "Is there a way to make it easier for people to consume news online?"
- *Point of view.* Design thinking next pushes the team to develop a point of view, or hypothesis, on those questions. For example, Pulse tried to depict news stories as square images with captions.
- *Prototyping.* Teams then build a rough version fast and watch what users do with it. Pulse developed a prototype and sold a $4 iPad version on Apple's app store.
- *Endless iteration.* The final process—it's not really a step because design thinking urges teams to loop through it repeatedly—is going out to people, getting their feedback on the prototype, and adapting the prototype in response to the feedback. For Pulse, this meant it quickly got 35,000 users; a figure that spiked to 250,000 after Steve Jobs praised Pulse at a developer's conference. It later used feedback to decide to give the product away in order to boost its user base, which quickly soared to 3 million users.

The Pulse example reinforces an important point that we saw first in the case of BrewDog: Entrepreneurs should seek to engage highly influential people. For Pulse, Steve Jobs's endorsement was critical to its rapid popularity spurt, and without Michael Jackson's influential endorsement, BrewDog would not have been as successful. But the product must deliver the endorser's promised benefit so that people who try it will keep coming back.

While the Launchpad approach would certainly apply to developing a product, it can also be used when it comes to raising capital. Instead of getting a list of big name VC firms and delivering elaborate business plan presentations, design thinking drives teams to think about how much capital they need and what kinds of mentoring will help boost their odds for success. At an early stage, this might mean that a Launchpad start-up raises $300,000 from a small group of angel investors with experience in sales and business development rather than raising $10 million at that stage from Sand Hill Road luminaries.

When it comes to raising capital, the power of influential endorsers is just as relevant. For example, if Steve Jobs and Bill Gates had been publicly clamoring to invest in Pulse or BrewDog, their interest would attract other investors. And even without that investment interest, Pulse's huge boost in traffic resulting from Jobs's endorsement of it would have spurred investors' ardor.

HUNGRY START-UP STRATEGY APPROACH TO RAISING CAPITAL

The hungry start-up approach to raising capital matches up the real-options approach introduced in Chapter Two to setting short-term goals to different sources of capital. Its purpose is to match different kinds of investors to the varying risks and rewards that a start-up faces at different stages of its development.

Figure 3.1 depicts the hungry start-up capital raising as a sequence of real options.

Three Steps for Applying the Hungry Start-Up Approach to Raising Capital

- *Bootstrap prototype.* The first step for a start-up is generally to use the founder's capital and "sweat-equity" to build a prototype of its product or service. This prototype should be good enough to show to potential capital providers and should ideally reflect several rounds of feedback and refinement from potential customers. If the start-up can build a working prototype that potential customers like, then it is in a better position to go on to step 2 in the capital-raising process.
- *Raise seed capital to build up customer base.* In step 2, the start-up makes a pitch for money to friends and family or angels. Positive customer feedback on the product—coupled with an estimate of the number of potential customers who might buy the product—can be an important

FIGURE 3.1   Hungry Start-Up Approach to Raising Capital.

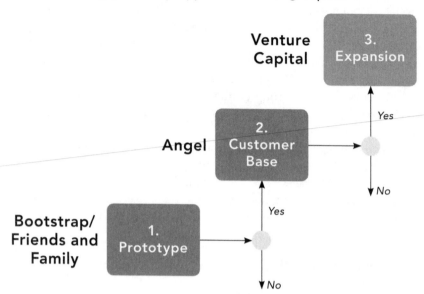

assumption used to calculate the start-up's value. Once that value has been negotiated, then the potential investor's stake in the company can be calculated (for example, if the start-up is valued at $1 million post-money and the investor agrees to provide $50,000, the company would exchange the cash for 5 percent of its shares). In general, the entrepreneur might raise the money from friends and family if no strategic guidance is needed but pick an angel if the start-up needs help with sales or distribution partnerships.

- *Seek expansion capital.* The successful completion of steps 1 and 2 is most likely to inspire venture firms to invest so that the start-up can expand. VC firms are more likely to invest in information technology and biotechnology start-ups and usually shun investing in most other kinds of companies. By contrast, banks almost never provide expansion capital to the start-ups that interest VC firms. However, as mentioned earlier, banks will lend expansion capital to start-ups in industries with what they consider to be valuable collateral. There are other options for expansion capital, including customers and suppliers, founders' deep pockets, grants from foundations, government loans, and business plan competitions. If a start-up has already generated significant sales, the expansion capital might be used to introduce new products or to branch out into new market segments, such as new geographies or client industries. Some start-ups—particularly those in biotechnology or medical testing—can raise money from VC firms without a product or a customer. It would be a misnomer to call this expansion capital but the amount raised at this stage can often be in the tens of millions as the company seeks to pass regulatory hurdles before the product can be legally sold.

Benefits of Hungry Start-Up Strategy Capital-Raising Methodology

This approach to raising capital offers two benefits to start-ups:

- *Maximized entrepreneurial control.* By delaying as long as practical the time when a start-up takes in outside capital, the entrepreneur can build frugally a version of its product that—if all goes well—can dazzle customers and investors alike. In so doing, the entrepreneur can present a compelling case for investing in the company while boosting its value high enough so that the capital providers will not be in a position to boot out the founder. Moreover, by overcoming the biggest start-up risks early, the entrepreneur can achieve greater negotiating leverage before seeking VC.
- *Linked capital raising to achieving key milestones.* If a start-up can build a compelling prototype without much capital, then it will be in a position to persuade capital providers to invest—helping the start-up generate its initial sales. And if the start-up reaches "critical mass" in that initial market, it can raise expansion capital. This approach enables the founder to present a compelling business case for capital at each stage.

RAISING CAPITAL: FIVE APPROACHES

I've identified five approaches to raising capital and the frequency of these approaches among those I interviewed is illustrated in Figure 3.2.

In order of frequency, the following list explains the five strategies I found in interviewing start-up CEOs:

- *Repeat entrepreneurs seeking "value-added" investors (45 percent).* The founders of companies in this category have previously started and exited new ventures—thus establishing themselves as investment worthy. They often can choose among investors and pick the ones with whom they have good chemistry who can help the start-up with

FIGURE 3.2 **Sources of Start-Up Capital, by Percent of Interviewees.**

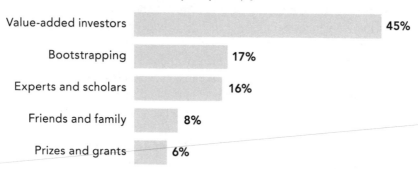

Value-added investors — 45%
Bootstrapping — 17%
Experts and scholars — 16%
Friends and family — 8%
Prizes and grants — 6%

critical activities such as recruiting, partnerships, selling, and product development.

- *Bootstrapping (17 percent).* The founders of companies that bootstrap invest their time and money to get the company off the ground. Often they do so because they have no previous start-up experience and are not in a good position to raise capital from investors. In some cases, they have worked with investors in previous start-ups and have decided that the benefits of maintaining control of a venture's destiny outweigh the cost of not getting investors' cash.

- *First-time entrepreneurs with talent-based connections seeking "value-added" investors (16 percent).* The founders of companies in this category have not previously started and exited new ventures—but thanks largely to their academic achievements they have access to top investors who have had success investing in companies from that school. They often can choose among investors and pick the ones who add value as described in the first item in this list.

- *Friends and family (8 percent).* Start-ups in this category persuade their friends and family to part with their cash in exchange for a stake in the venture. Entrepreneurs generally understand that the risk of not providing a return on these investments will strain their most important personal relationships. It is a measure of their belief in the venture and their desperate need for capital that this method of raising money is so common.

- *Business plan competition (6 percent).* Start-ups in this category are largely founded by student entrepreneurs who have won cash and services through a university business plan competition. Since some of the more prominent competitions are judged by local VC firms, the winners often find themselves in a good position to use the proceeds of their competition win to help build up their businesses to the point that they can raise capital from venture firms.

The remaining 8 percent of the companies I interviewed used other means for raising capital, as we will note.[97]

While not explored in-depth in the cases, another useful source of financing for start-ups is incubators. These are typically established by a city or region to provide office space for a high-potential start-up that either must raise or receive a grant of sufficient capital to develop a prototype of its product and raise more financing before it is required to leave the nest after six to 12 months.

An example of this is Worcester-based Massachusetts Biomedical Initiatives (MBI). CEO Kevin O'Sullivan explained that MBI is creating a breeding ground for biotech start-ups in the Worcester area. And it's not easy for a biotech company to get space at one of its Life Science Business Incubators (LSBIs).[98]

O'Sullivan notes that LSBIs have a 15 percent capture rate, meaning that for every 100 biotech companies that apply, only 15 get to operate in one of his labs. He picks the ones that are run by true entrepreneurs—the kind of people who, even though they may have young children, are so committed to the venture that they are willing to leave a secure job at a big company like Pfizer to start a company. He also wants the start-ups to have a good business and science plan, and a year of funding.

And he is always looking for new companies because he kicks them out after a year. During that time, he hopes the company will make enough progress within the LSBI to go off and get a bigger space to support more employees. About 75 percent of the companies that have left the LSBI are still standing, according to O'Sullivan.

We'll now examine the five most common approaches from my interviews—first focusing on the ones that are consistent with the hungry start-up approach to capital raising—bootstrapping, friends and family, angels/early-stage, and VC firms—and then examining business plan competitions.

Bootstrapping

Bootstrapping—operating a business with funds provided by the start-up's founders and/or the company's cash flows—is probably the most common form of venture finance. Its most obvious advantage is that it enables start-up founders to retain control—particularly as they try to prove that they can build a product for which customers are willing to pay.

But bootstrapping is also scary since there's a risk that the founders will burn through all their savings before they can come up with a viable prototype. As Charm told me, there are no hard and fast rules about raising start-up capital and that entrepreneurs should be open at any time to the chance that capital will become available thanks to a winning pitch to a potential investor.

Charm also raised another compelling idea: A venture does not necessarily need to target a billion dollar market to succeed. If an entrepreneur can raise only, say, $250,000 in capital, then he or she can build a business that generates an attractive return on that capital by targeting a smaller market or by outsourcing a critical activity, like sales. Instead of hiring a sales force, the start-up could form a distribution partnership which would use up less capital. And even though the start-up would get a smaller percentage of the sales, the lower cost would make the partnership more profitable.[99]

Bearing this in mind, entrepreneurs who are bootstrapping their ventures should make the following choices:

- Decide whether they ought to offer a high margin service as a way to finance the development of a product that may take time to gain market acceptance.
- If such a service does not make sense, consider the quickest and least expensive way to build a prototype of the product that can help the start-up get market feedback and customer acceptance.
- Take advantage of the widespread availability of inexpensive or free access to computing and marketing resources, such as cloud computing and social networking services, including Twitter and Facebook, respectively.

Here are examples of four bootstrapping approaches used by start-ups:

- *Self-financing: Tutor Vista.*
  Tutor Vista is my fourth venture. I got the idea for Tutor Vista after visiting the U.S. and finding that two of the biggest areas of concern in magazines and newspapers were that health care and education in the U.S. were in crisis. I spoke to 100 parents, teachers, and students in the U.S. asking them "Will they accept the service? Will it work? Will parents pay? Will they accept teachers from India?" The general reaction has been positive. Children were comfortable with having teachers from India. They thought it was cool. American parents had no reservations about Indian teachers. I was worried that they would have problems

with the Indian accents and their knowledge of U.S. curriculum. But they said that they were comfortable with their children learning academic subjects such as Math and Science from Indian tutors. I financed the company for the first six months to show that we could gain traction in order to raise venture capital.[100]

- *Profits from another business: Min.Us.* Founded in October 2010, Min.Us makes it easy for people to share pictures, and videos. Its cash comes in part from the profits of Cirtex, a global Web hosting company that John Xie, Min.us's CEO, founded a few years earlier. Those profits combined with an additional $200,000 Xie raised in early 2011 are keeping Min.us afloat.[101]
- *Internal VC: Critical Software.* This is an enterprise software company founded by a group of PhD students from Portugal's University of Coimbra. Since Portugal has virtually no VC industry, Critical Software financed itself from internal cash generation; it set up a $10 million internal VC fund to finance the creation of new technologies that can be the basis for creating new companies.[102]
- *Customer profits: TSI.* CEO Seth Burstein notes that TSI's cash flows make it nearly self-financing. Clients rent the equipment and pay up front. The high profit margins pay for the assembly and there is sufficient capital to pay for sales and marketing efforts.[103]

However a start-up chooses to bootstrap its business, the best way is to make the business inherently profitable so that it can operate without raising outside capital. The next best way may be to finance it with the cash flow from another business that the founder started. If a start-up is interested in growing very quickly, it may choose to bootstrap for a short period before raising larger amounts of capital from outside sources. However, TSI and Critical Software are examples of companies that appear quite content to bootstrap for the long run.

Friends and Family

Raising capital from friends and family is particularly common for ventures that are not going after technology-based market opportunities. This is not to say that many technology-based ventures do not start off raising funds from friends and family. However, if a technology-based venture has the potential to grow rapidly and its founders have prior entrepreneurial success, the odds are better that the venture will be able to raise VC.

But non-tech ventures generally do not interest VC firms because most venture investors do not perceive rapid growth in other kinds of ventures, for example, retailing.

One example from my own experience is a health club venture whose business plan I reviewed. I was convinced that the venture had a good chance to become profitable; however, its founders were clearly committed to taking the time to make sure each location was successful before expanding. While I agreed with their goals, I did not perceive the venture as offering the potential for high investment returns.

Venture investors often react this way to retail start-ups. Hence, their founders must turn elsewhere for funds. In addition to raising capital from friends and family, they try to follow the prescriptions that Stevenson offers—by seeking capital from customers and suppliers as well.

Here are three examples of start-ups that raised capital from friends and family:

- *Treca.* To finance Treca, a Peru-based retail store chain, Manuel Rizo-Patron Terrero could not go to Peru's banks, which do not extend credit to a money-losing start-up. So he turned to family and friends, and raised $250,000. Cordillera, his camping equipment store near Machu Picchu, has not exactly turned out as planned. It generated about $250,000 in sales—roughly half the level Rizo-Patron Terrero had expected. But the good news was that Rizo-Patron Terrero used his contacts from his previous job as a retail buyer—three years at Chile's Falabella one of South America's largest retailers—to get a better deal from suppliers North Face, Columbia, Merrell, Patagonia, and other brands. Instead of the "nobody" deal—no credit and a 35 percent margin—Rizo-Patron Terrero managed to negotiate a 40 percent average margin and sixty days of payment credit.[104]

- *Chattersource.* Chattersource gives college students discounts at local retailers. According to its co-founders, it has different "chunks" of revenue. Its housing guide is a good source of advertising revenue because housing management companies generally have regular cash flow. And it also generates revenues from operating its marketplace for buying and selling furniture and other items. Having sunk their own money and that of friends and family into Chattersource, co-founders Kristina Anderson and Amy Cooper next focused on whether to expand the site more deeply in Philadelphia—perhaps by hiring new salespeople to target new advertisers—or to open up new Chattersources in student-heavy cities like Boston, Chicago, and San Francisco.[105]

- *Orbit Baby.* A Stanford husband-and-wife team, Joseph Hei and Vivian Chiang financed this maker of innovative car seats mostly from friends and family because Hei understood that most VC firms prefer to invest in technology companies.[106]

Raising capital from friends and family is very common and these examples suggest that it is not as difficult as it might seem. The big challenge is to maintain good relationships with friends and family whether they earn an attractive return or lose their money.

Maintaining those good relationships depends heavily on how well the start-up CEO sets expectations for the investment's risks and potential rewards and the quality of the communication as to how well the business is doing compared with the plan. To do this well, entrepreneurs should:

- Ask friends and family what specific information they need to know about the start-up's activities and how frequently they need it.
- Propose a schedule of communication—such as monthly email updates and quarterly online meetings—to present results compared with expectations
- Get feedback on the communications processes from friends and families and adapt accordingly.

First-Time Entrepreneurs with Talent-Based Connections Seeking "Value-Added" Investors

Universities provide talent and capital networks that benefit graduating students and their wealthy alumni. Graduates have ideas, talent, and energy but are hungry for capital and business growth. The wealthy alumni have capital and experience and are hungry to stay in the start-up game that made them successful in the first place. Sometimes these talent-based networks result in financing deals.

Here are five examples of such start-ups.

Proven.com (Formerly WorkersNow)

Fuentes graduated from Stanford Business School where he made valuable contacts who helped financed the venture.

To finance Proven.com, Fuentes initially raised $1.85 million in two rounds. He tried to bring in investors who shared his vision for the company, provided blue-chip branding value, or offered their expertise generously to help the company grow.

These investors included Tim Draper of Draper Fisher Jurvetson, Lotus Development founder Mitch Kapor, angel investor Dave McClure, and a scion of the Bechtel family whom Fuentes knew from business school.[107]

Hearsay Social

Hearsay Social helps companies with many agents—such as insurance companies—use social networks in a way that enhances their brand. According to its co-founder, Clara Shih, a Stanford graduate, Hearsay became "cash-flow positive" in 2010 and subsequently raised a Series A round of financing from Sequoia Capital, famous for funding Stanford spin-off companies such as Cisco Systems and many others.

Hearsay later raised additional funding from other Silicon Valley VC leaders. For example, on July 28, 2011, Hearsay Social received $18 million in Series B funding. New Enterprise Associates, Inc. (NEA) led the round, with its partner Jon Sakoda joining Hearsay's Board of Directors. Sequoia Capital also participated in the round.[108]

Pulse

News reader app builder, Pulse, is an example of a company whose founders are well connected and appear to have access to top investors despite having no previous entrepreneurial experience. Pulse raised a $9 million Series A round from NEA, Greycroft Partners, and Lerer Ventures. As CEO Akshay Kothari said, "We used to sell Pulse for $4 per app, which allowed us to grow our team to four to five people. After the product went free in November, Pulse is financing itself through its seed round ($1 million) and Series A ($9.2 million)."[109]

Why did Lerer ventures invest in Pulse? It believes that Pulse has launched a way to read iPad-delivered news that connects with consumers. According to a Lerer statement, "The Pulse team understands product design and how consumers interact with mobile content. They essentially created the news reader category when they launched on the iPad, and are redefining how people consume news."[110]

According to Kothari, Pulse has received both seed and Series A funding from venture firms. As he said, "Our seed investors were mostly venture firms, who invested in us because we had a product with a lot of traction already. They each put $100,000 to $200,000 as a way to prototype a working relationship with us. Similarly, we got to work with some amazing folks."[111]

Six months into the relationship, Pulse decided to raise additional capital. As Kothari explained, "After six months or so, we decided to raise a bigger round ($9 million) since our product had grown rapidly, and we needed to ramp up the team. At this stage, we met with all our seed investors along with some new investors—and decided to raise money from NEA, Greycroft, and Lerer Ventures. This decision was made because these three investors were extremely complementary and made for the best fit for our company."[112]

Lore

Lore—an online social network for college courses known as Coursekit until April 2012—succeeded in raising seed capital on the strength of its CEO's relationship with a friend and coach. That friend introduced him to a seed capital provider that fit well with his goals for Lore, and applied valuable skills to the venture.

Specifically, in June 2011, Lore raised $1 million in seed financing from Founder Collective, IA Ventures, Shasta Ventures, and some angels. IA Ventures led the round. As Wharton drop-out CEO Joseph Cohen explained, he picked IA for three reasons:

- *Good connection.* His "good friend and coach" introduced Cohen to IA.
- *Shared vision.* Cohen believes that IA "understood the business."
- *Added value.* Cohen was impressed that IA assigned an associate with a Columbia JD/MBA to work for Lore and also appreciated IA's help introducing "great engineering candidates" to the company.[113]

Moreover, in April 2012, Lore raised an undisclosed amount from Pay-Pal co-founder, Peter Thiel, who used Lore to help teach *CS183: Startup* at Stanford to about 200 students.[114]

Sifteo

The founders of Sifteo have extremely impressive academic credentials and they developed a compelling and new idea. Turning that idea into a business took money. For that, Sifteo obtained a government grant and two rounds of venture financing.

The National Science Foundation (NSF) gave Sifteo an SBIR grant in 2009. In the summer of 2009, Sifteo raised $1 million from True Ventures—through a Mayfield Fellows introduction (an elite group of Stanford engineering students).

And in the spring of 2010, Sifteo raised $9 million from Foundry Group and True Ventures.[115]

These five examples reveal that entrepreneurs at the top of the talent pyramid—as chosen by professors at leading engineering programs—have special access to capital. However, they need to use their talent-based connections wisely to assure that they pick investors who share their vision for the company and can provide value beyond their checkbooks.

Repeat Entrepreneurs Seeking "Value-Added" Investors

When repeat entrepreneurs seek capital, they are often in the enviable position of being able to turn away capital providers who would like to invest; a start-up CEO's track record for success creates an investing fever that spreads via the venture grapevine.

To enhance that investment track record, a start-up CEO must choose wisely by conducting thorough due diligence on potential investors. And that due diligence should explore topics including:

- The investor's track record of helping previous portfolio companies grow through customer and partner introductions, helping hiring talent, and sound business advice
- Whether the investor helps solve difficult problems or panics
- How the investor has handled a situation in which a CEO needs to be replaced

Here are some examples of how the start-ups I interviewed applied this approach to raising capital.

Axcient: Capital Raising as Hiring Your Boss

Axcient, a service that lets small and medium-size businesses protect their computer systems from floods and fires for a monthly fee, is its CEO Justin Moore's third start-up. His first one was an online recruitment site he developed at Stanford. Next he built a telecom infrastructure company—MK Global—that "secured the rights to $1 billion in equipment surplused in the wake of the dot-com crash."

Axcient expected to end 2011 with eighty people and to have 150 on its payroll by the end of 2012. But all this hiring costs money—and for that Axcient had raised $18.5 million by September 2011. Its first round in September 2008 was for $6 million, its second in March 2009 raised $2 million, and in July 2010 Axcient raised another $10 million.

Axcient has been fortunate in that it has been able to pick its investors—what Moore calls choosing your boss. He picks investors based on whether his instinct tells him that there will be good chemistry and whether he believes the investor can add value in helping the company adapt effectively to "ups and downs and speed bumps." To figure that out, Moore talks to CEOs and others who have worked with the investors before.[116]

Dynamics: Importance of Chemistry

Dynamics—a service that lets people monetize their frequent buyer points—was founded by Jeff Mullen, who raised $5.7 million from Joel Adams of Adams Capital Management at the height of the financial crisis in September 2008. Mullen believes that Dynamics was able to raise capital because it solved "a seemingly impossible problem—offering a killer product that customers and consumers loved in the payments space while working with the existing infrastructure and existing players."

For his part, Mullen chose to work with Adams because of the trust that developed between them as they discussed Dynamics's business plan in Pittsburgh where they were both located. Adams invested in Mullen for two reasons: he was Poor, Smart, and Driven (PSD) and intellectually honest—meaning that he never tries to mislead him and he is always asking how he can do a better job.[117]

Evernote: Shared Vision, Value-Added

Evernote—a service that lets people store images, notes, and other information remotely has enjoyed the support of venture investors—to the tune of $165.5 million raised from Sequoia Capital and Morgenthaler Ventures, among others, in seven rounds since March 2006 (Evernote's last round raised $70 million in May 2012).

Evernote is CEO Phil Libin's third start-up and he now has the luxury of picking investors who share his vision of making Evernote a 100-year company. He also wants investors who can "add value" by helping Evernote deal with hiring and finding partners. For example, given Sequoia's deep tentacles into Silicon Valley, Libin anticipates that it can help introduce Evernote to people who can help it grow.

According to Libin, the VC model has changed substantially in the last decade so there are now VCs who are willing to invest without a short-term exit (in the form of an IPO or acquisition).

The reason for the change is the emergence of a variety of secondary markets for stock in start-ups. While Libin is not a fan of the likes of Second Market, a platform that connects start-up investors with sellers of pre-IPO shares, he points out that there are many VC firms that are interested in paying cash for other investors' equity stakes in start-ups.

This new way to realize investment gains is good for investors and for companies that prefer to operate over the long run without the pressures and costs of being publicly traded. As a result, capital providers can generate returns for their limited partners without putting pressure on portfolio companies to exit.

After Evernote's $70 million financing in 2012, Libin told me that he had a change of heart and probably would do an IPO—perhaps in 2013. But Libin wanted to manage the IPO in a way that would not disrupt Evernote's progress.

Libin accepted a lower valuation for Evernote from the investors he chose, because he has concluded that it is better to accept a lower bid from a rational investor than an extremely high price from an irrational one. The reason is that Libin "does not want a crazy person as a boss."[118]

Mocospace: Chemistry, Market Knowledge, Expansion Help

Mocospace, a provider of mobile coupons, did not want to take outside capital and initially turned down some offers from investors. The co-founders wanted to maintain control of the business. Eventually Mocospace saw the wisdom of taking on outside capital; they've taken a total of $10.5 million.

After initial funding from angel investors—including Launchpad co-teacher, Dearing—their first investor was General Catalyst ($3 million raised in January 2007 followed by a Series B round that September). Mocospace CEO Justin Siegel and his co-founder thought they had made smart mobile investments and they genuinely liked the partner they'd be working with.

Later they raised capital from SoftBank Capital ($3.5 million in 2010)—a firm with deep expertise in the Japanese gaming market—a capability that they thought would help them develop Mocospace's presence there.[119]

Oyster: Be Nice to Everyone, You Never Know Who Might Be Important

Oyster was able to raise money thanks to its CEO Elie Seidman's previous track record and contacts. By May 2011 Oyster had raised $20.4 million—including $8.5 million from Bain Capital Ventures in 2009 and $7.5 million from The Travel Channel and Bain in April 2011.

Seidman has found that when it comes to raising venture money, it helps to have built up good relationships with the people writing the checks. In his case, one of the Bain partners had turned him down when he asked for money for a previous venture. And another of the partners there had been Seidman's boss at a software company where he worked in the 1990s.[120]

These case studies illustrate the significant advantages that accrue to start-ups whose CEOs have a track record of success. Such a reputation enables entrepreneurs to pick capital providers with whom they are comfortable working and who have the specific skills that can help the ventures achieve their shared goals.

Business Plan Competition

While not among the most common capital-raising approach among my interviewees, business plan competitions provide company founders with the confidence that comes from competing successfully as well as a small, but helpful slug of capital. Often business plan competitions add professional services from lawyers, accountants, and other advisors as part of the package.

Winning business plan competitions depends on the specific factors that judges use to rank candidates. While these vary across competitions and over time, winners generally have original business ideas that target large markets;, and their founders demonstrate a deep passion for the business and a track record of doing what it takes to succeed.

Here are four examples of start-ups I interviewed that won business plan competitions:

- *Type-U.* This company helps people with diabetes improve their lifestyle and take their medicines on time. It has received $15,000 from winning a business plan competition sponsored by VC firm Highland Capital, and Type-U spent $1,000 of it to hire a Web developer who was helping build a prototype. Founder Mike Norwood anticipated that it would cost between $12,000 and $14,000 to get Type-U's prototype working well enough to attract investors.[121]
- *AfterSteps.* Bloomgarden said that DreamIt Ventures, along with winning HBS's Minimum Viable Product Competition, provided AfterSteps with the initial funds to build its Web site.[122]
- *Juntos Finanzas.* Juntos Finanzas uses cell phones to help Latinos to save money and plan for the future. Financing Juntos's growth is a challenge. Stanford graduate Ben Knelman, who founded the company, won $30,000 from a business plan competition—Stanford's Social Entrepreneurship Challenge. And he has also raised $40,000 from friends and family.[123]
- *Skycreper.* SkyCreper is a mall-based crepe retailer that won Babson College's Douglass Prize for its business plan. Its CEO, Matt Chatham, is a self-proclaimed foodie who has four Super Bowl rings. The prize included $20,000 in cash, plus $40,000 worth of "in-kind" services.[124]

These examples suggest that winning business plan competitions can be valuable for start-ups. While the money and services help to supplement founders' capital, the bigger benefit of winning is the message it sends to other potential investors. Since judges are typically venture capitalists, a business plan victory signals a stamp of approval that can give company founders an edge when it comes to raising additional capital.

HUNGRY START-UP CAPITAL-RAISING TACTICS

Following are tactics that entrepreneurs can follow to apply the *hungry start-up strategy approach to raising capital* described earlier in this chapter.

Bootstrap Prototype

When a venture is first formed, the founders must depend on themselves for financing. That can mean many different things, depending on their resources and how they choose to operate.

- *Resources.* Founders with prior track records of venture success may gladly lavish millions of dollars of their own money on hiring a talented staff and buying office space and equipment. At the other end of the spectrum are entrepreneurs with no spare cash who work without any pay out of their basements while charging expenses to multiple credit cards. And in between these two extremes are entrepreneurs who are willing to tap into their friends and family members to fund their prototype development stage.
- *Operating model.* As Charm pointed out, founders ought to adjust their initial stage operating model to the available capital. For example, if the start-up can only raise a few hundred thousand dollars, it should hire people in exchange for equity and no cash compensation and shun expensive office space. Moreover, with a lower capital base, the venture can afford to focus on a smaller market. That's because assuming that the typical start-up rarely gains more than a 10 percent market share, the investors will be able to generate an attractive return if the venture's revenues at the time of exit are comparably smaller.

However, regardless of how start-ups bootstrap themselves, at this initial stage, the founders should devote themselves to building a prototype of their product, getting feedback from potential customers, and refining the prototype.

And the ultimate goal of this series of learning loops is to develop a version of the product that customers are thrilled to use and recommend to others. If the founders can achieve this important milestone, then they are in a much stronger negotiating position when they seek to raise capital from others.

Here's a way for CEOs to bootstrap their start-ups to that end:

- *Assess founders' resources.* Here the founders count up all the cash, credit cards, and other assets that they may be willing to throw into the pot to fund the start-up.

- *Develop initial budget for bootstrapping phase.* Next the CEO should develop a weekly budget that covers all the operating expenses the start-up will need to develop a winning product. This budget should assume that it could take the start-up between five and ten learning loops to get the product right enough to gain popularity among users.
- *Estimate whether additional resources will be essential.* The start-up should then compare the founders' resources with the capital requirements detailed in the budget. If the founders have sufficient capital, then there is no need to raise more—as long as things go according to a budget that leaves room for plenty of mistakes.
- *If so, identify other capital sources.* If the founders lack the resources to fund the budget, they should seek additional capital. To do that, they should each list all their friends, family members, and trusted intermediaries—such as accountants, lawyers, bankers, and others—who might be able to introduce them to potential investors.
- *Attempt to raise additional capital.* The next step is to develop a business plan and present that plan to all the potential investors who are interested in it. At the seed stage, the business plan should be less elaborate than is required for a larger capital-raising process. However, it should answer basic questions that friends and family might have:
  - Why are you starting this venture and how committed are you to making it work?
  - Why do you think you can be successful?
  - Why do you think people will use your product?
  - Is the market for the product big enough that the company can grow to the point that I could get a return on my investment?
  - How will you use the money?
- *Revise bootstrapping budget according to the outcome.* If this process generates sufficient capital to fund your initial budget, then your bootstrapping capital raising is complete. If not, the start-up must fit the budget to the available resources. For example, Hygeia Therapeutics, a maker of products for menopausal women, was unable to raise capital in 2008 at the peak of the financial crisis so it cut staff and outsourced some activities.[125] Or in extreme cases, founders may decide that the start-up lacks sufficient capital and pull the plug.

Raise Seed Capital to Build Up Customer Base

If the start-up can build a product that customers are hungry to use and happy to recommend to others, then the CEO should assess whether more capital is required. If the product's value proposition is sufficiently compelling, it might require very little capital for the company to generate a substantial customer base.

A good example of this is New Relic, a company that makes software that helps Web site operators track real-time performance (for example, how quickly pages load when customers link to them). Its CEO, Lew Cirne, designed the product so that it was very easy for customers to see its value, to try it, and to get it working without a long sales process. As a result, New Relic's capital requirements for this second phase of its business were more modest than they would have been if a long sales cycle was required, as it had been with his previous company.[126]

However, not all start-ups can build up their customer bases with limited capital. Most of them need to raise a substantial amount of capital in order to hire the people who can build up the start-up's customer base. And in so doing, they should follow the same six steps outlined in the bootstrapping phase, as outlined previously.

Of course, there are some key differences. Most notably, the larger amount of capital the venture will require at this stage often means that the potential investors are no longer friends and family but so-called angel investors. These wealthy individuals can write six-figure checks—but the best are motivated by a strong desire to help out companies that they find compelling.

The nature of that help depends on the angel's interests, experience, and abilities. Elad Gil, whose start-up, Mixer Labs—a geolocation service—was bought by Twitter in 2008, offers many services a founder might want.[127] These include:

- *Hiring and firing.* Gil has found that most engineers who start companies don't have experience with hiring and firing and he helps them do both—initially, he may be asked to help with the more difficult task of firing an employee.
- *Fund-raising.* Gil helps start-ups find VC firms for their Series A and B rounds; assisting with negotiating key terms such as valuation and the rights of investors to appoint board members.
- *Product design.* Gil assists start-ups in designing more customer-friendly user interface and he monitors the effectiveness of their distribution strategies.
- *Organization structure.* Gil works with the founder once the company reaches, say, fifty people, to help analyze whether the reporting structure should be changed, and if so, how. And he helps start-up CEOs decide, for example, whether the venture should hire a vice president of marketing first and let the VP appoint people to perform, say, public

relations, product marketing, and advertising—or whether the start-up should hire those lower-level people first and later hire the VP.

- *Acquisitions*. Gil has assisted the leaders of a dozen start-ups to find the right acquirer, negotiate pricing, and determine the role of the founders and employees in the new organization.

While not all angel investors can offer so many valuable services to start-ups in exchange for the possible option to invest, this example should open entrepreneurs' eyes to the benefits of picking the right angel investor.

And as we saw earlier, CEOs should conduct extensive due diligence before bringing on angel investors. This means talking to CEOs of other start-ups who have worked with these investors to uncover information about how they behave in a crisis and how much they help companies seeking to gain market share.

Seek Expansion Capital

Ultimately, a CEO must raise capital to fuel the stage of growth that will lead to the start-up's initial public offering or sale to another company. While there are many CEOs who claim to be happy running the company as a going concern without such an exit, providers of expansion capital almost always demand such an outcome—and may expect it within two to three years.

If the entrepreneur is interested in cashing in, he must answer the following questions:

- How much bigger does the venture need to be in order to be attractive as an IPO or acquisition candidate?
- Can the venture reach that size by selling its existing product into new markets or should it try to add new product lines to sell to its existing customers?
- In either case, which additional people and other resources will the venture require in order to realize those growth strategies?
- How much capital will the start-up need to add the needed resources?
- How can the venture find the most suitable VC providers to achieve its expansion goals?

In many respects, the approach to answering these questions is similar to the approach a start-up should follow during its bootstrapping stage. However, working with VC firms presents unique challenges for an entrepreneur.

Here is a list of some of those challenges and suggestions as to how to handle them:

- *Finding a value-added VC.* While the term value-added gets used often, its definition is somewhat vague. Often it means that the VC tries to help the start-up achieve shared growth goals by providing more than capital—specifically, introductions to potential customers, partners, and employees; offering useful advice on strategy and operations during board meetings; and helping the venture through turbulent times. Finding such value-added VCs is best accomplished through introductions to them through trusted intermediaries—these might include entrepreneurs in which they have invested—such as bankers, lawyers, accountants, and professors.

- *Screening VCs.* If a start-up is at the stage where it can reasonably expect to raise capital in the tens of millions of dollars, it should have a track record that will make it attractive to many VCs. And before going too far down the road of talking with a VC, the entrepreneur should conduct due diligence on the partner who would likely be joining the start-up's board. As Moore said, taking VC means hiring your boss, so do it carefully. This means checking with other start-up CEOs who have worked with the specific VC partners you're considering, to find out how they operate when times get tough, the circumstances under which they have replaced CEOs, and how useful they are in board meetings.

- *Persuading a VC to invest.* Since VCs typically specialize in a specific industry or technology, a VC is more likely to invest if the partner already understands your industry. However, you will need to understand the criteria they use to screen their investments. Here are three common criteria:

  - *Team track record.* If all the members of your start-up team have a record of exceptional accomplishment, the VC will be more willing to bet on your start-up. If the team has already built a successful start-up, that conclusion is simpler to reach. If not, VCs look for evidence of outstanding accomplishment or entrepreneurial stirrings among the team members;

  - *Potential to build billion dollar company.* Venture capital firms like to invest in companies that they believe have the chance to be worth $1 billion. If the company sells to businesses, then VCs look for the start-up to target a market that will grow to be large enough to support a company that big. If the company is focused on consumers, the VC will need to imagine how it could become big—for example, when Google was launched, few investors could see the business potential of a world-beating search service as a way to attract Internet advertising revenue.

  - *Affinity for the team.* Entrepreneurs pick VC partners that they would like to work with, and VC partners invest in teams that they like.

There is no way to plan for such chemistry—it either exists or it does not. If not, the VC is not likely to invest.[129]

- *Structuring the deal.* Two common ways to structure an investment are as equity or convertible debt. Equity is generally better for aligning the interests of the founders and the investors. However, an equity investment requires the founders and investors to agree on the valuation at the time of the financing—this is often a difficult conversation. Convertible debt means that the investment is a loan that must be repaid over time or could be converted into stock in the start-up. While convertible debt defers the decision about valuation, it forces the founders and investors to agree later on how the debt converts to equity—another difficult conversation.

- *Negotiating key deal terms.* There are many deal terms that VCs may use to trick founders into unwittingly giving up control of their company. One common trick is a clause that lets the VC participate in the decision to appoint a so-called independent director. Often such clauses enable the VC to appoint a CEO who serves on another company in which that VC has invested. As a result, the VC in effect gets another board seat that may appear independent but is in fact in the VC's camp. And that may result in a board vote to replace the founders. To avoid signing contracts containing these tricks, start-up CEOs should hire advisors with experience negotiating with VCs.

If a start-up can do all these things well, then it will get the capital it needs on terms that align the founders' interests with those of the investors.

RAISING CAPITAL: DID YOU DO IT RIGHT?

The examples of different approaches to raising capital suggest some questions that can help start-up CEOs assess whether they have taken the correct approach. These questions include the following:

- Have you designed your business to make the best use of your limited capital?
- Are you sequencing your venture's strategic initiatives to strengthen your bargaining position with potential investors at each key stage of the venture's evolution?
- Are you getting introduced to potential investors through people you trust?
- Which capabilities do your potential investors need to add to your venture in order to help it grow?
- Do you trust your gut to tell you if there is going to be a good fit between you and the partners who might invest in your venture and serve on its board?

- If you are raising money from friends and family, have you explained the risks and opportunities and do you communicate with them regularly and clearly?
- Before accepting capital, do you conduct thorough due diligence on its providers?

If you have solid answers to these questions then your approach to capital raising is probably right. And if not, these questions may help you rethink those choices until you do have solid answers to them.

SUMMARY

Ideally, the hungry start-up CEO would never need to raise capital from VCs or angel investors. That's because if a venture can raise capital from founders, customers, and suppliers then the entrepreneurs can maintain tight control without questions from outsiders.

But this ideal outcome is not always feasible. When entrepreneurs need outside capital, they often go to friends and family, then angel investors, and finally VC firms. And since going outside means giving up control, entrepreneurs should be very cautious when selecting their capital providers: As entrepreneurs are hiring a boss, their survival and that of the venture depend on proceeding with care.

CHAPTER 4

Building the Team
Whom Do You Invite to the Table?

FOR A HUNGRY START-UP'S FOUNDERS the most pressing daily trade-off is between sleeping and getting stuff done. And if that start-up is bootstrapping itself, odds are good that they're burning through their own cash.

This means that unless those founders are spending their almost continuous awake-time getting the *right* stuff done, then their venture will never reach the point where it can raise the capital needed to hire help so the founders can get a bit more sleep.

Simply put, the people sitting around the start-up's table must produce more than they consume; otherwise the start-up will perish. This means that an entrepreneur has an insatiable hunger to invite only the right people to the start-up table—and make sure that no wrong people slip in.

My research reveals CEOs' possible answers to five key questions about how best to build the start-up team:

- *Is it in the venture's best interest to invite friends onto the founding team?* There is no clear answer to this question. Often it's a bad idea for friends to start a company together unless the friends have business skills that both complement each other and will help the venture grow. For example, if two friends—one a salesperson and the other an engineer—co-found a tech venture; there's a chance that their combined skills will help the start-up succeed. However, if they disagree on strategy, the venture and the friendship could end.
- *What is the right mix of skills in the founding team to boost the venture's chances for success?* The answer to this question depends, to some extent, on the industry in which the venture hopes to compete. For example, a medical products company would benefit from a founding team that includes a technical innovator, a CEO with prior medical products operational skills, and an R&D executive with experience

taking a technology from concept through regulatory approval. More generally, as Charm explains, a start-up team needs a leader who can create the right vision for the company and inspire others to follow, and a manager who can set goals, chart schedules, create budgets, and manage people on a daily basis.

- *What values must the team share to make the start-up a success?* In general, companies with strong cultures have a better chance of succeeding. However, values must fit well with the requirements for gaining and sustaining market share in the start-up's selected markets. Moreover, over time those values can restrict how well a company reacts to changing technology, evolving customer needs, or upstart competitors. Nevertheless, many of the start-up CEOs I interviewed consider setting those values to be critical to the venture's prospects for success.

- *How should a start-up CEO apply the venture's shared values to hiring people?* Start-up CEOs should decide on specific values that reflect what they believe will be important to the start-up's ability to gain market share. And the start-up should use these values to screen potential employees, to decide who should be promoted, and who should leave the company. Such values are particularly important when a new CEO comes in to turn around a start-up.

- *What is the right mix of skills to boost the venture's odds for success?* My interviews suggest that quite frequently, the idea for a start-up's product comes from an engineer with strong technical skills who hopes the product will be so good, that it will sell itself. Sooner or later, the engineer realizes that the venture needs a CEO who can sell, set direction for the company, and build and motivate a team. While the skills needed for a venture to succeed vary by industry and the stage in the venture's development, my research reveals that resisting the urge to hire friends, and instead deciding what skills the venture needs to grow, is vital.

- *How should the founder share equity with other team members?* Founders should avoid the easy decision—dividing the shares by the number of founders and giving each an equal share. While this has the short-term benefit of avoiding a messy fight at the beginning of the venture, it creates huge problems later. That's because early in a venture it is generally unclear who will stay and who will leave, and the roles of those who stay are often undefined early on. Therefore, the division of equity should not happen until the founders figure out how they will divide up the responsibilities of running the start-up and the contract that does the dividing should anticipate different scenarios—such as a founder leaving—and how that will affect the equity split.[128]

BUILDING THE TEAM

The experts I interviewed provide more details on these ideas.

The Experts Weigh In on Ways to Build the Team

Charm: Don't Hire Your Friends

Charm offers an interesting general perspective about how start-ups ought to build teams. He points out that most entrepreneurs hire their friends and people like them. In their minds, this lowers the risk of hiring a stranger. But it can be bad for the start-up if the team does not have the skills—say, in sales or product development—that it needs to build a sizable business. As noted earlier, Charm also believes that start-ups often need a combination of a leader and a manager. Many start-ups fail because they lack both skills.[130]

Launchpad: Network to Close Skill Gaps

Launchpad encourages start-ups to apply design thinking to organizational design (see Chapter 4). Design thinking pushes start-ups to apply those principles through the following steps:

- Analyze the founders' strengths and weaknesses.
- Identify the skills that the start-up will need to excel in the future.
- Find the gaps between the founders' strengths and the future needs of the business.
- Hire people who can close the capability gaps. This could be done by
  - Developing profiles of the kinds of people they need,
  - Sending these profiles out to people they know to suggest individuals that might fit the bill
  - Picking out such people via their LinkedIn profiles[131]

IDEO: Diversity Works

IDEO believes in creating multidisciplinary teams because the creative tension among those disciplines leads to faster development. In working with Yoomi, IDEO assembled such a team, including product designers, an ethnographer, a branding expert, and an entrepreneur.[132]

Stevenson: Don't Let "I-Strain" Kill Your Venture

Stevenson offers a more fundamental observation about start-up teams. If a start-up CEO is too egotistical, people will feel disrespected and perform at less than their potential, or simply quit. So once a CEO has a team in place, he or she must make people feel that they're making progress.

As Stevenson quipped, "More companies are killed by I-strain." For such companies, his prescription is less "I am" and more "We can." He said that the most successful entrepreneurs use the word "we" a lot. Stevenson believes it's important to make people in a start-up feel that they are making progress. And achieving this depends on consciously designing a firm's culture so it's clear that people should be treated well, respected, and rewarded for skill and honesty rather than luck.[133]

HUNGRY START-UP STRATEGY APPROACH TO BUILDING TEAMS

Start-ups should build teams that are hungry to change the world and that match this hunger with a powerful will to win that makes them eager to be part of a team with complementary skills. Consistent with these principles, entrepreneurs should apply the five-step *hungry start-up team-building approach* summarized in Figure 4.1.

Here is an expanded explanation of the five steps:

FIGURE 4.1   **Hungry Start-Up Strategy Team-Building Framework.**

- *Analyze skills needed to prove start-up concept.* The start-up founders should take an objective look at the skills that the venture will need in order to prove that the concept can work as a viable business. To do this, it helps to look at successful competitors in the market the venture is seeking to enter.[134] If there is a common bundle of skills that the most successful competitors have within their founding teams, the start-up should consider whether it should follow suit.

- *Evaluate founders' skills and adjust accordingly.* Once the founders have identified the skills required, they should take a hard look at whether the current founding team has those skills. If so, the start-up should get to work. If not, the founders should reconstitute the team to add needed skills and shed ones that are not adding value. Although it is painful, this reconstitution boosts the venture's odds of succeeding.

- *Agree on roles and goals.* Once the founding team has been assembled, each member should agree on his or her role and set goals—along the lines we discussed in Chapter 1. While these role and goal definitions will not be permanent, they should help the venture grow to the point where it needs expansion capital.

- *Create culture.* Many start-up CEOs perceive that they ought to define their culture in ways that will help them to hire. To that end, entrepreneurs should develop a set of core values—either unilaterally or in collaboration with other stakeholders. The goal is to agree on shared values to build the team and boost its effectiveness as the company grows.

- *Use culture to hire, promote, and purge.* Finally, the start-up should use these core values to hire people. To that end, it should devise processes to find candidates and screen them that explicitly incorporate those core values. In that way, start-ups can limit the number of hiring mistakes they make. Moreover, entrepreneurs ought to use the core values to decide whom to promote and who does not fit.

Benefits of Hungry Start-Up Strategy Team-Building Methodology

This approach to building the team offers a start-up two benefits:

- *It minimizes start-up risks.* This approach to building the team helps to strip out many of the risks inherent in getting a venture off the ground. If the founding team has the right mix of skills, agrees on goals and values, and hires the right people, then the venture can focus on finding a viable business model and expanding it.

- *It boosts team productivity and adaptation to change.* If a start-up can create the right team, then it will be more likely to work productively and have the level of initiative needed to identify important signals of change in the competitive environment and adapt to them accordingly. These benefits will help keep the venture going through inevitable turbulence.

BUILDING TEAMS: FOUR APPROACHES

The start-ups I interviewed take four approaches to building their teams (Figure 5.2). But these approaches vary most significantly by the ventures' source of capital. Specifically, companies that are bootstrapping make do with the efforts of their co-founders, and, if they can scrounge sufficient capital or persuade them to work in exchange for very little cash or noncash inducements, the bootstrapped ventures selectively outsource.

Once a venture has raised significant capital, its CEO typically ramps up hiring. And among the companies I interviewed, many entrepreneurs are more interested in hiring people for specific sets of skills that they believe the venture needs to grow. However, many of these CEOs place a great emphasis on building a strong culture—one that hinges on using values to hire, promote, and fire people in the company.

These four categories are described more specifically as follows:

- *Hiring teams to provide complementary skills (37 percent).* The founders of companies in this category believe that in order to boost their venture's market share, they must hire people with specific functional skills that are critical to building and selling the product. Such entrepreneurs

FIGURE 4.2 **Four Approaches to Building Start-Up Teams, by Percent of Interviewees.**

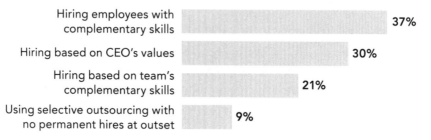

respond to rising market demand by analyzing how many people with varying skills—such as engineering, marketing, sales, and customer service—that the company will need to enhance the venture's competitive position.

- *Hiring based on CEO values (30 percent).* The founders of companies that hire based on CEO values believe that the start-up's success depends on a strong culture. To that end, they develop a list of personal attributes that embody the employee traits (for example, belief in the venture's mission, persistence, or a passion for extreme sports) that the start-up CEO believes are essential for the organization's success. In most cases, these two categories are not mutually exclusive: Start-ups in the first category hire based on values and those who hire based on values also seek out complementary skills. However, my interviews suggest that CEOs focus primarily on one or the other.

- *Original team, complementary skills (21 percent).* The founders of these companies lack sufficient capital to hire more people. The lack of capital could be due to the very early stage of their product development process or their inability, after significant effort, to operate the business in a way that interests potential investors. These companies are being run by a group of co-founders and their odds for success rise dramatically if the strengths of each co-founder satisfy two criteria: (1) As a team, they give the venture most of the important skills the business needs to prove out its business concept, and (2) the co-founders' strengths do not overlap.

- *Original team, selective outsourcing (9 percent).* The final category of start-ups I interviewed enlists people to work with the venture in a loose relationship. This loose relationship can take many forms—unpaid internships, compensation based completely on sales commissions, or even very scant cash compensation—with the unspoken promise of a possible full-time position once the venture gets funding.[135]

Let's take a closer look at each.

Hiring Teams to Provide Complementary Skills

Start-up CEOs can't do everything their venture needs to assure its success. Indeed, the difference between a start-up's survival and bankruptcy can often be a founder's timely recognition that the start-up needs different skills from those the founder can provide and must hire people with the needed skills.

Here are four steps to achieving this:

- Analyze the founders' strengths and weaknesses.
- Evaluate the capabilities of leading competitors in the start-up's market.
- Identify the gaps between these capabilities and the start-up's strengths.
- Hire people with missing strengths to close the capability gap.

Here are two cases where founders hired teams to provide complementary skills.

Embrace

Embrace's mission of saving the lives of low-birth-weight babies is extremely compelling for many talented people who are willing to work on its behalf for what is likely less pay than they could earn in a purely for-profit enterprise.

Thanks to its compelling mission of saving babies, Embrace has attracted extraordinary talent. Among its staff of twenty-five are a PhD in Electrical Engineering who is an expert on fiber optics, an aerospace engineer, and a computer scientist with a string of entrepreneurial successes in his wake.[136]

And during 2011, Embrace intended to hire twenty-five more people in engineering, quality assurance, manufacturing, sales, and marketing. Embrace's ability to hire these people reflects a cool-headed analysis of the skills needed to serve more families with its products. And its mission will probably help persuade those skilled people to contribute to Embrace's growth.

CEO Jane Chen is a big believer in the idea of assembling and motivating a team of people who can work together to achieve an organization's mission. As she explained in an essay in 2010, "My three core values as a leader include empowering my team, open communication, and leading by example."[137]

She explained her thoughts about how an organization can be strengthened by a team of people with complementary skills. "I strongly believe in the power of teams, and that any great organization begins with a unified team that is empowered to best use their skill set to contribute to a mission."

As Embrace's CEO, she has assembled a diverse team and helped them work together. "I realized this through my role as CEO of Embrace. I work with a team of incredibly talented individuals. I constantly try to best leverage the talents of each individual within my team, because I know the whole is greater than the sum of the parts."

And the team's credentials are impressive. As she wrote, "My co-founding team consists of a PhD in electrical engineering, an aerospace engineer, and a computer science master's from Stanford. [In the summer of 2010, Embrace had] twenty-three MBA and engineering interns from Stanford and Harvard universities. I hope that the work we do will continue to inspire others to strive to improve humanity, to use their skills to leave the world a better place than it is today."

Chen is likely to evaluate the skills Embrace needs based on its ambitious goals to spread itself around the world and to introduce "twenty new disruptive technologies" that help people at the bottom of the pyramid. Accomplishing this goal will require Chen to attract more such talented people with the relevant relationship building and technology development skills.

Sonatype

Open source software company Sonatype was founded by Jason van Zyl, an engineer who built most of the core open source software for developers. After burning through most of Sonatype's first round of financing, the company raised a second round.[138]

One of Sonatype's investors made its investment contingent on convincing van Zyl to accept hiring in a CEO who could complement his skills as a software innovator.

As Hummer Winblad Venture Partners' Ann Winblad explained, she saw Sonatype as a technical leader when HWVP decided to invest. However, she concluded that van Zyl—while a "rock star developer"—could only do part of the job needed to expand Sonatype.

Initially, van Zyl was was quite skeptical about the importance of salespeople, but he saw the company burning through cash and not getting any closer to being able to sell its products.

So van Zyl—realizing that he lacked the sales skills needed to build the company—agreed to hire a CEO with the technical know-how, sales ability, and a successful start-up building track record.

After interviewing and rejecting eighteen previous candidates, van Zyl hired as Sonatype's CEO Wayne Jackson, who led intrusion detection software maker SourceFire to a 2007 IPO and in 2000 sold mobile infrastructure maker Riverbed for over $1 billion. Nearly two years later, van Zyl believed that Sonatype was on track to become a public company in part thanks to his engineering skills combined with Jackson's CEO capabilities.

Hiring Based on CEO Values

Many of the companies I interviewed believe strongly in the importance of creating a corporate culture. At the core of such cultures is a clear set of values—ones that the CEO believes the start-up people should use as a guide for their daily actions.

Such CEOs build strong start-up cultures through four steps:

- Decide on the start-up's core values—either unilaterally or in conjunction with the company's co-founders and/or employees.
- Communicate the core values frequently when interacting with the company's employees, investors, customers, and other stakeholders.
- Develop a hiring process that screens for employees who act in accordance with those core values.
- Link promotions and rewards to how well people follow the start-up's core values—and counsel or dismiss workers who do not live by the start-up's core values.

Here are five examples of companies that use core values to build their teams.

Axcient

Axcient is hiring at a rapid clip. Axcient decides whom to hire based on a combination of the skills it needs in order to grow and the values that its people must embody to fit in there.

In 2010, Axcient had twenty-five people and Moore expected eighty by the end of 2011. But he did not think that would be enough people to meet demand for Axcient's service—so by the end of 2012, he expected the company to have 150 employees. He started Axcient in 2006 to solve a problem that he faced when he was running his previous start-ups.[139]

And he is passionate about Axcient's culture. Moore has developed a very specific collection of values—integrity, teamwork, inspired product development, partnering with customers, and getting results—and he hires and promotes people who live by them. He prides himself on offering jobs to a mere one out of 50 or 100 people who interview at Axcient.

When he hires, he's looking for people with aptitude, cultural fit, agility, and out-of-the-box thinking. He has interviewed "thousands" of people and hired about 80 at Axcient. He starts off every interview by asking potential employees to tell him the values they would like to see in the company where they work. Moore then discusses Axcient's values. If there's a good match there, the candidate is likely to proceed. If not, Axcient is not likely to pursue the process.

Moore uses Axcient's values to decide whom to hire, whom to promote and whom to "manage out of the company" (a new way of referring to firing someone).

In October 2011, Moore hired an entry-level salesperson who accepted a position at Axcient after turning down an offer of 25 percent more from another company because he wanted to be part of Axcient's team.

Moore has gotten burned in previous start-ups when he lost good people to offers of higher salaries. He is determined to keep that from happening; he thinks that if employees come to work just for the money, they will not stick around when times get tough or if they get offered more money somewhere else.[140]

Hearsay Social

Hearsay Social's approach to building its team combines knowledge of the functions it needs to support demand growth with a commitment to core values. Hearsay Social employs thirty people and is hiring aggressively in marketing, sales, engineering, and recruiting functions.[141]

Hearsay has a very strong culture and only hires people who fit. To that end, it uses three hiring criteria:

- *Raw intelligence.* What Hearsay co-founder Steve Garrity calls "processing speed."
- *Get Stuff Done (GSD).* Hearsay does not just want brains; it wants people who can use brains to solve problems effectively and quickly.
- *No asshole rule.* Borrowing a philosophy from Stanford professor, Bob Sutton's book of the same name, Hearsay wants people who work well with others. And it screens outs people who don't pass this test by talking with applicants' previous managers, peers, and direct reports.

Main Street Hub

Main Street Hub (MSH) helps small businesses manage their social media reputations. MSH's approach to building its team reflects two distinctive values of its founders: an emphasis on getting fast feedback from customers and a well-tuned ability to empathize with customers. And as of June 2011, MSH was expanding its twenty-seven-person team that was organized into functions: engineering, sales, and account management.[142]

MSH has a strong culture. It wants to hire people who are "passionate about building a company to make a huge impact for small businesses" and who share its design thinking values. This mind-set derives from Launchpad and emphasizes building prototypes and getting fast feedback by observing how customers behave with them.

MSH also wants to hire people with high Emotional Quotients (EQs) because the company will be most effective if it can empathize with its customers who suffer when their online reputations are at risk.

Oyster

Oyster believes that people who have succeeded in large companies may not be able to work effectively in a start-up. Moreover, each person added to the team could either help the company in important ways or ruin the company's ability to function well.

Therefore hiring people well is a critical skill. To do that, Seidman has realized that he needs people who have succeeded in previous start-ups and that it could be dangerous to hire people who worked in large companies.[143]

How so? Seidman believes that start-ups are inherently more emotionally volatile than large companies where the idea is to develop and follow standardized routines. Seidman wants to hire people who have demonstrated that they can adapt well to a start-up's inherent ups and downs because they are self-starters and self-critical.

He also wants to hire people who will handle the emotional stresses of a start-up by working with others to solve problems rather than blowing off the stress by getting belligerent with co-workers.

Grockit

Grockit helps students study in groups for standardized tests, such as the Graduate Management Admission Test (GMAT). CEO Roy Gilbert took over from the company founder, Farb Nivi, who stayed with Grockit. Gilbert thus faced an important challenge of changing the company while retaining the services of its founder.

Nivi moved into the role of chief product officer and in October 2010 handed over the CEO reins to Gilbert, a Stanford MBA. Before Grockit, Gilbert spent seven years at Google. He led its Global User Operations, where he was responsible for all of Google's non-advertising functions, including search quality, consumer and ads policy, localization, book scanning, and product support. And before that he led Google's India operations and launched Gmail's business operations.

Before taking on his new role at Grockit, Gilbert worked with Nivi to agree on how they would collaborate. As Gilbert told me before he started working there, he and Nivi took personality tests and worked with a leadership coach who facilitated a discussion about how each perceived the world and their respective approaches to resolving conflicts. Nivi and Gilbert communicate frequently and address their occasional conflicts efficiently.

To that end, Gilbert wants to build Grockit's twenty-five-person organization around five values. To decide what those were, he worked with Grockit people to develop this set of values by exploring questions such as "Whom do we admire?" and "Why do we admire them?"

Based on people's answers to these questions, Grockit articulated the values that Gilbert uses to help decide whom to hire and whom to let go.[144]

These examples suggest that clearly articulated core values can help a start-up to grow by attracting new people who share those values. If the CEO uses the core values to hire and dismiss people, he or she can assure that everyone is rowing in the same direction. Ultimately, a values-driven company will succeed only if the values are consistent with what it takes to win in the start-up's selected market.

Original Team, Complementary Skills

Many of the start-ups I interviewed are still working with their original teams—with aspirations of hiring more in the future. How well the original team members complement one another is one of the key factors in determining whether these start-ups will develop enough to raise the capital required to augment their teams.

If team members have different strengths—and in combination those strengths are essential to the venture's success—then the original team may have a greater chance of raising the capital needed to build the team. If the founders' skills do not complement one another or don't help the venture grow, then its prospects may be weaker.

Here are three quick examples of start-ups that are trying to follow this approach:

- *Venuetastic*. This company helps match venues with excess space with people looking for somewhere to meet. Venuetastic is the brainchild of a math and neuroscience graduate of MIT, Helen Belogolova, who got bit by the start-up bug. This bug bit when Belogolova was in San Francisco trading on Barclay's money market desk. She was hanging out with MIT alumni in the Bay Area and was talking with an MIT classmate, Christine Yen, a computer science major who worked at Google and Aardvark, in August 2009. Belogolova brings considerable organization and data analysis skills while Yen manages the software development for Venuetastic.[145]
- *TSI*. Burstein and his partner, Ian Framson, co-founded the company. Between Burstein, who handles marketing, and Framson, who's a great salesman, TSI's team is able to meet customer requirements, develop new products, and achieve Burstein's growth targets.[146]
- *Bionée* develops skin care products for women. Its founder, Eva Asmar, aspires to supplement Bionée's team with mothers who like the product and want to make a living selling it. Bionée is seeking capital for its venture and has a team of four. This includes Asmar who is in charge of

marketing and product development, working in France, a public relations person in Paris, a business development person, and a marketing
assistant. Asmar is also assembling a board of advisors.[147]

Original Team, Selective Outsourcing

If a start-up's original team is making progress with its business model, but
still lacks the capital required to hire workers to expand that model into new
markets, the venture can try selective outsourcing. This often means finding
a way to offer potential workers something of value that does not require
significant cash payments.

Here are three examples of start-ups that are supplementing their original team with selective outsourcing:

- *Kembrel.* This company enables upscale retailers to reach college students. Kembrel has devised a clever way to persuade students to work
  for free in exchange for helping them get a leg up on the fashion industry. Kembrel is currently operating on founders' capital and has a team
  of seven people—including a head of business development, who is a
  former fashion designer. An important part of Kembrel's strategy is to
  involve students as "models, writers, curators, and campus ambassadors." Kembrel thus provides opportunities for students to get valuable
  exposure to the fashion and start-up world, while ensuring the site's
  authenticity and further strengthening its presence on campuses around
  the country."[148]
- *UniEats.* This company offers college students 10 percent discounts at
  local restaurants. UniEats is a good example of a concept that is so successful that students at other universities are willing to help launch the
  concept on a pure commission basis. In fact, UniEats was in such great
  demand during the 2010–2011 school year that it launched on five new
  campuses in the fall of 2011—Harvard, MIT, Columbia, Northwestern,
  and Cornell. To get things off the ground at these campuses, CEO Liz
  Wessel hired people who were smart and well connected on campus
  and pays them commissions. And those campus managers hire salespeople assigned to sell the discount cards to students.[149]
- *Type-U.* In 2011, Type-U received $15,000 from Highland Capital and
  decided to use part of that to outsource the development of its prototype—spending $1,000 of it to hire a Web developer to do that. Nor-
  wood anticipated that it would cost between $12,000 and $14,000 to get
  the prototype working well enough to attract investors."[150]

Selective outsourcing is a good temporary solution for many start-ups. Ultimately, if it helps the start-up to prove the viability of its business model, the start-up may be in a stronger position to raise sufficient capital to hire a more permanent team. Other start-ups may continue to employ selective outsourcing as a way to keep costs low and continue to operate without raising outside capital.

HUNGRY START-UP TEAM-BUILDING TACTICS

The best approach to building a start-up team depends on its growth stage. Specifically, as Xirrus CEO Shane Buckley suggested, the needed team changes as an organization grows from $0 to $10 million, between $10 million and $50 million, from $50 million to $100 million, and over $100 million.[151]

If a venture is trying to get to that first $10 million and has already assembled its core team, the founder should apply the hungry start-up strategy approach to building teams by using the following tactics.

Analyze Skills to Prove Business Model

If the founding team is thinking about how best to prove its business model, it needs to consider whether it has the right skills to do that.

The first step in that process is to think broadly about the most critical skills that a start-up in the team's industry needs to build a product that customers will want to use—and ultimately buy.

To do this, the founding team can follow six steps:

- Assess the unmet needs of the start-up's target customers.
- List the key capabilities needed to satisfy those unmet needs.
- Identify the most respected rivals in the industry.
- Analyze the key capabilities that helped those rivals prove the viability of their business model.
- Determine whether rivals' key capabilities add to the initial list of capabilities.
- If so, add them to the list of capabilities the start-up needs in order to prove its business model.

It is important to emphasize that as the start-up grows, so will the demands on its capabilities. So at each stage in its development, its board and top executives should rethink the venture's required capabilities.

Evaluate Founders' Skills and Adjust Accordingly

Sometimes the people who form the initial start-up team can keep working together for years. Other times, it becomes clear that a group of friends who decided to work together because they thought it would be fun discover that it's not working.

In general, the most effective founding teams tend to consist of people who complement one another. For example, the CEO might be a technology visionary and sales aficionado whose business partner loves to oversee the details of hiring people, keeping a project on schedule, and creating and meeting budgets.

If the founders have a harmonious working relationship, then there may be no reason to change the founding team.

However, if a core team is not working out as well as the founder had hoped, she might need to take a step back and evaluate whether the venture has the right team. To do that, the founder may need help—possibly from an objective outsider—to figure out the skills the start-up needs to achieve its sales targets.

For example, the venture might have three great engineers who are the founder's friends, but their skills all overlap and they fight all the time over the product. And the venture may lack a top-notch "hunter"—the sort of sales person who can make 100 phone calls a day and travel 500,000 miles a year finding, qualifying, and closing sales with customers willing to take a chance on your product.

In this case, the founder might have to decide to part ways with some of those engineers and hire the best available hunter.

Making those departures happen is likely to mean starting a painful series of conversations.

And after that has occurred, the remaining founders will need to figure out the skills and roles needed to get the venture off the ground.

Here are five steps an entrepreneur can apply to evaluate founders' skills and adjust accordingly:

- List the key skills, such as product development, sales, manufacturing— required to achieve the start-ups goals.
- Make an inventory of the skills of each of the start-up's founders. For each skill, list two or three examples that illustrate the founders' passion and achievement in performing it.
- Compare the founders' skills with one another and with the skills required to achieve the start-up's goals.

- Identify overlaps and gaps and investigate two questions:
  - Do the skill overlaps among founders create more conflict than valuable insights?
  - Does the start-up's survival depend on closing the capability gaps?
- If the answer to these questions is yes, consider taking the following actions:
  - Of those with the overlapping skills, remove the less valuable founder from the start-up team.
  - Hire a person who can perform the needed skills at a world-class level.

Taking either of these actions will surely be disruptive to the start-up. Therefore, before taking such actions, one founder must be confident that the conclusions about gaps and overlaps are founded on solid evidence.

The conversation to persuade one of the founders to leave day-to-day operations is extremely difficult. To do this most effectively, the CEO should meet with the soon-to-be-departing founder, explain the conclusion, cite the reasons for the decision, and explain that the departing founder's stake in the start-up is likely to be more valuable if he or she leaves the venture.

Agree on Roles and Goals

If initial pruning of the founding team occurs, the next step will be to decide which management roles remain unfilled. For example, imagine a start-up with two co-founders, both of whom were technical visionaries who could not agree on a shared vision. Suppose that one of the two founders was forced out, leaving a need for a chief operating officer (COO) role.

Then the remaining founding team would first define the specific duties of the COO role and possibly any other important top management team roles. To that end, the start-up CEO should conduct best practices analysis and then tailor the key findings to help the venture compete, as follows.

- Make a list of likely competitors.
- Rank the competitors by their relative growth rates.
- Analyze the resumes of the competitors' key people.
- Determine whether similar skills and experience would help the venture.
- Develop idealized job descriptions and qualifications for the people the start-up needs to hire.

When start-ups are small, people tend to have functional specialties—such as product development and sales—but also be able to make decisions that affect the entire company.

To that end, the start-up team should meet and agree on the most critical short-term goals that the venture must achieve in order to survive. Then each team member should come up with his or her own specific goals that will help the venture achieve what the team agrees are right for the venture.

Create Culture

Before hiring additional employees, CEOs should define the start-up's culture in conjunction with key members of the start-up team. Culture is simple in concept—it's a list of about five values that are important to the founder and will help the start-up compete. For example, as mentioned earlier, Axcient's values include getting results, integrity, teamwork, building inspired products, and putting partners and customers first.

However, many start-up CEOs do not recognize culture's significance as a tool for attracting people who will fit well within the venture and thus contribute to higher productivity, lower turnover, and ultimately faster growth.

Axcient's Moore believes that to create a start-up culture, the entrepreneur must answer the following questions:

- Who are you?
- What's important to you?
- What behaviors do you want to see in people in your company?
- How do you want your employees to act and make decisions?

Then CEOs should use the answers to develop a list of fifteen to twenty-five values and then whittle them down to a number that people in the company can remember; Moore believes that number is five, and that CEOs should run the company based on those values.[152]

Use Culture to Hire, Promote, and Purge

In theory, the start-up is now well-positioned to actually start hiring people. Here are some basic steps that the CEO should take to boost the odds of hiring the right people:

- Send job descriptions to people you know who are well-connected among potential employees who can recommend candidates.
- Search for candidates with the desired skills on LinkedIn.
- Create a process for initial fifteen-minute telephone interviews to screen out candidates who will not fit well.

- Invite candidates who survive the phone screening to take a basic test of their ability to do the job, for example, their software-writing productivity or their ability to manage teams.
- Invite candidates to a social get-together, and ask questions to determine their fit with the culture of the company and to observe whether their informal personality is consistent with the one they demonstrated during the productivity test.
- Conduct detailed reference checks—especially with references who are friends of the candidates—in order to get an objective assessment of their skills.
- Consider hiring candidates for a consulting assignment to see what they are really like to work with before offering a permanent position.

The entrepreneur should also use values to assess how people are doing. Moore has "skip lunches" with people—meeting with people who report to his management team—on a regular basis. He has all-hands meetings every six weeks and holds cross-functional team meetings every two months to make sure the different functions communicate with one another.

Moore also has a compelling argument about the value of "team first." He believes that putting the team first is "not you being altruistic." Instead, Moore sees it as "being selfish. If you meet your sales quota but your team fails, then the company fails, your stock goes to zero, and you are out looking for a job. But if your team succeeds, the company is successful, and you make money."

So what does Moore say to CEOs who are working on their company culture? First he explains why culture is so important to achieving great results. But to develop a culture, a CEO must start with creating a set of values that become the basis of what people in the company do.

When Moore tried to do this the first time, he was grateful for the help of a mentor who had taken three companies public.[153]

But culture is not all fun and games. If, after being hired, employees do not fit, it is easier to persuade them to leave by pointing out the mismatch between their conduct and the company's culture.

BUILDING THE TEAM: DID YOU DO IT RIGHT?

The examples of different approaches to building the team suggest some questions that can help start-up CEOs assess whether they have taken the correct approach. These questions include the following:

- What skills does your venture need to get off the ground?
- What are the founders' skills in leading competitors?
- Does your founding team have the needed skills? If not, how will you get them?
- Does your start-up have a clearly defined culture and a set of core values?
- Do you use those core values to hire and incentivize people?
- Do you know the number of people you'll need with specific skills in order to achieve your start-up's growth goals?

If you have solid answers to these questions, then your approach to building the team is probably right. And if not, these questions may help you rethink those choices until you do have solid answers to them.

SUMMARY

From the beginning, the people who work for a start-up have an enormous effect on its destiny. If the start-up's founders have the right mix of skills, that combination boosts the chances that it will be able to prove that its business model works on a small scale.

And if that team can persuade investors to finance the expansion of that business model, the founding team will need to hire people to achieve the venture's growth goals. If so, many entrepreneurs believe that an important part of their job is to define the start-up's culture—setting core values and using them to pick whom to hire, whom to promote, and who does not fit.

CHAPTER 5

Gaining Share

Satisfy Your Customers' Cravings

THERE IS NO MORE IMPORTANT HUNGER for a start-up than the one for getting and keeping customers. Because potential customers are reluctant to risk doing business with an unproven company, it's a challenge for start-ups to attract and keep those deeply needed customers.

Start-ups must find a problem to which customers crave a solution. More specifically, a start-up's ability to feed its profit-hungry coffers depends on satisfying customer cravings for a solution to a painful unmet need. Unfortunately for their cash flows, many start-ups I interviewed have found that not only do customers want those problems solved, they want these valuable solutions at no charge; I call this a "quantum value leap" (QVL).

My research reveals that delivering QVLs must be done with a clear answer to the question: Who is the customer? Sometimes, the start-up's customer is just the product's user. Some start-ups decide that both distributors and end users are their customers; others even add suppliers into the mix of their customers.

Whoever a start-up's customers are, the only way for the start-up satisfy their craving is by feeding them a QVL. This raises some important issues for start-up CEOs seeking to gain market share (findings from my research on these questions are given as follows):

- *How can the start-up discover the specific, ranked criteria these participants use to pick a winning supplier?* A start-up CEO must listen to key participants in the value network to uncover the criteria they use to select suppliers. More specifically, entrepreneurs should identify and rank the measurable criteria that customers use to compare suppliers. Interviews should focus on discovering their customers' "pain points," important needs that vendors are not satisfying. Identifying these pain points is a crucial starting line in the race for market share.

- *How do start-ups design and deliver products that gain market share?* The start-ups I interviewed seem to tackle this question in two ways. First, some start-ups get off the ground by developing a product that relieves their own personal pain points. Once the founders have developed a product that removes the needle from their proverbial paws, they believe that others will feel that same pain relief. A second common way is to build a prototype of a product quickly and get feedback from customers; in other words, many start-ups conduct frugal experiments quickly to discover how much their product must improve performance to win users.

- *How should the start-up set prices to encourage product adoption while also covering its costs?* Many of the start-ups I interviewed have adopted a freemium pricing strategy. The idea is to eliminate the financial risk for customers of using the product, in hope that these users will like and recommend the product to their networks. If that happens, the product can grow virally and potentially become the de facto standard in its category. But this is only part of the freemium pricing approach. In addition, the start-up generally offers a more powerful version of its product and charges customers a monthly fee for that more powerful version. For example, Dyn, a company that allows people to host Web sites and email on their own computers, had around three million individuals as customers, only a few hundred thousand of whom were paying $35 a year for a more powerful version of its product. But that was enough to keep Dyn cash-flow positive.

GAINING SHARE

Offering customers a QVL is essential to gaining market share. To do this, entrepreneurs must find a solution to a problem that pains customers.

The Experts Weigh In on Gaining Share

Minimize Risk of Adoption

Charm offers an interesting general perspective about how start-ups ought to gain market share. Charm points out that start-ups need to convince companies and individuals to try their products in a way that is not too risky for the customers.

For example, it is usually easier to convince a company to try for free a piece of software that solves a big problem for the company. By contrast, it is often impossible for a start-up to convince a company to try any kind of software, the failure of which would shut down that customer's operations.

Focus on the Next 10

Charm thinks that the best way to frame a start-up's effort to gain market share is to talk about how to get the next ten customers rather than to set a goal of gaining 5 percent market share. The more down-to-earth market growth goal is easier to communicate and achieve.[154]

The reason for this is fairly straightforward—many sales compensation plans give bonuses to salespeople for adding new accounts, not for boosting market share. The effect of adding new accounts is increased market share; denominating it for salespeople in terms that affect their bonus motivates them more effectively.

Target a Well-Defined Piece of a Big Market

Stevenson shares this idea. In his view, start-ups gain market share by picking their customers carefully and serving them better than competitors do.

Stevenson believes it's important for start-ups to think about getting 100 percent of a particular customer's business rather than to set broad market-share goals (for example, getting 1 percent of a $1 billion market).

A start-up generates revenues only by finding customers who need what it can do differently—and better—than its competitors. When Stevenson helped start investment firm Baupost Group, for example, he was looking for customers who wanted to preserve and grow capital over a long time rather than seeking to beat short-term market averages.

This decision to target customers who were focused on long-term results enabled Baupost to distinguish itself from private equity firms that sold winning investments quickly in order to justify the high short-term performance they needed to raise more capital from investors.

Stevenson presented Baupost as a firm whose investment managers would put their own money in the same partnerships as its clients. Therefore, the clients and Baupost would share the same objective: to generate long-term capital gains.

As a result of these different incentives, Baupost positioned itself to hold on to winning investments for the long run rather than selling them quickly to spike short-term performance statistics.

Another example of picking customers well is a home oil delivery service that seeks to win the business of a cluster of homeowners in a specific neighborhood who need deliveries on the same day.

In Stevenson's view, this approach to customer selection reflects the economics of delivering oil: It is cheaper to deliver to a limited area all at once than to drive to geographically distant parts of a city on different days.

Hence, if an oil delivery business can capture 100 percent of the business in a particular neighborhood, it will have lower costs than competitors and may choose to pass these lower costs on to customers in the form of lower prices; this strategy helps it close delivery deals with more homes in a neighborhood.

Create Wide Awareness

Another way that start-ups gain share is "to know and be known." Stevenson points out that this elegant formulation was developed by Myra Hart, one of his graduate students. It means that an entrepreneur needs to have industry-specific knowledge and must meet and develop the trust of influential people within that industry.

Stevenson suggested three principles for gaining market share:

- *Figure out how to serve each customer.* One of Stevenson's favorite entrepreneurs was Landmark Communication's late chairman and CEO, Frank Batten. Batten's basic philosophy was to serve the customer at a profit, not to maximize shareholder value. Batten believed that profit was a constraint—you needed enough of it only to serve the customer—which was his goal.

- *Know your economics.* An entrepreneur must know the factors that drive a company's prices, costs, and profit. For example, the savvy oil delivery company we mentioned earlier knows that costs decline and profits rise if each oil truck leaves full, drives to a neighborhood, and transfers the entire load into the oil tanks of homes in that neighborhood. Stevenson notes that too many companies delude themselves by thinking that they can make up losses on each unit sold by selling more units.

- *Obsolete yourself or your competitor will.* Over time, new technologies are invented that create a QVL for customers. Stevenson's idea is that rather than let a competitor introduce the new, QVL-generating product, the maker of the old technology should introduce its own version of the new technology. As Stevenson pointed out, Batten saw that Monster.com was taking over his newspapers' help-wanted advertising, Angie's List was swiping its classified advertising, and others were taking away its automobile listings. Moreover, Batten saw that more people wanted to get their weather information from the Internet. In response, Batten started Auto Trader to capture some of the lost auto listings, and

Landmark—which then owned the Weather Channel—bought Weather. com to serve customers using the Web.[155]

Launchpad encourages start-ups to apply design thinking (Chapter 4) to gaining market share. One important way to gain market share is setting the right price.

Test Pricing Strategies in Parallel

Launchpad's approach to gaining market share is based on the idea that the start-up cannot predict which pricing strategy will prove to be most effective. Therefore it makes sense to try different possibilities and see which one works the best.

Here's how Launchpad advises start-ups to gain market share:

- Develop a hypothesis for pricing—such as charging one-third of potential customers $1 for the product, another third $2, and giving away the product for free to the other third.
- Introduce these hypothesized pricing strategies to customers.
- Monitor the number of customers who use the product under each of the different pricing strategies.
- Analyze the results of the hypothesis test and either adopt the pricing strategy that works well or develop new hypotheses that will yield better results based on analysis of the results of the previous ones.[156]

Never Stop Experimenting

IDEO believes in maintaining a permanent sense of experimentation in order to gain market share. Hulme suggests that the only way to gain market share is to think of a company as being in "permanent beta mode." In other words, companies must always be doing experiments in which they build prototypes, observe how customers use them, and adapt accordingly.

IDEO urged Yoomi to keep its manufacturing local and its assembly in house so it could shorten its "learning cycle time."[157]

HBS Professor Joe Lassiter offers his own professional experience as a way to illustrate what a start-up must do to gain market share. And he echoes the importance of managing with great uncertainty as an intrinsic element of rapidly growing companies.

After earning his PhD at MIT, Lassiter joined test equipment maker Teradyne when it had $50 million in sales. After he joined, that number immediately dropped to $20 million, and when he left twenty years later, total sales approached $1 billion. Over that span, Lassiter ran about 25 percent of the company.

This experience taught Lassiter that he liked working in new companies that are experimenting and growing fast. He is intrigued by making decisions in the light of incomplete and inadequate information, and designing the lowest-cost experiments that can test those decisions. But once he has built a new venture that hits 200 people, he tends to want to move on to a new one.[158]

HUNGRY START-UP STRATEGY APPROACH TO GAINING SHARE

The *hungry start-up strategy approach to gaining share* urges entrepreneurs to take the following initiatives:

- *Offer customers a low-risk way to try the start-up's product.* CEOs can boost the chances that a customer will try a start-up's product if it relieves the customer's pain much more effectively than competing products do. However, in many cases, those customers will be reluctant to pay for a start-up's product—at least initially. That's why many start-ups offer customers a free version of the product so they perceive that they are getting an irresistible value.
- *Encourage customers to recommend the product.* There is tremendous value to a start-up in encouraging satisfied customers to recommend its product to members of their social and business networks. Such referrals can lead to very rapid, viral growth in the number of users. Instagram, a mobile photo-sharing service, achieved this kind of growth—leading Facebook to acquire it in April 2012 for $1 billion despite having no revenue and only thirteen employees.
- *Raise the start-up's price as the product's perceived value rises.* If the start-up's product delivers on its promise and the company survives long enough to deliver an improved version, it should implement a strategy that allows the start-up to generate positive cash flow.
- *Expand customer and geographic scope.* Once the start-up has established that it can serve a group of customers within a specific industry or region, it can gain market share by applying its competitive strengths to a new market. The start-up can choose to maintain its focus on the same industry and find new customers in different countries, it can apply its skills to new industries in the same region, or it can expand in both directions.

Hungry Start-Up Strategy Market-Share-Gaining Methodology

How do these start-ups find the customer pain and relieve it?

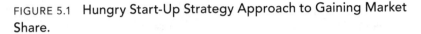

FIGURE 5.1 Hungry Start-Up Strategy Approach to Gaining Market Share.

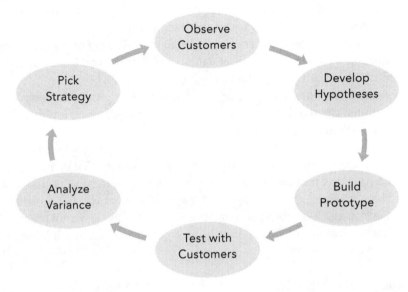

The following list details the approach recommended in Figure 5.1:

- *Discover details of their unmet needs.* Entrepreneurs must observe the customers in pain that they choose to target. To do that, they should develop a set of interview questions, meet with these suffering customers in the environment where they're suffering, and listen to what they say when you ask them the questions. Through this listening, start-ups must discover more details about the nature of their pain—and try to assess what kind of product would encourage them to become customers.
- *Develop hypotheses.* Using the observations of customer needs and the start-up's vision of the technology, it should make educated guesses about the most important product features likely to lead to wide customer adoption. Moreover, the start-up should make a numeric estimate of the number of customers it thinks will use a prototype with those features.
- *Build a prototype solution.* The next step is to develop a quick and inexpensive prototype with those features. The first version is not likely to meet the customer's unmet need but it should help the start-up focus

quickly on the specific product features that it must improve to get customers to use and ultimately pay for the product.

- *Test with customers.* The start-up must then give the prototype to customers; keep track of how many customers actually use the product; and ask them what they like and don't like about it. The general objective of this step is to learn and collect data that will either confirm or disconfirm the hypotheses developed earlier.

- *Analyze variance.* The start-up should compare the expected outcome with the observed results. This comparison will generate insights that shape the start-up's strategic positioning.

- *Pick strategy.* Better-than-expected results are likely to confirm that the start-up will gain market share if it turns the current version of the prototype into a product and markets it aggressively. If the results are worse than expected, the start-up must learn from what did not work and develop another prototype. And it should iterate and test until observed results exceed expectations, or until it becomes clear that it's time to shut down the business.

Benefits of Hungry Start-Up Strategy Market-Share-Gaining Methodology

This approach to building the team offers a start-up four benefits:

- *It discovers reference customers.* Start-ups need to find potential customers who like to be the first in their industry to try something new. Even those customers will not bother with a start-up if its product does not satisfy a burning unmet need. By focusing on alleviating customer pain, start-ups can lower customers' reluctance to switch vendors because no other companies are solving that problem.

- *It reveals the start-up's business model.* Many start-ups get going without knowing how they will generate revenues. If they start off with an explicit acknowledgment of this reality, then the odds rise that they will see the need to figure out their business model early. Such as discovery process may involve significant trial and error in an effort to hit on a product that customers will initially use and ultimately pay for.

- *It focuses the founders.* When a start-up is in its early days, there are probably hundreds of different things that the founders could do with their time every day. How do they decide what subset of things they ought to do in those early months? By focusing on alleviating customer pain, the founders and their colleagues have a way to make that decision.

- *It helps create the conditions for additional financing.* Finally, a focus on alleviating customer pain creates a learning process that is quite valuable for potential investors in future rounds. If the start-up can discover such pain and develop a product that relieves it, then the start-up's founders are in a far better position to go to investors and convince them that there is demand for their product.

GAINING SHARE: THREE APPROACHES

Start-ups I interviewed take three approaches to gaining market share. But these approaches all share a common principle: They identify customer pain and relieve it with a product that delivers a QVL. And each approach delivers a very compelling value proposition to its varying stakeholders.

While sharing this common thrust, each of the three approaches targets different stakeholders. As Figure 5.2 illustrates, the companies I interviewed targeted their QVLs to three sets of stakeholders.

These groups are described in more detail below:

- *Superior performance on most important customer purchase criteria (CPC) (64 percent).* The founders of companies in this category gain market share by homing in on the biggest pain point of one customer in the industry value network and delivering those customers a QVL on that specific criterion. Several start-ups I interviewed offer business customers much higher Internet technology (IT) productivity and in so doing are able to generate a very swift payback on the investment in the start-up's product.
- *Superior value to consumers and distributors (20 percent).* The founders of companies in this category strive to create QVLs for both consumers and the businesses that distribute products or services to them. This approach is quite common for companies seeking to accumulate millions of consumers who visit frequently with the hope of attracting advertisers seeking to reach those consumers. Pinterest, an online scrap-booking service that attracted 10 million users faster than any of

FIGURE 5.2 **Approach for Gaining Start-Up Market Share, by Percent of Interviewees.**

Aiming for superior performance on top CPC — 64%

Offering superior value to consumers and distributors — 20%

Providing superior value to suppliers and consumers — 16%

its competitors by December 2011, is an example of a start-up that has created superior value for consumers and likely aspires to do the same for advertisers seeking to reach them.

- *Superior value to suppliers and consumers (16 percent).* Start-ups in this category strive to create QVLs for the companies that supply them products and to those products' consumers. Many retail start-ups I interviewed seek to give suppliers of high-end clothing access to, say, students at top universities at discount prices. These retailers offer consumers great bargains on prestigious brands while offering the clothing suppliers a chance to develop long-term customer relationships with students who are likely to become top earners who will pay full price in the future.

Let's take a closer look at each of these groups.

Superior Performance on Most Important Customer Purchase Criteria

The simplest way to gain market share is to find one group of customers and deliver an overwhelmingly better way to solve a problem that ails these customers. To do this, start-ups should do the following:

- Based on their own experience, find an unsolved problem that afflicts customers.
- Interview those customers to identify the criteria—such as price, service, quality, or others—that they would use to pick suppliers of a product that would solve the customer problem.
- Ask the customers to rank those criteria in order of importance.
- Develop a product that excels in satisfying the most important CPC.

Here are three examples of how the start-ups I interviewed apply this approach to gaining market share.

ASSIA

ASSIA, which makes software for providers of high-speed Internet service over copper wires—known as Digital Subscriber Line (DSL)—controls a whopping 90 percent of the U.S. market for DSL management software. Of its seventeen major deployments, all but five are outside the United States, according to CEO John Cioffi.

The reason for its dominance is that Cioffi believes that ASSIA's software creates between $50 million and $100 million each year in added value for each of its DSL provider customers, and ASSIA charges them a small fraction of that value to license its software. ASSIA also offers its software as a cloud service to smaller carriers.[159]

ASSIA's technology is far superior to competing ones. As Cioffi pointed out, hardware providers have tried and failed to replicate ASSIA's technology.

At the core of ASSIA's technology is software that keeps its customers' customers—DSL consumers—happy. More specifically, ASSIA's software monitors each consumer's DSL service quality—for example, packet loss, a measure of how much transmitted information does not reach its recipient on the first try.

ASSIA's software adjusts what Cioffi referred to cryptically as "customer stability knobs," to make sure that the rate of packet loss and other quality measures remain below a threshold, so that the customer stays happy enough not to bolt to a competing service, and may even be willing to pay for a higher quality of DSL service.

ASSIA's ability to offer its customers a measurably superior return on the investment in its software assures it of future market-share gains.

iZettle

iZettle allows anyone with an Apple iPhone to take chip-card payments. iZettle is the European equivalent of U.S.-based mobile payment service, Square, founded by Twitter co-founder Jack Dorsey. Square gives away a device that attaches to a mobile phone so people can accept credit card payments with a swipe of the card's magnetic stripe.[160]

In Europe, the credit cards have chips instead of magnetic stripes. Founder and CEO Jacob de Geer's wife, who imports products from Asia to Sweden, wanted to use Square to speed up her payments but Square showed no signs of responding to her request.

Dorsey was probably wise not to enter the European market because the technical requirements for accepting payment from a chip card are very different. But as de Geer told me he was not about to let down his wife so in April 2010 he started iZettle.

Within two months of its August 2011 launch, iZettle had gained 10,000 users within the Swedish mobile payment market; that included 450,000 companies with between one and nine employees who were formerly paid by invoice or cash.

iZettle's free iPad, iPhone, and iPod touch app and mini chip-card reader launched in Sweden in August 2011 and "became an instant hit in the App Store; it rocketed to number one in the finance category and number four in the overall App Store."

iZettle offers huge advantages over other systems that let businesses accept chip-card payments. For example, de Geer told me, if a company wants to accept chip cards, it needs to pay almost $4,000 for a chip-card reader along with a technical support fee and transaction fees.

iZettle's tangibly better return on its customers' investment in the service is the best way for it to keep growing.

Xsigo

Xsigo saves companies capital expenditures by making much more efficient use of their networks. By February 2012, Xsigo had between 250 and 260 customers around the world and it was growing fast—it then had 150 people, 50 more than the year before. One recent "customer win is Salesforce.com that paid under $200,000 for its first Xsigo 'kit,' a combination of input/output hardware and server virtualization software—and saved over $1 million in capital expenditures in the bargain," according to CEO Lloyd Carney.[161]

At the heart of its growth is the irresistible deal Xsigo makes to potential customers. To understand the offer that companies can't refuse from Xsigo, you need to know about data center switches that connect storage devices in an air-conditioned floor where companies store their ever-growing piles of data.

Established switch vendors—such as Cisco, Hewlett Packard, Juniper, and Brocade— sell switches that use only 5 percent of their potential capacity, according to Carney. Their typical switch has 100 switch ports—where cables attach.

Each of their cables has the potential to carry 10 gigabytes (GB) of traffic, but by Carney's calculation Cisco's technology leaves 9.5 GB of that data-carrying capacity unused. Through the use of so-called "switch virtualization," Xsigo makes much more efficient use of a switch's data-carrying capacity while enabling companies to buy relatively cheap commodity servers—instead of expensive, closed-system Cisco switches.

As a result, Xsigo's product saves companies the capital they would spend on those inefficient switches, to the tune of a 50 to 60 percent reduction. That's because Xsigo can make one cable with 40 GB of capacity act like forty-eight of the 10-GB cables that its competitors sell.

Not only does that save companies capital expenditures; it also saves them on power: 10 watts per cable, according to Xsigo customer NTT, the Japanese telecom giant. In Carney's estimation, companies that are buying twenty or more servers will get a speedy payback on the cost of Xsigo's switch virtualization software.

Xsigo created so much customer value that on July 30, 2012, Oracle acquired it for an undisclosed sum.

Superior Value to Consumers and Distributors

Many start-ups choose to deal with more complex industries in which they can only gain share if they create superior value for other industry participants. For example, if the start-up hopes to reach the end user of its product, it must also make a compelling economic case to distributors or partners.

Simply put, such start-ups offer products that are so valuable to consumers that they draw more of them into the distribution channel or retail store that the partner operates. If the new customers bring additional profit to the distributors, then both participants are better off.

Here are two companies that use this approach.

Bionée

Bionée has eight products for three related groups of people, among them, acne and anti-stretch–mark products for pregnant women, a postpregnancy slimming product for women taking care of their babies, and protective body lotion for babies.

Bionée's products are certified as safe and organic by France's Ecocert. As CEO Ewa Asmar pointed out, there is no dedicated regulatory body in the United States that certifies cosmetics. This makes it easier to introduce new products quickly but it also leaves consumers open to products that might not be suitable for consumption.

For Bionée's direct marketing force, Asmar wants to recruit mothers who like the product and who would like to make a living selling it. To do this, she is working with networks of midwives and *doulas* (who help women as they deliver babies). Doulas tend to work with mothers on a volunteer basis, and they believe strongly in the importance of "natural and holistic birth."

Hence, if they like Bionée's products, Asmar expects them to be compelling advocates. Rather than holding Tupperware parties, Bionée has "playdate advocates." According to Asmar, "Bionée believes in creating awareness through engaging by emotions. The company wants to give moms a lot of freedom to express themselves in a way they feel comfortable with, and wants to bring forward their talents and skills." She continued, "The playdate structure has therefore an educational angle, which makes the purchase a unique experience. Playdates around a parenting or pregnancy theme are a unique change to the traditional corporate way of selling at home."[162]

If Bionée can deliver better products to moms and more cash flow to doulas, it has good growth prospects.

Kayak

Kayak creates compelling value for consumers and people trying to advertise to them. As Kellie Pelletier, Kayak.com's VP of communications, explained, "Co-founders of Orbitz, Travelocity, and Expedia created Kayak.com to provide consumers with more comprehensive travel options in one place."

The site searches more than 100 different travel sites and provides real-time prices and availability for hundreds of airlines, 158,000 hotels, all leading rental-car companies, and 17 cruise lines. Kayak.com displays more choices of available itinerary/price combinations than any other travel site. Kayak.com even offers consumer comments and professional reviews to assist with trip-planning decisions.

Kayak.com is a travel search engine or "meta-search site" and not a retailer, so the site does not sell anything. Kayak.com is especially helpful because it links travelers directly to the airlines, hotels, and rental-car companies to make their reservations, which means users avoid paying the high service fees charged by online agencies, and benefit from incentives offered on supplier sites such as reward points and upgrades, according to Pelletier.

This strategy has yielded tangible results in terms of market share and return on advertising investment for travel advertisers. As Drew Patterson, Kayak.com's VP of marketing, explained, "According to Compete.com's December 2008 survey, we are the seventh-largest online travel site. We are in the search marketplace, and we get our revenues from travel advertisers. Our conversion rate is 10 to 15 percent, and we get paid per click—which represents 100 percent of our revenues. And we see ourselves at being really good at travel consideration—which is helping people absorb large bodies of information so they can make sense of it.[163]

By July 2012, Kayak.com completed an initial public offering as Kayak Software. Its May 2012 prospectus indicated that for the first quarter of 2012 it had over $73 million in revenues, 39 percent more than the year before, and its profit was $4.1 million. Moreover, in the first quarter of 2012, Kayak had 3 million downloads of its mobile software, representing growth of 43 percent.[164]

This suggests that Kayak generated value not only for consumers and advertisers but also for its investors.

Superior Value to Suppliers and Consumers

Many of the start-ups I interviewed position themselves between their suppliers and their customers. And in so doing, they create value for both in a way that puts into action the original meaning of the French word entrepreneur—someone who *takes between*—or as I would interpret this—someone who finds and profits from a market opportunity between two participants at different stages of the industry's value network.

Suppliers will not allow a start-up to take their existing customers. They will be glad to work only with a start-up that provides new customers, thus boosting their profits.

Here are three case studies of start-ups that create superior value for suppliers and customers.

Cardlytics

Cardlytics gives $100 to $200 in discounts every year on products that they advertise on the back of customers' bank statements. Cardlytics service benefits the product suppliers, the product consumers' banks, and the consumers.

CEO Scott Grimes explains: "We sell to good-sized banks. We've reached 10 million households and are targeting a market of 75 million households. The product benefits all our stakeholders: Consumers with average card usage save $100 to $200 a year—with no cap to what they can save, banks get a free program that drives more visits to their Web site and retailers only pay for ads when consumers use offers."

Grimes continued, "We can adapt much more quickly to market opportunities than large competitors. Our secret sauce is making the system work for the conservative banking industry while it also appeals to cutting-edge advertisers. We've expanded into mobile devices through the banks and are looking to social networks next and into global markets in 2011."[165]

If Cardlytics continues to deliver value to consumers, banks, and advertisers, its growth should follow.

Coolspotters

Coolspotters has grown fast, and in the process, has benefited product suppliers, advertisers, and consumers.

As Aaron LaBerge, CEO of Fanzter, Coolspotters' parent company, explained, "The Coolspotters platform gives entertainment lovers a true 360-degree view of whatever they're passionate about. As a result, we've been lucky enough to see our usage go from about 30,000 monthly unique users our first month (May 2008) to about 350,000 unique users as of January 2009 (and growing fast)."

Coolspotters gets revenues—from advertising and e-commerce—from the online-retailing industry, which it believes to be valued at $300 billion.

According to LaBerge, "Most of our revenue comes from commerce transactions and brand advertising. Currently they are about equal, but commerce revenue continues to grow quickly. It's very clear that celebrities and public figures have a huge influence on a consumer's purchasing decisions."[166]

If Coolspotters keeps generating consumer enthusiasm and demand for suppliers' products, it should keep growing.

Value Retail

Scott Malkin is outcompeting the world's malls in sales per square foot. How? He has created a company operated by retailers who serve the fashion brands and the women who love them, while his competitors think of outlet malls only as another form of real estate development.

After graduating from HBS, Malkin started Value Retail in 1992. As Malkin said, Value Retail has married Freeport, Maine (famous for its L.L Bean Store and hundreds of other outlet stores), with locations in Europe like Disneyland Paris.

Nineteen years later, Value Retail had about $2 billion in revenue, growing at 20 percent a year, and it operated nine Villages in the major tourism markets of Western Europe. At $1,950 its Bicester Village, outside Oxford, England, had the highest sales per square foot of any mall in the world.

At $2,250 per square foot, this was far better than Value Retail's portfolio average of about $1,200 per square foot (growing at about 15 percent per year) and several times better than the high end regional mall industry average of $500 to $700 per square foot.

A big reason for Value Retail's superior performance is its corporate mind-set. While its competitors are construction and finance guys who understand how to build retail space, Value Retail is a company run substantially by women who are creating an environment that appeals to women shoppers.

Value Retail focuses on a very specific group of customers—people who are traveling or have a traveling mentality. It offers discounts on popular brands in destinations near major cities. More specifically, its Villages give consumers discounts of up to 70 percent on roughly 100 brand-name fashion boutiques on year-old, retail items from raincoats to purses.

Its Villages are retail destinations near European capital cities. And with their sense of place, they are what Malkin called "an antidote to the Internet."[167]

If Value Retail continues to find new destinations for its target consumers and perseveres in offering them attractive discounts on brand-name products, its growth should persist.

HUNGRY START-UP MARKET-SHARE-GAINING TACTICS

Here are steps that a CEO can follow to apply the *hungry start-up strategy approach to gaining market share*.

Discover Details of Customers' Unmet Needs

To gain share, entrepreneurs need to gain greater insight into why customers' unmet needs are important to them and what would constitute a compelling solution. To that end, the start-up team should take the following steps:

- Develop an interview guide to structure the conversation with customers. For example, a start-up selling to companies might create an interview guide including these topics:
  - Who the key decision makers are
  - What unmet needs are most pressing and why
  - How those unmet needs will hurt the organization in the future if they are not resolved
  - What an ideal solution to the problem would look like
  - How much the company would be willing to pay for that solution and why
- Conduct the interviews.
- Analyze the results, highlighting both a statistical analysis of the answers to the questions and interesting quotes and observed behaviors that illustrate the key findings.

Develop Hypotheses

The start-up team must next brainstorm possible ways to solve the most pressing unmet needs they discover in the previous step. This process should generate hypotheses—or informed guesses—about the product attributes that will make customers enthusiastic and how many customers will use the product.

To that end, the start-up team—possibly using the CEO as facilitator—should take the following steps:

- Review the analysis of the customer interviews.
- Write each team member's two most significant findings on a sticky note.
- Ask team members to discuss why they picked their findings.

- Vote as a group on which customer findings it considers most important.
- Encourage each team member to develop three to five new product ideas that would solve these key customer problems.
- Team members present their two best ideas.
- Team votes on the two or three best ideas.
- Team estimates how many customers will use each of these products.
- Team picks the product idea that it believes will be the best received.

Build a Prototype Solution

The start-up team must next develop a prototype—an inexpensive version of the product idea selected above—with a minimum of time and money. The nature of the product determines how to accomplish this.

For example, it will require much more time and money to build a prototype of a robot for disarming improvised explosion devices than to build an iPhone app that lets people view news stories from their favorite sources.

Regardless of the prototype, start-up teams can take the following steps:

- List all the features of the proposed prototype from the customer's perspective.
- Rank these features based on their perceived importance to the customer.
- For the most important features (for example, how long an iPhone app takes to load), estimate the specific measure (for example, 10 milliseconds) that a customer will use to determine whether the product works well.
- Agree on the three to five most critical features of the prototype and the specific success measures that customers will use to decide whether each is a success.
- Set a specific and very ambitious time frame to build a prototype and put all available resources to work to meet the deadline.

Test with Customers

Once the start-up decides the prototype is ready, it must observe how customers use it. To that end, the start-up team should follow these steps:

- Identify potential customers and ask them to try the prototype.
- Observe how they use the prototype. Depending on whether the product is physical or virtual, such observation could take many forms, including
  - Videotaping the customers as they use the prototype

- Tracking their key strokes as they use the prototype, measuring how much time they spend using it and what specific aspects consume most of their time
- Letting them use the prototype on their own and asking them questions about it afterwards
- Counting the people in their network to whom they recommend the product

- Compare the actual feedback from customers using the prototype to the hypothesized reaction.
- Highlight results that were better and worse than expected.

Analyze Variance

The start-up must next analyze the reasons for the gaps between expected and observed results. In general, if the outcome is much better than expected in all areas, then the start-up should take encouragement and consider how to turn the prototype with its current features into a more robust product. If the outcome is worse than expected, the start-up must learn why.

Regardless of the outcome, the start-up must investigate positive variances to gain insight into why customers liked the prototype and if the variances were negative, the start-up must find out why customers did not like the prototype and figure out what the next version should do in order to generate better results.

The best way to do this is to ask those tested to describe their reactions to the prototype. The start-up should explore the following questions:

- What features did you like, and why?
- Which features did you not like, and why?
- How would you envision improving these features so you would be enthusiastic about the product?
- Which features did you not use, and why?
- What missing features are critical to your decision to use the product? Why are these features important to you?

Pick Strategy

If the prototype does not excite the customer, the start-up should develop a new hypothesis. In so doing, the team should use the results of the analysis of variance to minimize the risk of failure in the next version of the prototype. (The start-up must do this while recognizing that it is rapidly running through dwindling resources.)

And if the prototype achieves a positive reaction, the start-up should use the insights gained from the learning loops we've described to set its strategy by making choices in key dimensions including

- Product features
- Price
- Distribution channel
- Sales and marketing
- Manufacturing

As we'll explore in Chapter 6, if the strategy results in market-share gains for the start-up, the profits that flow from that success represent a blessing and a curse. Success feeds the start-up's hungers to change the world and pay its stakeholders. But it also has the potential to produce complacency that ultimately dooms its long-term survival.

GAINING MARKET SHARE: DID YOU DO IT RIGHT?

The examples of different approaches to gaining market share suggest some questions that can help start-up CEOs assess whether they have taken the correct approach. These questions include the following:

- Can you name ten potential customers for your product and their pain points?
- Are there competing products that are relieving those potential customers' pain?
- If so, are you confident that a customer would try your product and conclude that it does a better job than competitors'?
- Are you convinced that potential customers are willing to pay enough for your product to generate sufficient profit to keep your start-up afloat?
- If you are selling to other industry participants—suppliers or distributors—can you offer them a compelling value proposition?
- In comparison to competitors, are your capabilities better when it comes to delivering that value proposition to these potential customers?
- Are your incentives for employees better aligned with customers' economic interests than those of your competitors?

If you have solid answers to these questions then your approach to gaining market share is probably right. And if not, these questions may help you rethink those choices until you do have solid answers to them.

SUMMARY

Start-ups with no revenues or customers are born hungry. In order to survive, they must find the right customers and offer them an irresistible reason to try their product. The right customers are similarly hungry for a solution to a problem that matters to them. If your start-up's product solves that problem well, then take the steps needed to lower customers' risk of trying it to deliver a QVL.

Once this has been achieved for a small number of customers, the start-up must find more in order to grow. Picking customers wisely means knowing that there are enough of them who will be willing to pay for the start-up's solution. And finding that out often depends on asking potential customers whether your product will be valuable to them and how much they are willing to pay for it.

CHAPTER 6

Adapting to Change
Don't Let Others Eat Your Lunch

DESPITE THE MANY RISKS they face, hungry start-ups enjoy at least one big advantage over their larger rivals: They make decisions faster. But as start-ups enjoy success, they run the risk of becoming like their bigger peers: slowed down by the conflict between protecting their profitable products and adapting to market shifts.

In order to prevail, start-ups must respond to change and they must do that in spite of their initial success. The irony is that by filling their bellies with market share, capital, and people, start-ups are at risk of losing their hunger to change. And if they lose that hunger, they will become vulnerable to other hungry start-ups seeking to eat their lunch.

To adapt effectively to external threats and opportunities, entrepreneurs must answer difficult questions. These questions and my findings follow.

- *What part of the start-up's business strategy should change over time?* The answer to this question varies by start-up. Based on my interviews, the most common change is to the company's product. In general, start-ups offer customers new versions of their product, get feedback on those versions, and make the next version better. Start-ups commonly build new partnerships and expand into new countries as a way to tap the profit they expect to follow from their product advantages over competitors in these markets.
- *In observing changes in technology, evolving customer needs, and upstart competitors, how do entrepreneurs pick out the signal from the noise?* Most commonly, entrepreneurs filter these changing market messages— either signal or noise—through the lenses of their customers. If they decide that not responding would cost them customers, then they take the change as a signal. If the same change would have no impact on the start-up's ability to get new customers and retain older ones, then the

entrepreneur treats the change as noise. Simply put, the start-up adapts to signals, and does not respond to noise.

- *Should an entrepreneur make changes that realize the company vision or should the venture adapt to market feedback?* Both approaches are common. The start-up CEO with a clear vision of what the company needs to be able to do to achieve its goals will seek to build new capabilities—such as partnerships or acquisitions—that bring that vision closer to reality. However, many entrepreneurs track different market signals, such as net promoter scores (a way of measuring how many customers recommend the company's products), viral coefficients (that track whether new customers are replacing old ones), and other measures of customer satisfaction. If these market signals are getting better, the start-up will stay on its current trajectory. If not, it will try to change so these market signals improve.

ADAPTING TO CHANGE

The most critical point about adapting to change is the willingness to admit to failure quickly and move on. Ironically, this attitude toward failure is one of the big reasons that start-ups succeed while their larger peers stumble.

The Experts Weigh In on Adapting to Change

Fail Fast, Learn, Grow

How so? In large firms, admitting failure can be a career ender. Often the blame for a failure is placed squarely on the shoulders of the person with the least amount of political power, even though the failure has been parented by a top executive.

This leads to a culture of intellectual dishonesty that makes it nearly impossible for a larger firm to assess how well, compared with competitors, it is satisfying the needs of its customers.

By contrast, if a start-up tries a business strategy that fails, it must do so quickly and at the lowest possible cost. Given its limited cash flows, the start-up needs to come up with a better strategy and get it working fast before it runs out of money.

As a result, the start-up is likely to find its way to a successful strategy far more quickly than the larger firm that can afford to ignore its failure long enough to scapegoat someone that nobody likes anyway.

Eric Ries, the author of a book on lean start-ups, offers an interesting perspective on this topic. Ries graduated from Yale and worked as a programmer. He rose to the job of chief technology officer at IMVU—a social networking site whose members use 3D avatars to meet new people—founded in 2004.[168]

Before IMVU, Ries worked during the dot-com boom at a start-up that failed, and at the heart of the start-up's failure was that people didn't want its product. Ries referred to it as "a science fiction product that was a commercial failure."

But Ries's experience taught him that many ventures struggle to find a viable business model. What he noticed is that in that struggle, ventures should find a way to make meaningful, inexpensive stabs at finding many business models as possible before they run out of money.

To that end, Ries was interested in the ideas of Steve Blank, a Silicon Valley start-up guru, that a company should talk to customers and continuously release new versions of its product—as many as fifty times a day. Using customer feedback on these new versions of the product, companies could discover what works and what doesn't.

At the time, Ries believed this was a radical notion—far different from the traditional approach of engineers working in isolation to perfect a product before releasing it to the market. As I pointed out to Ries, however, this idea has been around for decades. I first wrote about it in my 1997 book, *The Technology Leaders*.

And I got the idea from Franz Edelman, the late RCA operations research guru with whom I had the honor of working in 1982 when I was employed by Index Systems, an IT consulting firm founded by four former MIT Sloan School professors.

Regardless of the origins of the idea of prototyping, Ries was making investors "giddy" with "how much stuff we got done" using the approach. And investors raved about how it made employees "supernaturally productive" and thought Ries "was a genius."

Ries observed that people were very resistant to the idea of rapid prototyping. He saw them as being "invested in the heavy psychological burden of believing that everything you ever did in the past is right."

But Ries realized that old ways of thinking about managing were linked to the ability to plan the future with confidence, as General Motors did when it dominated the automobile market in the 1950s.

Ries knew that start-ups could not do that kind of planning—they lived in a world that was the opposite of 1950s GM. So he began with the principle that start-ups needed a management discipline that would help them deal with extreme uncertainty.

Ries concluded that the idea of "lean manufacturing"—cutting costs such as inventories so that a company spends only on creating customer value—could be applied to start-ups.

The resulting lean start-up methodology imparts insights as to what customers value through cheap, fast experiments, which steer the start-up to a viable business model.

Ries discovered that while lean manufacturing advocated small batch sizes (a batch is a part of the manufacturing process that gets completed before it goes on to the next step), this mind-set did not work for start-ups.

To illustrate this idea, Ries provides the example of a person sending out, say, fifty resumes. The batch approach would tell the person to follow these steps: (1) print out all fifty letters, (2) fold them all, (3) stuff them into fifty envelopes, (4) seal all the envelopes, (5) put stamps on them, and finally (6) dump them all into a mailbox.

But Ries points out that it's faster for the job seeker to perform all these steps at once—print, fold, stuff, seal, and stamp—for each letter sent—rather than in separate batches. This is the key to the series of frugal experiments that will help a start-up find a viable business model.

To measure whether that business model yields growth, Ries uses a viral coefficient (K) that tracks whether new customers outnumber ones that drop away from a service. If K is growing fast—and exceeds 1.0—as it did with Facebook, for example—then the start-up is learning effectively.

And that means that even though it might not be generating cash flow, a VC firm might be wise to invest to make sure that the start-up has the resources to monetize its growing K.

Be Tough-Minded about Failure

Stevenson has a simpler idea for how start-ups ought to adapt to change. In his view, start-ups need to be very tough minded about failure.

More specifically, Stevenson believes that start-ups should be intellectually honest and should make their people understand that life will go on after failure. He thinks that intellectual honesty—the ability to recognize when something is not working and to cut your losses—can be taught.

He also believes that for a bet to succeed, many things have to go right at the same time. So if failure happens it's important to learn from it by recognizing which specific factors went wrong—and right—and then move on.[169]

But to appreciate Stevenson's view of how start-ups adapt to change, it helps to understand how it fits into his broader thoughts regarding entrepreneurship, which he defines as "the pursuit of opportunity beyond the resources you currently control."[170]

This is an important distinction because it is far easier to target an opportunity than it is to build a company to take advantage of it. And a key entrepreneurial skill is the ability to persuade people you don't control to give your venture the resources it needs to seize that opportunity.

While Stevenson cites a long list of HBS entrepreneurs, one stands out: Batten. Batten ignored those who said it was impossible for a channel on weather 24/7 to survive. And if July 2008's $3.5 billion acquisition of the twenty-six-year-old channel reaching 96 million homes is any indication, those naysayers were wrong.

Stevenson served twenty years on the board of Landmark Communications. From this perch, Stevenson was able to observe three traits that made Batten such a great entrepreneur:

- *Serving the customer.* Batten continuously invested in boosting the value that the Weather Channel created for its customers—the viewers, cable networks, and advertisers.
- *Unique approach to results.* Batten wanted to encourage people to take risks and to treat people well. As a result, he rewarded a manager who ran a business that lost $60 million because Batten thought, without him, that the business would have lost $100 million. And Batten fired the manager of his most profitable business because he treated people badly.
- *Trusting people.* Batten did not spend his time making sure that managers are not cheating him. He told them, "I trust you but if you cheat me I will prosecute you to the full extent of the law."
- *Loyalty toward people.* Batten took care of many of his people. As Stevenson pointed out, there were a few hundred shareholder-employees who did well and were all able to retire very comfortably—"some in the eight figures."

A quote from one of Stevenson's students reflects an important lesson HBS hopes to impart: "You taught me to define an opportunity for me." To Stevenson, this comment has two important implications. The first is that HBS helps students envision a future state of the world that's different from the current one, by illustrating many alternatives. The second is that HBS gives students the belief that such an end state is possible for them.

Composting to Learn from Failure

Launchpad builds on the idea that entrepreneurs must be good at learning by encouraging start-ups to take the emotion out of analyzing failure.

Some Stanford students enter school with the idea that people are either failures or successes. Design thinking busts that myth, by teaching that successful people can try and fail and that value can be extracted from analyzing the failure.

Co-head Dearing calls this analysis composting. For example, a venture wanted to produce fuzzy slippers from animal fur. Its founders thought the fur producers were farming the fur and then found out the producers were killing the animals instead of shaving them. When the venture's founders learned this, they shuttered the business. Composting helped them learn from the failure and use that learning in a future venture.

The emotional aspect of design thinking—where Perry Klebahn, Launchpad's other co-head, takes the lead—vies in significance with its cerebral component, Dearing's primary bailiwick. Stanford students tend to excel at the cerebral part and feel discomfort when Launchpad forces them to act before they believe they're intellectually prepared .

Forcing Stanford students to take action before they have the "right answer" goes against their grain. But Dearing and Klebahn have developed ways to push them into the water. While Dearing focuses on showing them that the worst outcome of a failed prototype is not that bad, Klebahn gives them emotional reinforcement for taking action.

And if that bias for action can help people who like design do's and don'ts to get comfortable with business building, Launchpad will ultimately turn more of them into entrepreneurs.[171]

Let Start-Up Board Adapt to Change

Charm offers an interesting general perspective about how start-ups can adapt to change. Charm points out that start-up CEOs are usually too engaged in the day-to-day of building a product, thinking about getting office space, raising capital, hiring, and so on to think about longer-term trends.

Charm believes that start-ups should have board members who can filter out all the market noise to focus the CEO on the most important market signals to which the start-up should adapt; a leader such as the CEO is more likely than managers to develop an effective approach.[172]

Boundaryless Company Development—the Hungry Start-Up Strategy Approach to Adapting to Change

Most large companies use incentive systems that encourage them to resist change and they don't adapt until the costs of that resistance get very high. Moreover, they develop products through a relay-race approach whereby engineers develop a blueprint and throw it over the transom to manufacturing, which builds the product, then calling on the sales force to find customers.

Such large companies also operate with a "not-invented-here" (NIH) syndrome—meaning that if a new product comes along and it was not developed by the company, then its significance is dismissed. When in the 1980s Ken Olsen, CEO of minicomputer giant DEC, noticed the growing popularity of personal computers (PCs), he resisted selling them, presenting strong symptoms of the NIH syndrome.

DEC ultimately got gobbled up as PCs overtook it.[173] But since start-ups run out of money unless they are on a path to positive cash flow, it is vital that they change a failed strategy before it's too late.

Hungry start-ups cannot afford to wait before they adapt to change. The relentless pressure to meet the staged goals we discussed in Chapter 1 motivates entrepreneurs to reinvent their companies. Start-ups, like all organizations, need to do that in order to survive over the long term. Specifically, they need to engage in an ongoing process I call the "value cycle" (Figure 6.1).[174]

The value cycle consists of three transformations:

- *Value creation.* To create value, companies listen to customer needs and develop products that meet those needs better than their competitors. In a sense, they transform their insights about unmet customer needs into products that satisfy those needs. As we discussed in the section on alleviating customer pain, start-ups have a unique way of creating value.
- *Value capture.* To capture value, companies set their prices and costs at a level that enables them to earn superior profits. Here, companies transform the value they create for customers—also known as "willingness to pay" (WTP)[175]—into returns for their shareholders. As we'll discuss in this section, start-ups change the way they capture value over time. Initially, they may set prices at or near zero—giving away most of the WTP—and over time; they raise prices as customers acknowledge the benefits of their products.

FIGURE 6.1 **Value Cycle.**

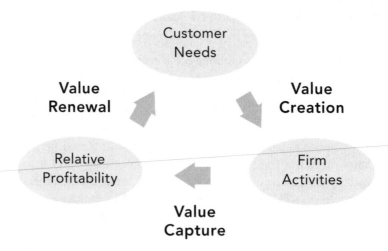

- *Value renewal.* Customer needs, technology, and upstart competitor strategies change. To continue to gain market share, companies must adapt to these changes. Long-term survivors do this through value renewal, applying a learning mind-set to these changes and adjusting the company's competitive strategy accordingly. Value renewal is how companies adapt to the changes in customer needs, technology, and upstart competitor strategies. Start-ups have a unique approach to value renewal, using "boundaryless company development" (BCD)[176] as a way to focus the ongoing reinvention of their products, pricing, and marketing.

Boundaryless Company Development Methodology

As depicted in Figure 6.2, BCD is a fairly simple concept. The idea is to build a team of people from different disciplines—both inside and outside a company—who can help reinvent the company so it maintains its market leadership instead of resting on its laurels.

This team would follow an iterative process quite similar to the one discussed in Chapter 5. However, the scope of the team's work would extend beyond the development of the first product to rethink key elements of the start-up's overall growth strategy. Specifically, this team would follow this six-step methodology:

- *Map out the start-up's value network.* The value network connects all the links in a company's business system from its most basic suppliers to its product end-users. For example, the value network for a semiconductor

FIGURE 6.2   Boundaryless Company Development (BCD) Methodology.

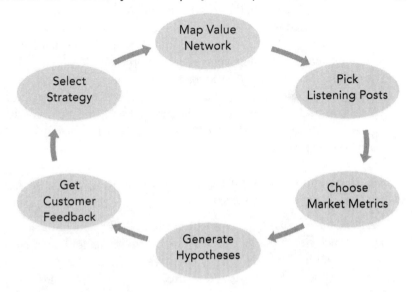

maker would start with suppliers of the raw materials for a computer chip and connect all the industries from there to the end user of the device that contains that chip. BCD begins with mapping the value network because it helps to identify all the potential sources of key signals to which the venture must adapt.

- *Identify the critical listening posts.* By sending members of the BCD team to different places in the value network, the venture must decide which ones are most critical. More specifically, it should focus on the participants in the value network who represent its most significant threats and opportunities.

- *Pick market feedback metrics.* The next step in the BCD process is to pick feedback metrics—for example, the viral coefficient that measures growth in customers or the conversion rate for online advertisers—to determine whether the venture's business model needs to change, and if so, how.

- *Generate business model hypotheses.* Based on the market feedback, the BCD team must develop hypotheses about the venture's business model. More specifically, the team should use the market feedback to pinpoint what parts of the business are working well and which ones are faltering. This input should fuel a brainstorming process for a new business model.

- *Get market feedback on hypotheses.* Next the BCD team should try out the new business model hypotheses with a sample of its customers, and gather market feedback. The venture should use this market feedback either to implement the hypotheses with the best market feedback or to use that feedback to develop a new set of hypotheses.
- *Refine business model based on market feedback.* In the spirit of value renewal, the team should continue to seek out feedback, develop new hypotheses, and adapt based on market feedback. Indeed, ventures large and small must persist in the BCD process because to let up on it is to sacrifice their future viability.

Benefits of Boundaryless Company Development
Here are three benefits to start-ups of BCD:

- *It keeps the start-up alert to change.* BCD values healthy paranoia, learning, and diversity. It places a premium on thinking about how a company fits within a broader business ecosystem, and takes functional experts outside of their narrow domains. By forcing companies to see themselves as they appear to customers, BCD keeps a start-up highly attuned to change.
- *It sustains customer loyalty.* Even though start-ups need to add customers in order to grow, they must also take steps to keep their existing customers loyal. BCD is a way for start-ups to stay close to discover their customers' gripes about products and to identify new needs. If a start-up responds effectively to this feedback, it can keep its customers loyal, a far more profitable path than turning over customers and scrambling to recruit new ones.
- *It maps a growth path.* BCD helps companies chart a course for higher sales. The new sales will come from getting existing customers to pay more for new products or services;, finding new customers to buy a product, and opening up new countries as markets for a company's product. As such it creates the conditions needed for the company to reach critical mass so investors can realize a return on their investments.

ADAPTING TO CHANGE: THREE APPROACHES

Start-ups I interviewed take three approaches to adapting to change. These approaches all share a common principle: They all involve picking the corporate equivalent of the North Star and using that fixed point to navigate a start-up's massively uncertain waters.

While sharing this common thrust, each of the three approaches picks a different North Star, as illustrated in Figure 6.3, and explained as follows:

- *Fill capability gap to implement CEO's vision (36 percent).* Start-up CEOs in this category have a very clear vision of the capabilities the firm needs to prevail in the long term. Companies in this category seek opportunities to acquire companies or hire people who can fill in the gaps between this vision and the start-up's current capabilities. These CEOs build relationships throughout the industry and try to create opportunities to fill these capability gaps in order to accelerate the realization of their vision.
- *Track market feedback (35 percent).* The founders of companies that track market feedback are effective at measuring and observing leading indicators of change in their industries. By picking the right measures—for example, changes in the rate at which existing customers are recommending their product to others—such start-ups can anticipate opportunities and threats. By getting a lead on competitors, they are better positioned to change strategy to avoid the threats.
- *Boost performance on key customer need (20 percent).* The founders of these companies seek to stay ahead of competitors by continuing to make their product more valuable to customers. This approach is characteristic of Apple, for example, which introduces an initial version of its product and then adds new features, often creating so much perceived additional value that customers line up outside its stores to upgrade to the latest version. If start-ups are targeting groups of customers whose basic needs remain constant, this approach can help start-ups keep growing over time.[177]

Let's take a closer look at each of these three approaches.

FIGURE 6.3 **Start-Up Approaches to Adapting to Change, by Percent of Interviewees.**

Closing the capability gap — 36%

Tracking market feedback — 35%

Boosting performance based on key customer needs — 21%

Fill Capability Gap to Implement CEO's Vision

The most common way to adapt to change is to compare a start-up's current state with its CEO's long-term goals for the venture. For example, to adapt to change, a start-up with the goal of becoming a large public company pinpoints the capabilities—for example, product development, manufacturing, and sales—required to reach that goal and adds the missing ones until the goal is met.

This is an excellent approach if the entrepreneur knows the industry well enough to have the right vision for the capabilities that the start-up must add. Here are three examples of companies that are getting this right.

Yesware

Yesware makes a browser extension to Google's Gmail that lets salespeople report on their activity more accurately, so public companies can make more precise sales predictions. Yesware's CEO, Matthew Bellows, wants to turn it into a big company that creates value for customers, investors, and employees. He does not want Yesware to become just another company, typical in Boston, which gets acquired by a California firm. To do that, Bellows wants Yesware to have millions of users in the next year or two.[178]

Accomplishing this will depend on four strategic initiatives:

- *Outbound marketing.* Bellows expects Yesware to use direct response online marketing. This approach to marketing will help Yesware to grow rapidly with a minimum of added cost while creating customer loyalty.
- *Viral growth.* He is seeing "significant viral adoption," as salespeople push their organizations and peers to use Yesware. Such viral adoption will turn its customers' salespeople into Yesware evangelists who push more companies to adopt its product.
- *Inbound marketing.* Yesware will interest potential customers who are searching for a solution. More specifically, Yesware's Web site will make it easy for potential customers to try its product and to get in touch with Yesware salespeople if they have questions about how to get the product working well within their organizations. Such inbound marketing is how Bellows wants to get new customers to try its product.
- *Expanding platforms.* Yesware is initially targeting people who use Google Apps with the Chrome browser. The company started supporting Firefox in June 2012. In this way, Bellows expects to become the leading company in its market segment by offering its product to the most popular email platforms.

Antenna Software

To stay competitive, Antenna Software—a Jersey City, New Jersey, provider of a mobile service that lets companies put paper product catalogs onto an iPad—has a fairly unusual strategic planning process. Its managers write a *Forbes*-like article about the company, dated three years into the future.

This imaginary article details the company's revenues, number of employees, number of products, and what customers are saying. Antenna management then communicates that vision to employees and investors and uses it as a guide to actions the company should be taking to realize the vision, including making acquisitions to obtain skills or technologies that its customers need.

If a change in the competitive environment emerges—for example, a new technology, an upstart competitor, or evolving customer needs—CEO Jim Hemmer can decide whether the change will upset Antenna's ability to realize that three-year vision. If so, Antenna will adapt accordingly.[179]

Antenna's three-year plan includes growth by expanding its product capabilities and adding to customers. Hemmer knew the CEO of a Boston-based firm in the industry with a slew of great customers.

So in 2010 Antenna bought the company Vaultus, a maker of mobiScaler, software that lets companies deliver services to consumers' mobile devices. Hemmer concluded that Vaultus's product complemented Antenna's. Moreover, Vaultus—with customers such as E-Trade Group, State Street, Prudential, and Genzyme—could boost Antenna's market penetration.[180]

Antenna demonstrates that if the CEO has the right vision for the capabilities that a start-up needs, then it knows when to seize opportunities—such as acquisitions—to realize that vision.

Pyxis Mobile

A business conference producer's challenge is to coordinate the logistics of getting all the speakers and attendees on airplanes and to the venue, on the same day. A speaker cancels and has to be replaced at the last minute, a hotel runs out of rooms and a new one has to be found fast, reports and presentations are being tweaked and changed up until the last minute.

Everyone involved— speakers, food service companies, meeting attendees, and everyone else—needs to be updated on the latest changes so they can get to the right places at the right times. Since most of the people involved are walking around with smartphones and tablets, it is vital to have the ability to make these changes and send them instantly.

Thanks to Waltham, Massachusetts-based Pyxis Mobile, a company can spend a mere $80,000 for a software platform that lets them build and update its own mobile applications instead of hiring an outside firm to do it for them, according to CEO Steve Levy.

Pyxis Mobile and Levy have gone through some changes since the company was founded in 1998. Originally, Pyxis Mobile made an application for those long-disused Palm Pilots that let salespeople synchronize their handheld devices with their company's customer relationship management (CRM) systems.

Over time, customers asked Pyxis Mobile to customize its applications for each client. After a while, Pyxis Mobile developed a software application that made it very quick for the company to implement the customized changes that customers requested. Eventually, Pyxis Mobile decided to change its focus and sell its platform to companies instead of building customized applications.

To continue to make a difference for companies, Levy wants to fill in the missing pieces in its value chain through acquisitions and partnerships. If it can find companies that help it to design, build, deploy, and manage the mobility platform for its customers in a way that will deliver quick benefits to customers, Levy will acquire or partner with them.[181]

From these examples, start-ups should take away an important lesson. An entrepreneur must develop a clear vision of the capabilities that a venture needs in order to grow by adding new products and customers. These new capabilities can come from acquisitions or from hiring people with the needed skills.

Track Market Feedback

Many of the entrepreneurs I interviewed do not have such a clear vision of the future. Instead, they believe that it's wiser to reinvent their venture based on market feedback. They use many different kinds of market feedback—from end users, intermediaries, and other business partners.

And they seek out quantitative measures of that feedback. For example, customer feedback might come in the form of net promoter scores and the viral coefficient. Intermediary feedback—for example, from advertisers—might measure the percentage of customers who buy an advertised product after viewing an online ad. They also measure distribution partner feedback by monitoring trends in sales and profits that the start-up generates for the partner.

If the start-up is intellectually honest in evaluating this feedback, it should recognize quickly when its business strategy is working and when it's not. And if market feedback suggests the start-up is failing, the entrepreneur must use this feedback to help inspire brainstorming about a new business model that it can implement to turn that market feedback from negative to positive.

Here are two examples.

iZettle

iZettle's de Geer has a very clear north star by which he navigates the company. As de Geer works toward his vision of expanding iZettle into Asia, Latin America, and Europe, he also aspires to provide his customers a way to analyze their huge quantities of transaction data.

In pursuit of that long-term goal, iZettle is likely to face unexpected changes. But de Geer will adapt by listening to users through social media and in-person conversations as a way to identify the changes that require iZettle to respond.[182]

iZettle is applying this approach of listening to users in its geographic expansion. De Geer sees 20 million small businesses in Europe that could potentially benefit from iZettle's service since they accept only cash. And in the United Kingdom alone, iZettle perceives a large opportunity: There are 1.2 million point-of-sale systems and 10 million iPhones.

For example, in February 2012, when iZettle introduced its product in Denmark, Norway, and Finland, de Geer told GigaOM that he expected to find that merchants in each country would adopt iZettle in different ways, especially since many small businesses that used traditional Chip-and-PIN readers would view iZettle as a lower-cost alternative.[183]

As he told GigaOM, "We'll see totally different usage patterns. The cost of a reader without the PIN pad is much lower, which makes it appealing for smaller merchants like chiropractors, carpenters, or anyone still bound to cash, checks, or invoices."

Boost Performance on Key Customer Need

Many of the start-ups I interviewed place themselves between suppliers and their customers. And in so doing, they create value for participants at different stages of the industry's value network.

Needless to say, the suppliers will not allow a start-up to take its existing customers. Instead, it will be glad to work with the start-up only if it provides the supplier with new customers, thus boosting its profits.

Here are three case studies of start-ups that have adapted by boosting their performance on key customer needs.

ET Water Systems

If you've ever driven by a company that's dousing its big lawn with huge quantities of water in the middle of a rainstorm, then you understand the reason that ET Water Systems is in business. ET Water Systems builds systems that make far more efficient use of water. It has received $10 million in three rounds over fifteen months and employs twelve people, a pool it hopes will grow as the company grows.[184]

According to CEO, Pat McIntyre, "Our customer is the end user responsible for the water bill for a municipality or landscape management firm. Their pain point is wasting water and money and polluting water."

Thanks to its investment in R&D, ET Water Systems is improving its service to give customers more of what they want. And that improvement is boosting its growth. As he said, "We are growing through investing in R&D which is what our investors want us to do to stay ahead of competition. This results in systems accessible by smartphone that reduce 20 to 50 percent of wasted watering and generates customer payback in under two years—yielding a 230 percent return on investment. Our designers work in the field with customers to understand their activities. With this insight, our designers can develop new products that boost customers' water use efficiency."[185]

AlgoSec

CEO Yuval Baron believes that AlgoSec, a service that helps banks make changes to their information security settings much more quickly than do competing products, is growing faster because its technology saves money and time for customers and because of its "obsession to make the customer happy."

Baron bills himself as AlgoSec's Chief Customer Service Officer (CCSO)—a role that involves reading customer satisfaction surveys, calling customers six months after they have signed on, fixing any problems that come up, and refunding the money of any customers who are not happy.

AlgoSec is adapting to change. For example, when the 2008 recession hit, AlgoSec changed its product and marketing message to focus on the cost savings and efficiencies that its technology can provide companies that are trying to keep their lights on.[186]

CloudFlare

CloudFlare "makes sites twice as fast, protects them from attacks, ensures they are always online, and makes it simple to add Web apps with a single click," according to co-founder and CEO Matthew Prince and co-founder

Michelle Zatlyn. CloudFlare is big: Prince claims that 10 percent of the Internet passes through its network.

CloudFlare offers a big benefit to customers compared with competitive products: It requires no hardware or downloaded software to do its job. Not only that, but most users pay nothing for the service. However, CloudFlare does offer tiers of service that involve extra features for which it charges monthly subscription fees starting at $20 per month.

Early in CloudFlare's development, its founders interviewed Web site owners to understand their unmet needs. Specifically, they sent out 500 surveys and got responses from 25 percent of them. They learned that the challenge of securing their site was "a huge pain point," according to Zatlyn. As one customer told her, "Web spamming makes me believe in the death penalty."

Originally, CloudFlare offered "a firewall in the sky," but the technology it created to implement that concept also ended up making Web sites "twice as fast." And Prince referred to these two features as "a killer combination."[187]

HUNGRY START-UP TACTICS FOR ADAPTING TO CHANGE

Six Steps for Implementing Boundaryless Company Development

To implement BCD, here are six steps that start-up teams should follow.

Map Out the Start-Up's Value Network

Consider, for example, the value network of the book industry. It consists of all the subindustries—including the publisher/marketer, retailer, and reading device maker—that connect the author with the reader.

To follow through with this example, here are some steps that the CEO of an e-book start-up might take to get greater insight into the industry value network. To get these insights into the value network, the start-up CEO can send members of the BCD team out to

- Find the fastest growing competitors.
- Identify the reasons why they are growing so fast.
- Assess whether key partnerships—for example, with very popular authors—can help to boost market acceptance.
- Determine whether changing key technology components might enhance the e-book's performance and boost demand.
- Search for specific groups of readers that are more prone to use e-books than others, why, and how they pick among products.

Pick the Critical Listening Posts

At this point, the CEO should listen to the BCD team's findings and decide which listening posts are most critical for identifying important changes in the competitive environment that could represent threats or opportunities.

Continuing to use the e-book start-up as an example, these listening posts could include:

- Current and potential customers
- Distributors
- Authors
- E-book competitors
- E-book component suppliers
- E-book software providers
- Book reviewers
- E-book industry journalists and consultants

There are two ways that start-up CEOs can choose to filter the listening posts. These include:

- Assessing whether they help or threaten the realization of the entrepreneur's vision for the start-up
- Assessing whether they boost or threaten to reduce growth in user demand

The start-up CEO could use either or both of these filters to decide which of the listening posts the BCD team ought to monitor.

Analyze Market Feedback Metrics

Next, the start-up team should pick and analyze feedback metrics—for example, the viral coefficient that measures growth in customers or the conversion rate for online advertisers—to determine whether the venture's business model needs to change, and if so, how.

Continuing with the e-book example, here is a list of possible metrics that the start-up's BCD might monitor:

- Viral coefficient for users of the start-up's e-book
- Viral coefficient of competitors' e-books
- Changes in e-book journalist and consultant assessments of the start-up's e-book
- Changes in the flow of talented product developers among e-book competitors

If all these metrics are getting better—for example, the start-up's viral coefficient is improving and competitors' are declining; journalist and consultant opinions toward the start-up's product are improving, and the industry talent is flowing toward your start-up—then there is probably no big rush to change the start-up's business model.

However, if these metrics are getting worse, then the start-up CEO must conduct a more in-depth evaluation to discover why. For example, if all the metrics mentioned above were deteriorating, here are some of the questions that the BCD team might investigate:

- Why are customers not continuing to use the start-up's product and not recommending it to others?
- Why are more users choosing competitors' e-books and recommending their colleagues to use them?
- Why are journalists and consultants lowering their opinions of the start-up's e-book?
- Why is industry talent leaving the start-up and going to work for faster growing competitors?

Generate Business Model Hypotheses

The answers to such questions should fuel the BCD team to generate ideas on how it might improve the start-up's business model. If the market feedback is not favorable, it should give the start-up insight into the specific areas that might be improved.

To that end, the CEO should assemble the BCD team for a brainstorming session that incorporates this feedback, to consider whether that start-up should keep or change the following key elements of its business model:

- Product features and price
- Target customers
- Distribution channel
- Suppliers
- Manufacturing
- Sales and marketing
- Customer service

Get Market Feedback on Hypotheses

Next the BCD team should try out the new business model hypotheses with a sample of customers, and gather market feedback. The venture should use that market feedback either to implement the hypotheses with the best market feedback or to start with a new set of hypotheses based on the feedback.

Refine Business Model Based on Market Feedback

And in the spirit of the value cycle, the team should continue to seek feedback, develop new hypotheses, and adapt based on market feedback. Indeed, ventures large and small must persist in the BCD process because to let up on it is to sacrifice future viability.

ADAPTING TO CHANGE: DID YOU DO IT RIGHT?

The examples of different approaches to adapting to change suggest some questions that can help start-up CEOs assess whether they have taken the correct approach. These questions include the following:

- Is adapting to change an important part of the founder's job?
- Has the CEO assembled a cross-functional team to help the start-up adapt to change?
- Has the team mapped out the key listening posts in the start-up's value network?
- Has the team tracked key market feedback indicators that are important to the start-up's key stakeholders?
- Is the start-up getting ever-improving results in these key market feedback indicators?
- If not, does the start-up know why some of the indicators are deteriorating?
- Is the start-up developing hypotheses about how it can boost the performance of these indicators?
- Is the start-up getting helpful feedback from the market on the prototype of this new business model?

If you have solid answers to these questions, then your approach to adapting to change is probably right. And if not, these questions may help you rethink those choices until you do have solid answers to them.

SUMMARY

If start-ups achieve a level of success, they must remain hungry to survive. This is particularly difficult because it is in the nature of organizations that as they become successful, they tend to invest more effort in protecting their past practices rather than in ruthlessly ripping out past practices that impede their ability to adapt.

In fact, if a start-up loses its hunger, it also loses its ability to grow. Hence, the most successful start-ups put in place mechanisms that keep them from losing touch with the markets on which their growth depends. At the core of these learning mechanisms is the ability to pick out the market signals from the much more cacophonous noise.

And as long as it persists in gathering objective market feedback, acknowledges failures efficiently, and brainstorms, tests, and implements new business models that respond to the feedback, the start-up's odds of surviving will rise.

PART TWO

Implications for Stakeholders

CHAPTER 7

Straight Talk from Start-Up Capital Providers

HUNGRY START-UP STRATEGY argues that start-ups should delay raising outside capital as long as they can. Moreover, as we saw in Chapter 3, when entrepreneurs do seek out capital providers, they view it as both a risk and as an opportunity.

The risk is that the founder could lose control of the venture if there is a dispute with the investor. And the opportunity is that the founder can hire a boss who's a "servant leader"—helping the founder achieve the shared goal of turning the venture into a market pacesetter. Naturally, the founder will attempt to minimize the risk and maximize the benefit.

Despite the love-hate relationship between entrepreneurs and capital providers, the two have hungers that only each other can satisfy. The start-up needs the capital to pay its bills and the providers need the start-ups to generate a great return on their investment.

But since hungry start-up strategy is about helping entrepreneurs, I want to help them satisfy their hunger for control and capital by showing entrepreneurs how their start-ups look through the lens of the capital provider.

This chapter shows how capital providers try to feed their hunger to generate returns for their investors, by answering six key questions. These questions, my findings, and the So What? for entrepreneurs are described below:

- *What kinds of start-up candidates do capital providers consider?* Capital providers work with start-ups that can benefit from their expertise. This conclusion reflects the experience of the investors I interviewed who worked as start-up founders and executives before becoming investors. Ultimately, capital providers focus on start-ups in industries they understand who need their expertise in specific functional skills.

- *So what?* Entrepreneurs should seek out capital providers who understand their business at least as well as they do.

- *How do capital providers identify and initiate discussions with these candidates?* Capital providers are open to many sources of possible deals. They are most comfortable working with the people they trust the most to introduce them to entrepreneurs who fit the profile of start-ups in which they seek to invest. However, they also consider start-ups that take the trouble to seek out the capital providers through people they know as well as new ones whom they find at industry conferences.
  - *So what?* Entrepreneurs should network their way into meetings with the right capital providers by getting "warm" introductions to people in the VCs' trusted networks.

- *How do capital providers screen the candidates?* Quite often capital providers screen candidates based on common criteria: the quality of the start-up team, the size of the market that the team is targeting, and the capital providers' perceived ability to help the company. Needless to say, how each capital provider applies these criteria varies depending on their talent and experience.
  - *So what?* Entrepreneurs should have well-thought-out answers to questions that VCs will ask them about the quality of their team, the size of the market, and their start-ups' plan to take market share.

- *What kind of due diligence do capital providers conduct before investing in the start-ups?* Capital providers are thorough in their due diligence. In many cases, this diligence can be streamlined by working with entrepreneurs who are known to trusted members of their professional networks. Capital providers conduct thorough interviews with many people who have worked with the entrepreneurs and must probe deeply to get details, such as how well entrepreneurs have performed in stressful situations.
  - *So what?* Entrepreneurs with blemishes in their past should communicate them early to investors because due diligence will reveal hidden flaws. And an undisclosed discovery is likely to kill the opportunity for the entrepreneur to secure an investment.

- *How do capital providers structure the terms of their investment in start-ups?* In general, start-up investments tend to be structured as either equity or convertible debt. With equity investment, the most challenging decision for the capital provider and the entrepreneur is how to value the firm at the time of the investment. With convertible debt, that decision is deferred until the time that the debt is converted to equity. However, at least one of the investors I interviewed prefers equity investing because he believes it is a better way to align the interests of investors and start-up executives.

- *So what?* Entrepreneurs should favor capital structured as equity rather than convertible debt because the equity investors are more likely to support the venture if it runs into trouble.

- *How can capital providers help the start-up to grow beyond simply providing capital?* Capital providers compete primarily on their ability to help start-ups grow by providing specific skills—including building teams, negotiating financial terms with later-round capital providers, developing the product, and finding partners.
  - *So what?* Entrepreneurs should seek out capital providers who are well known for providing these value-added services and do their own due diligence since getting outside capital means hiring a boss.

HOW CAPITAL PROVIDERS INVEST IN HUNGRY START-UPS

My interviews with start-up capital providers suggest that entrepreneurs must understand how investors answer two fundamental questions when faced with choosing to invest in two or three companies from as many as 2,000 candidate companies each year:

- Is the start-up candidate targeting a market that is now small—and, therefore, not attracting attention from other investors—but is likely to grow very rapidly to become large in the next three to five years?
- Can its founder grow into a CEO who will turn the start-up into that market's leader?

Beating the odds in start-up investing means finding the one or two candidate companies every year for which the investor believes firmly that the answer to these questions is a resounding yes.

Before they invest, capital providers seek answers to specific questions regarding the market opportunity and the founders, as depicted in Figure 7.1.

Capital providers seek to invest in entrepreneurs that are great CEOs—and to satisfy this screen, start-up CEOs must pass the tests outlined in Figure 7.2.

FIGURE 7.1   Four Tests of an Attractive Emerging Market.

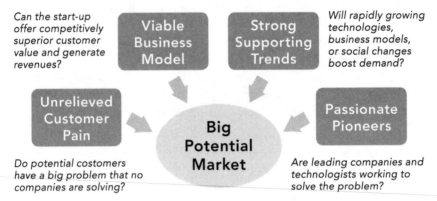

FIGURE 7.2   Five Tests of a Great Start-Up Founder.

The thing that separates the most successful start-up investors from their peers is an ability to tap networks of smart people with answers to these questions and apply a savvy "gut" to all the information that flows to the investor through the network.

Making these two decisions "correctly" represents perhaps 1 percent of the genius required to make a venture investment pay off. After that, the investor must work with the start-up to help it achieve its longer-term goals.

WHERE CAPITAL PROVIDERS COME FROM AND WHAT THEY DO

Entrepreneurs seeking to raise capital must understand what capital providers do. The remainder of this chapter presents insights from interviews with nine capital providers, which will help start-up CEOs understand capital providers' career backgrounds and how they find, screen, invest, and work with start-ups.

Capital Provider Career Backgrounds

Many venture capitalists have prior experience building companies and realizing profits for their investors. Entrepreneurs must seek out specific VC partners whose background and interests best fit with those of the capital providers.

By taking responsibility for finding a good fit, a start-up CEO can boost the odds of finding a capital provider who can also serve as a good boss to help the start-up grow and achieve the entrepreneur's long-term goal.

We'll now discuss four individuals who demonstrate a variety of VC backgrounds.

Peter Bell

Peter Bell is a general partner at Highland Capital Ventures. Before that he was CEO of StorageNetworks, a storage service provider. When he took it public in July 2000 it yielded a peak first-day valuation of over $9 billion when its shares jumped from $27 to $102.

By 2012 Bell had switched to investing in enterprise-focused technology start-ups. Among the valuable insights he offered was a list of five things that turn him off in the first three minutes to an entrepreneur's pitch for capital.[188]

After a childhood in Minnesota, Bell went east to Boston College. He then joined EMC, where he worked with its co-founders Richard Egan and Roger Marino, in late 1986 when it had eighty people, and spent five years there before entering HBS in 1991. Bell went back to EMC for three years after completing his MBA.

Several years later, with Bill Miller, he started StorageNetworks and grew its sales to $120 million by 2001. In 2003, Electronic Data Systems acquired its software business, and Storage Technology acquired its services business.

Bell then spent years teaching entrepreneurship. He taught at Boston College for seven years and at MIT's Sloan School of Management for four years. In addition, he started investing in start-ups on his own—through Stowe Capital in Newton, Massachusetts—before Highland Capital Partners hired Bell as a venture partner in early 2006. Bell moved out to the Bay Area with Highland in 2010.

Gil

Gil has long wanted to make a positive difference in the world. And thanks to his work with Silicon Valley start-ups he's achieving that altruistic ambition and making a profit to boot.

Gil has impressive academic credentials. Among his degrees are a BA in mathematics and a BS in molecular biology from the University of California, San Diego, and a PhD in biology from MIT. While at MIT he got involved with the $100K Entrepreneurship Competition and concluded that he could have more of an impact on the world working in start-ups than as an academic.[189]

Gil went out to Silicon Valley after earning his PhD and worked at a number of start-ups, including a short stint as a market-seeding consultant to Plaxo with Sean Parker. He next went to Google where he started its mobile wireless team, helped acquire Android, and worked on AdSense, leaving there in 2007. In 2008, he started Mixer Labs, a service for helping developers build geo-location applications that Twitter acquired in December 2009. In 2012, he was working there as director of corporate strategy and by that July he left to consult to Twitter and plan his next venture.

Gil enjoys helping his friends with their start-ups. He brings to this an ethos that inspires many programmers to devote a huge amount of time to developing open source software: a desire to give back to a community that they believe has given them tremendous value.

Kevin Hartz

If you can't learn from the past, you're doomed to repeat its errors and to miss its brilliant insights. That's one of Kevin Hartz's credos.

With a master's in British history and political philosophy from Oxford, a bachelor's of arts and sciences (BAS) from Stanford, you might be tempted to conclude that Hartz would not get much traction among the hard-core geeks of Silicon Valley. But his success there begs to differ.[190]

Hartz first broke into Silicon Valley as a product manager at Silicon Graphics (SGI); the former high-performance computing leader gave Hartz a view into the future of personal computing.

His experience there also informed him how Silicon Valley's talent flows to the most exciting companies. Over the last decade he's seen talent flow to places like PayPal, Google, and Facebook.

After SGI, Hartz co-founded Connect Group, providing hotel guests with high-speed Internet access that LodgeNet acquired in 1998. While at

Stanford, Hartz met Peter Thiel—then a law student with a reputation as a brilliant intellect. Thiel's reputation was one reason that Hartz decided to plow his Connect Group profits into Thiel's company, PayPal; eBay acquired it for $1.5 billion in 2002.

From there, Hartz went on to found Xoom—an online-to-offline money transfer service that lets people send money overseas. His view into PayPal informed Xoom's strategy: Build on top of a fast-growing payments platform (PayPal), create a "drop dead simple" service, be resilient to audacious fraud attacks—all while working within the confines of a heavily regulated industry.

Hartz next went on to found Eventbrite, a platform that makes it easy to plan and sell tickets to events of any size or type. By May 2011, Eventbrite had helped "over 120,000 event organizers in 150 countries host more than half a million events. Over 20 million people [had] attended an event ticketed by Eventbrite." Eventbrite has raised $80 million—including $20 million in October 2010 and $50 million in May 2011, led by Tiger Global.

But for Hartz there is even more work to be done; he attributes his work ethic to his mother who grew up on a farm and whose workday started at 5 a.m. Hartz is now giving back to Silicon Valley through his work as an entrepreneur and an angel investor.

Asheem Chandna

An experienced investor in technology-intensive start-ups, Asheem Chandna has been evaluating hundreds of companies a year and investing in "a handful or less." After doing this for years, he has five pieces of advice for those newly minted Facebook, LinkedIn, and Groupon millionaires who might want to invest in start-ups.

Chandna is a general partner at Greylock Partners in Menlo Park, California. He grew up in Mumbai but moved to Canada before enrolling at Case Western Reserve where he earned a BS in electrical engineering and an MS in computer engineering in 1988.[191]

Chandna took his networking expertise to AT&T Bell Labs in 1988 and spent the next fifteen years in a variety of large and small companies as a product management executive. In 1991, he joined SynOptics, a Silicon Valley–based networking company. While there, the company grew in revenues from $175 million to $900 million.

Chandna also had a great run at Check Point Software where he "was part of the core management team for 6.5 years" starting in 1996—during which time its annual revenue grew from $10 million to $550 million.

During his time at Check Point, Chandna tried his hand at investing in start-ups. And he was so successful at getting into new companies before the big VC firms that they were asking "who's that guy in our deals?"

Eventually, he decided venture investing and helping entrepreneurs build companies was "the right full-time passion for him." Chandna joined Greylock Partners in 2003, where he has invested in "over a dozen companies."

And some of those have ascended to VC heaven; that is, successful exits. According to Chandna, several have been acquired by the likes of Cisco, Intel subsidiary Secure Computing, and Websense.

These background sketches of start-up capital providers should spur entrepreneurs to consider the following ideas:

- *Raising capital is personal* **and** *business.* A start-up CEO must build a successful relationship with the individual representing the capital. This means that the entrepreneur must learn about the partner's background as a prelude to figuring out whether there is a good fit.
- *Finding a fit is essential.* Chemistry between a start-up CEO and the venture capitalist is important. While much of that chemistry comes down to shared business goals, industry knowledge, and common work interests, it also depends on how well the two get along. The entrepreneur should take responsibility for finding a good fit in order to secure the start-up's future.

Find Possible Investments

VCs all seek to explore many investment opportunities and invest in a tiny fraction of the companies at the top of their investment funnel. It is critical that entrepreneurs understand this process in order to have realistic expectations of the odds that any particular capital provider will write their ventures a check.

VCs get possible investments from different sources, including their professional networks of entrepreneurs, other investors, lawyers, accountants, and other professionals. Entrepreneurs who know members of the capital providers' networks have a much better chance of getting their attention than through a cold call. Hence, entrepreneurs must be good at networking.

Here are three examples that illustrate ways that capital providers find possible investments.

Dearing: Seeking Exceptional Entrepreneurs

In addition to teaching at Stanford, Dearing is an angel investor—he invested in fifty-six start-ups between 2001 and 2006. In 2011, he estimated that he had looked at 2,800 business ideas and selected a mere 2 percent of them for investment. And the most important question he asks in making that choice is this: Is the entrepreneur exceptional?[192]

He does not shun first-time entrepreneurs, but before he meets them he studies whether they have demonstrated exceptional accomplishment in either work or school.

Even though he turns down 98 percent of the ideas he sees, he does not consider them to be a waste of time because they give him useful context. He talks to many different teams to pick just the few that he wants to invest in. He also consciously avoids talking to competitors of companies he is working with.

Dave Whorton: Network of Respected Entrepreneurs and Executives

Dave Whorton is a partner at Tugboat Ventures, which does what he calls "life cycle investing" (LCI), whereby a capital provider starts working with a start-up as early as when the founder comes up with the business idea. At that point, the investor provides both capital and help—in the form of advice on key choices like developing the product, building the team, and finding partners. Life cycle investing winds down when the start-up has grown to the point where the company either completes an IPO or sells itself to a larger firm.

Over the years, Whorton has gotten to know and respect many entrepreneurs and executives, who have introduced him and his partner, Dafina Toncheva, to other promising entrepreneurs. Of the 500 to 600 start-ups to which they are introduced each year, they actually invest in only two to four.

Chandna: Pitches and Network

Some may think you need to turn over many rocks to find the rare golden coin. Chandna views it differently. As he explains, "It's the process that's just as important as the result." That's because he gets email pitches from well over 1,000 start-ups a year. And Chandna is not counting the cold pitches—people in his network refer over 1,000 start-ups he evaluates.

Chandna is often the first email or call young engineers make when looking to capitalize on their expertise through a new venture. He encourages these founders (often futilely) to send him their complete "slide deck" rather than just the executive summary "to ensure he isn't wasting the entrepreneur's time."

Founders are generally reluctant to give him their entire presentations, believing they can make the sale if they can just get a personal meeting.

Chandna is able to whittle down those more than 1,000 requests to the roughly 200 founders with whom he meets in person.

Screen Candidates

Entrepreneurs must understand how the capital providers they are talking with screens candidates. VCs use different techniques to whittle down to a small number all the possible candidates about whom they will conduct due diligence. With insight into the process, entrepreneurs can prepare their best case for why their start-up should stay in contention.

Four examples of different screening approaches are presented below.

Bell: Knock Out Candidates in Three Minutes

Within the first three minutes of meeting an entrepreneur, Bell decides whether "the next fifty-seven minutes are going to be excruciating" or he will "want to spend four more hours" with the person.

Here are five tests that Bell uses to knock out a start-up CEO from contention in the first three minutes:

- *Poor communication.* Bell has spent decades in the technology business so he knows his stuff. Therefore, if an entrepreneur can't get across a clear description of what he is doing, Bell is turned off.
- *Not a winner.* Bell bets on people who he believes have the potential to become CEOs. In order to do that, however, he needs to see that the person has a track record of winning. If the person appears not to know how it feels to win, Bell will lose interest.
- *Poor team builder.* One key skill of winning start-up CEOs is the ability to attract and motivate an excellent team. If Bell meets a founder with a poor start-up team, he seriously questions the founder's judgment and quickly shuts off to the rest of the pitch.
- *Asking for too much money before a market exists.* Bell believes that founders should take a rigorous approach to analyzing the markets into which they are selling. That means before they ask him for an investment of, say, $10 million, they should be able to demonstrate the market is big enough to generate a return on such a big initial investment. Bell passes on founders who have not done enough homework to prove that.
- *Business potential too small.* In order to make it worthwhile for a venture-size investment, the founder must present a credible plan that demonstrates the start-up's potential to become a market-leading company in a billion-dollar market. If Bell is convinced that the start-up

cannot become that big, he advises the entrepreneur to seek other sources of funding.

Levchin: Use Trends to Screen

When Levchin began to invest in start-ups, he decided to apply three tests to decide where to invest. The tests include the following:

- *Does Levchin have a deep understanding of the company and its product?* Initially, he would pass if he was not well-versed in a start-up's industry. Now, he is more open to putting capital into start-ups even where he does not have deep expertise.
- *Does Levchin believe he can add value?* If he does not think he can help the start-up with its strategy, its product development, or its team building, he will decline to invest.
- *Does the start-up take advantage of what he thinks the world will look like in five years?* Every year, Levchin likes to look at key trends and identify themes that help him predict how the world will be different five years into the future. Then he tries to invest in start-ups that have interesting ideas about how to take advantage of those themes.[193]

What are Levchin's themes for 2012 to 2017? In addition to being interested in so-called big data—the notion of extracting useful insight from lots of data, which has become pretty popular among the technologically sophisticated—here are three others that struck me as unique:

- *Data collectors and sensors.* According to Levchin, "the proliferation of cheap data collectors and sensors (and rapidly falling costs of storing and processing such data) is exciting. Examples include "accelerometers in phones and on wrists and hips; GPS receivers in every car, watch, and phone; cameras in practically everything; and indeed simple and ultra-cheap ID devices like RFIDs that help us track things." Levchin seeks applications that use all the data that these sensors collect in a way that's profitable for start-ups and their customers.
- *Valuing data.* Levchin is also interested in businesses that can find data that have value to people. In thinking about this, he distinguishes between data narratives and data that companies, for example, would pay for. For example, an insurance company might be able to pay $1 for a potential customer's driving record. If that potential customer ended up buying insurance from that company, then the $1 might be well spent since it would help the insurer set a profitable rate. If the driver went to another insurer, the money would be wasted. Levchin is

seeking start-ups that can turn now "worthless" data into valuable information.

- *Misallocated resources.* Levchin sees all kinds of waste in the world, and, thanks to the ability to gather data inexpensively at the periphery and analyze it deeply at the center, he believes that markets can be created that slash this misallocation of resources. One example of this is in automobiles: Some people have two cars in their garage that they never drive and others don't have cars but need to travel twenty-five miles back and forth to work every day. Levchin believes that a market could emerge that would match up the people without cars who need them with people who have them but don't drive too often. Similarly, Levchin sees an opportunity to create a service that brings trucks loaded with commonly purchased groceries to locations inferred from consumer location data, to maximize both convenience and sales.

Levchin's ability to invest profitably in such trends highlights the importance of being able to "see around market corners."

Gil: Screen by Team and Market

Gil tends to invest in companies that pass three tests:

- *Team track record.* If all the members of your start-up team have a record of exceptional accomplishment, it passes Gil's first test. If the team has already built a successful start-up, that conclusion is simpler to reach. If not, Gil looks for evidence of outstanding accomplishment or entrepreneurial stirrings among the team members. He also looks for whether the team's product people have been working on the problem for a long time and whether the people work together well.
- *Potential to build a billion-dollar company.* Gil likes to invest in companies that he believes have the chance to be worth $1 billion. If the company sells to businesses, then Gil looks for the start-up to target a market that will grow big enough to support a company that will be worth $1 billion with a reasonable market share. If the company is focused on consumers, Gil needs to imagine how it could become big, even when others can't; for example, when Google was launched, only a few investors could see the business potential of a world-beating search service as a way to attract Internet advertising revenue.
- *Affinity for the team.* Just as entrepreneurs should pick VC partners that they would like to work with, simply put, Gil invests in teams that he likes. Lacking this chemistry, Gil is not likely to invest.

Ping Li: Invest in Big Markets and CEO Stars

Accel Partners managing director, Ping Li, seeks to invest in companies with the potential to lead big, emerging technology markets whose CEOs can build and lead teams with outstanding people. Two companies that exemplify Li's approach to investing are Cloudera and Lookout, a mobile security company.

In the case of Cloudera, Li met with Facebook's chief data scientist Jeff Hammerbacher years before Li first invested in Cloudera. Hammerbacher taught Li how he was using an open source database program, dubbed Hadoop, to help extract valuable insights from the enormous amounts of data produced by the social network.

Hammerbacher and his co-founders saw before others—inspiring Li— how Hadoop could be used to tackle big data problems not only at large consumer Web sites but "at any enterprise or industry."

With Lookout, Li was very impressed with its CEO/co-founder, John Hering. Li and everyone else knew that mobile was and would continue to be a huge market. What made Hering unique in Li's view, however, was that he had grown up with mobile platform and devices.

This "native" mobile heritage set Hering apart from other entrepreneurs pitching Li mobile start-up ideas; they were PC-centric and always talked about how mobile was different from PCs. Moreover, the others couldn't provide the kind of specific answers to key questions—such as which underlying "mobile market drivers" to focus on, mobile technology's likely evolution, and specific mobile product features—that Hering did.

Ultimately, start-up investing comes down to taking a risk. Li likes to invest in entrepreneurs that look at a big opportunity in a different way. Rather than making Li nervous that they will not be able to handle unexpected outcomes, these entrepreneurs appeal to Li because they have really thoughtful answers about the risks their start-up will encounter.

These examples suggest the following three important things to add to entrepreneurs' agendas:

- *Refine the art of the pitch.* As Bell articulates, it is incredibly easy to turn off a potential investor in a very short period of time. The entrepreneur should strive to do the opposite of the bad things Bell uses to screen out potential investments.
- *Prove you have a billion-dollar company.* Similarly, start-up CEOs must be able to answer all the questions needed to persuade capital providers that their company is going to be worth at least $1 billion in the next several years. Doing that effectively means coming up with carefully

researched and clearly articulated answers to the four tests of an emerging market that we outlined in Figure 7.1.

- *Show why you're a leader.* Entrepreneurs should come to a meeting with venture capitalists demonstrating how, based on their experience, they pass the five tests of a great founder, as depicted in Figure 7.2.

Choose Investments

If a candidate makes it to the short-list, a VC firm's partners are likely to conduct a deep investigation of a start-up's people, technology, and market opportunity. Odds are small that any individual start-up will make it past this process. However, if a start-up tries to hide blemishes, its reputation could be damaged far beyond the mere disappointment of not getting capital.

Therefore, the entrepreneur must prepare for due diligence by imagining that the start-up is about to be vetted for a high-level government appointment and that every past blemish will be uncovered.

This mind-set will push entrepreneurs to prepare how they would respond to any negative information that might be discovered during due diligence, including disclosing these problems up front, to boost their credibility.

Below are three examples of how venture firms conduct due diligence on candidates before deciding to invest.

If a start-up CEO passes all these tests, Bell scrutinizes it even further. He asks himself whether he would phone a very good friend and say, "You really should check out this company." He also makes some quick calls to people who know the market to see whether they think the team and product are excellent.

If all these checks are positive, Bell conducts more in-depth due diligence. To that end, he examines other factors, including the venture's

- Ability to attract and motivate excellent people
- Business model robustness
- Success at winning customers
- Product development roadmap solidity
- Customer value creation relative to competitors
- Capital requirements

Last, Bell considers whether Highland will be able to earn an attractive return on its investment.

Chandna: Bet on the CEO

Despite meeting "dozens of great teams, and companies that most likely will be quite successful," Chandna knows he has only "enough cycles to invest in less than a handful of companies a year." He seeks to "partner with founding teams that he is convinced can build disruptive technology, can be industry thought leaders, and can attract great teams."

If a company is beyond the start-up stage, Chandna evaluates all the factors listed previously, and adds one more: Since a significant amount of his investment is likely to be applied to building sales, he wants to be comfortable with the venture's sales productivity. Specifically, he will be more comfortable investing if the start-up's sales productivity is as high or higher than the competition's—and "if management views this as a focus area."

Chandna's investing experience has taught him some useful lessons about the characteristics of start-ups with above-average odds of success:

- A CEO who is both frugal and humble while able to get customers to "believe that the start-up represents the next generation and deserves to earn their business"
- A good fit between the market needs and the start-up's product and technology capabilities—they must be better than competitors'
- Strong missions, excellent founders, and the ability to recruit talent
- An ambitious, yet realistic, product roadmap
- Ability to deliver a "minimally viable, awesome product" and to "iterate rapidly" in response to customer feedback

Hartz: Bet on High IQ Entrepreneurs, Targeting Big Markets with Multiplatform Services

When it comes to picking his investments, angel investor Hartz has learned from history, which has taught him that if a start-up passes three tests, he will be excited to invest in it.

- *High IQ, strong work ethic, first-time entrepreneurs.* He believes that a start-up needs extremely bright, highly driven first-time entrepreneurs. From PayPal's success, he learned that such entrepreneurs are often first-generation immigrants eager to take advantage of the opportunities that America affords them.
- *Attacking big markets with profitable incumbents.* Hartz is also very interested in investing in start-ups that are attacking big markets that are dominated by large, profitable companies that he believes are vulnerable to attack. Such incumbents' core business profits will inhibit quick, innovative responses to shifts in the market.

- *Building multiplatform services.* Finally, Hartz likes to invest in companies that make their services available on many different platforms so they do not become too dependent on one big player that might decide to backward integrate or take other steps that could slow down their growth.

Help Start-Ups

Investors contribute based on the start-up's needs and the investors' specific skills and experience. These value-added services include

- Helping to design the firm's culture
- Hiring and firing staff
- Designing organizational structure
- Developing the product and planning future versions
- Forging partnerships and providing customer introductions
- Advice on acquisitions
- Assistance with raising later rounds of funding

For entrepreneurs, this approach to investing should guide them to finding capital providers whose skills match their needs. Following are three examples of how venture capitalists deliver value-added services to start-ups.

Gil: Soup to Nuts

Gil tailors his help depending on the needs of each start-up. Here are five of the services he offers them:

- *Hiring and firing.* Gil has found that most engineers who start companies don't have experience with hiring and firing, and he helps them do both. Initially, he may be asked to help with the more difficult task of firing an employee. And he helps start-ups establish hiring processes that include testing candidates for their productivity, checking their references, and finding out how they behave in an informal setting.
- *Fund-raising.* Gil helps start-ups find VC firms for their Series A and B rounds, assisting with negotiating key terms such as valuation and the rights of investors to appoint board members.
- *Product development.* Gil assists start-ups design more customer-friendly user interfaces, and he monitors the effectiveness of their distribution strategies.
- *Organization structure.* Gil works with the founder once the company reaches, say, fifty people, to help analyze whether the reporting structure should be changed, and if so, how. He helps start-up CEOs decide,

for example, whether the venture should hire a vice president of market-ing first and let the VP appoint people to perform, say, PR, product mar-keting, and advertising, or whether the start-up should hire those lower-level people first and the VP later.

- *Acquisitions.* Gil has assisted the leaders of a dozen start-ups to find the right acquirer, negotiate pricing, and determine the role of the founders and employees in the new organization.

Dearing: Financing and Marketing

One of the interesting things that Dearing's experience has taught him is that it's better to invest in the stock of a new venture than in so-called con-vertible notes—loans with an option to be converted into stock.

Dearing has found that these two kinds of financing produce very dif-ferent investor behavior. Since convertible notes are often sold to many investors in small denominations, when the start-ups face challenges and need more help, the absence of a lead investor makes it harder to organize them to help out the company when it's distressed.

Dearing also argues that the economic interests of the debt holders are not aligned with the goal of maximizing the start-up's valuation—and thus its conversion price per share.

Dearing has found that if investors own equity, they will help out the company in a jam. As he said, "If it goes poorly or sideways, I want all hands on deck to help. If investors buy debt and it's not going well, they'll say, 'I'm out of here.'"

Why have some of Dearing's investments succeeded? "Entrepreneurs are heroes. They create something out of nothing. The common thread is resilience and good fortune." Successful entrepreneurs demonstrate resil-ience through iterative product development—as he mentioned, this means building prototypes, figuring out what works and what doesn't, and trying again.

One of his companies, AdMob, which was sold to Google for $750 mil-lion, benefited in part from luck. But AdMob's management was also "smart enough to see the opportunity in mobile advertising." And they were for-tunate to be in business at a time when the whole landscape of devices and apps for smartphones and tablets broke in AdMob's favor.

Why did others fail? They couldn't generate cash flow from operations or they couldn't convince investors to provide more cash. The inability to get customers to pay for the product results from a "product/market mismatch."

A failure to persuade investors to reinvest might have been due to the financial crisis in 2008 or 2009; however, by 2011 investors would likely turn down the CEO if they perceived that the start-up was not growing fast enough.

Given the low capital requirements for many consumer Internet start-ups, coupled with what Dearing calls "high velocity," investors can quickly see whether the number of users of a start-up's product is growing very rapidly, or not.

Ultimately Dearing has found that there are many different ways to succeed as a start-up investor. However, it is critical that investors are "true to their nature." Some investors want to be active, engaged, and helpful to their portfolio companies. Others want to be passive and leave entrepreneurs on their own to generate a return on their investment.

In order to be "internally consistent," investors should logically link their view of the world, what makes them happy, and their investment strategy.

What makes Dearing happy is working with small start-up teams on projects that matter to the world, targeted to people who are underdogs. As well, he likes to invest in a small number of deals and develop a collaborative relationship. He tries to create an environment where "smart people are happy to work hard and make good things happen."

Dearing also observes that the skills he developed by working with consumer Internet companies could help portfolio companies in other industries to thrive.

For example, Heroku, a platform service for developers building and deploying apps in the cloud, benefited by applying strategies and tactics to the developer market that they had observed in the consumer software market. Salesforce.com bought Heroku in 2010 for $210 million.

Luck is always a factor in venture investing. While Dearing observes that people "accidentally pick up skills that are surprisingly useful later on," his success with start-up investing offers valuable lessons for others.

Whorton: Trusted Advisor

Whorton believes that LCI investors should be willing to serve as trusted advisors to the founders for a decade into the future. This means not only writing checks, but also serving on the board of directors of the start-up, being a "trusted and highly available sounding board," and mentoring the CEO "proactively" in product development, strategy formulation, distribution, team building, and compensation strategies.

Amazon CEO Jeff Bezos looked for such a relationship, in the person of John Doerr, and both Bezos and Amazon investors benefited greatly from Doerr's service as a trusted advisor and provider of insights, ideas, and experience.

Levchin: Strategy, Office Space, Capital, Getting Out of the Way

Of the roughly fifty companies in which he has invested, one that best exemplifies Levchin's approach to start-up investing is Yelp, the local business social review site of which he owns 13.2 percent, with an estimated $165 million value as of July 30, 2012. He first invested in Yelp in the summer of 2004 after meeting with two "really good technical guys he knew."

Back then, Levchin was convinced that local search would become enormously valuable. People in San Francisco, for example, would want to find the best sandwiches nearby and would not care, for example, about the best sandwiches in say, San Jose.

Another theme that interested Levchin was wikis. He was fascinated by the way that Wikipedia was able to take something that was free—the willingness of people to refine Wikipedia entries without pay—to create something valuable and proprietary.

Yelp started off by licensing local yellow pages. It was able to tap into the same concept that helped Wikipedia grow: People in different locations volunteered to give their reviews of the local places they visited. Over time, Yelp's user reviews dwarfed the value of the Yellow Pages content.

Levchin helped Yelp considerably. In addition to writing checks, he shared office space with the company in its early days and let Yelp share his computing resources. At the time, Levchin's initial investment was to him a really big risk, but he wisely helped the company, and then got out of its way.

These examples send entrepreneurs a simple message: Figure out which skills your start-up needs from a capital provider and pick the one that best delivers those skills.

SUMMARY

Entrepreneurs and capital providers are both hungry. The entrepreneurs want capital and help to grow their start-up. The capital providers want to generate high returns for their limited partners and to work with great entrepreneurs to prove to themselves that their experience is valuable.

Entrepreneurs should seek out capital providers that fit well with their needs for capital and advice. To do that, entrepreneurs must build relationships with capital providers based on shared experience and interests.

Their start-ups have to pass stringent tests. (See Table 9.3 for a framework to help entrepreneurs see their start-up from the capital provider's perspective.) These tests help speed up the matching process so entrepreneurs and capital providers can satisfy their mutual hungers.

CHAPTER 8

Can Big Companies Train Entrepreneurs?

MANY UNIVERSITY STUDENTS are drawn to entrepreneurship but they're not ready to start companies while still in their senior years. These budding entrepreneurs are hungry for information to help them decide whether to start their companies.

Some students conclude that, thanks to their ability to subsist on Ramen noodles and an absence of financial obligations to others, graduation is the perfect time to start a company. Others decide in college that they will always need the structure of a big company and hope to find one that encourages some degree of innovation. Still others know that they want to start a company but believe that they need big company experience before they jump into entrepreneurship's bracingly chilly waters.

While everyone is different, most aspiring entrepreneurs can get useful advantages from big company experience, including

- Acquiring knowledge of an industry
- Learning how to make effective business decisions
- Developing contacts that can help provide access to customers, capital, and talent
- Finding a specific business problem that they are uniquely qualified to solve

For those who do not start companies right out of college, the big question is what kinds of companies are the best training grounds for start-ups. Any company that is a leader in its industry is a good candidate for delivering knowledge, contacts, and opportunity.

Those who want to learn how to make effective business decisions can learn the most from big companies whose CEOs have made well-considered decisions to change their corporate strategy and organization, to encourage innovation while also preserving and strengthening their core.

The reason is simple: Such companies give an aspiring start-up CEO a chance to experience the benefits and the substantial resources of a big company, along with a directed effort to overcome the barriers to innovation. Seeing both of these going on in the same company will provide a uniquely rich training ground for aspiring entrepreneurs.

My research suggests that two companies—Procter & Gamble and Intuit (seller of TurboTax and founded by a P&G alumnus)—are great places to learn how to make effective business decision making. But one bad decision about a succeeding CEO could make either of these companies a less great place to train for leading start-ups.

This chapter explores the general characteristics of companies that make the best entrepreneurial training grounds. Let's examine the questions that would drive CEOs to inject their big companies with a dose of start-up-ness,[194] and my findings on the answers:

- *What is motivating the CEO to lead a change in the organization?* Quite frequently, CEOs of large organizations want to encourage start-up–like behavior after being stung by a growth problem. For example, one CEO decided that the company needed to implement a design-thinking capability after he took over from a CEO who seriously neglected customers and drove the company into a ditch. To his credit, the new CEO understood the long-term benefits of this capability. Only a very small number of big company CEOs can preserve the best of the start-up mind-set even after their little ventures become corporate Goliaths.

- *Is the CEO willing to create a new entrepreneurial unit with a different strategic intent, culture, and so on from its core business?* My interviews reveal that big companies use one of three organizational approaches. In the first, they create new divisions responsible for creating innovative businesses with distinct strategic intent, culture, and performance measures. A second approach is to make innovation a small part of everyone's job—and they provide a strategic architecture to encourage frugal experimentation. The third approach is to create an internal capability that helps the core businesses to apply the start-ups' new business development strengths.

- *Will the CEO directly oversee both the company's entrepreneurial unit and its core?* One of the researchers I interviewed believes that the CEO or general manager of a business unit—depending on the magnitude of the entrepreneurial business—must oversee directly both the core and the entrepreneurial units. Otherwise, he argues, the political clout of the managers who run the core will sideline the less powerful start-up unit.

- *Can the CEO create performance measures and incentives to encourage both parts of the company to work together?* The few CEOs who have taken on this dual responsibility have figured out incentive systems that encourage both parts of the business to collaborate. These CEOs tie the bonuses of the executives in the core business to the success of the entrepreneurial one, and vice versa. Moreover, such CEOs are able to persuade the executives in both units of their high value to the company.
- *Will the CEO apply best practices from the entrepreneurial unit into the core business?* Expert opinion appears divided on this topic. Some argue that a core business should be managed to encourage exploitation of a big company's advantages and the entrepreneurial one should be charged with the distinct mission of exploring new business opportunities. However, the few CEOs who have initiated this ambidextrous approach to leading a company have concluded that some of a start-up's greatest strengths—such an ability to learn very quickly as they seek opportunity—can be incorporated into an established business.

BIG COMPANIES AS START-UP TRAINING GROUNDS

So what should aspiring entrepreneurs look for in a big company that could train them as entrepreneurs? According to interviews with eight experts, aspiring entrepreneurs should look for big companies that do the following:

- Self-cannibalize to create QLVs for customers.
- Operate dual organizations that blend the strengths of a start-up with those of a large company.
- Focus on extreme customers and learn from failure.
- Make decisions at industry-leading clock speed.
- Create a cocoon of start-up-ness by tasking highly motivated managers with limited resources to build fast prototypes, get customer feedback, and learn.

The Experts Weigh In on Big Companies as Training Grounds

Stevenson: Eat Your Lunch Before Someone Else Does
Stevenson argues that start-ups are different from "administrative" companies (ACs) in six important ways. Those six ways give ACs an advantage over start-ups in wars of attrition. Conversely, start-ups win by targeting markets for which an AC response would cannibalize its core.[195]

Interestingly for ACs, Stevenson offers two examples of companies that have found their way out of this problem—Landmark Communications, and International Business Machines under Lou Gerstner.

In Stevenson's view, ACs and start-ups differ in six critical ways:

- *Strategic orientation.* Start-ups pursue opportunity with resources that don't match the task; although they may have one or two critical ones such as a product idea or access to an experimental customer, they lack all the resources required to win. ACs have become so successful that they have resources—such as factories and distribution channels that they need to decide how to use. In a war of attrition with a smaller company, these resources can provide a decisive advantage. However, if a start-up offers customers a product that obsoletes the assets, this limits the AC's strategic flexibility.

- *Style of resource commitment.* While a start-up is quick, agile, and adapts to change; the managers in a successful AC study an investment opportunity before committing resources. And if the manager who makes that study turns out to be wrong, he tries to "reinvent reality" to make sure that he does not take the blame for a bad prediction.

- *Decision-making approach.* Whereas a start-up does frugal experiments to prove its business model in stages—so it can demonstrate the progress needed to attract additional resources—an AC studies that decision and then commits its current resources all at once.

- *Attitude toward asset accumulation.* Start-ups use other people's resources: people, money, and machines, and they almost always shun spending on resources that are not essential to their mission. By contrast, ACs reward middle managers according to how many people report to them and the amount of assets they control.

- *Management structure and style.* Start-ups manage a network of relationships with people and organizations that they don't control; whereas ACs appoint bosses and make decisions from the top down, for most of them, authority must equal responsibility.

- *Approach to rewards.* Start-ups give almost all their key employees a chance to get rich if the company succeeds—while leaving them with next to nothing if it fails. By contrast, ACs give individual promotions and rewards, often ensuring that the "top dog takes all the dog food."

These differences give ACs the edge in wars of attrition. For example, it is unlikely that a start-up will succeed in taking on Wal-Mart directly in the retailing business with an everyday-low-price strategy, nor will a start-up office operating system designer make much headway against Microsoft. These ACs' greater resources will exhaust resource-poor start-ups.

By contrast, if an AC fears cannibalization, the start-up enjoys a competitive advantage. As Stevenson pointed out, there was nothing in theory to stop a newspaper from inventing Angie's List—the online local business review site. However, the fear that such a site would cannibalize the newspaper's classified advertising business deterred the move.

Stevenson cites Batten as the rare example of an AC CEO who was able to run a big company in some ways more like a start-up, and hence avoid the strategic paralysis resulting from the typical AC's fear of cannibalization.

Batten took a different approach to the six dimensions outlined above:

- *Strategic orientation.* Batten focused on how to exploit resources to create new businesses. To that end, Landmark decided to "obsolete itself or the competition would." So it went from print to cable, to the Internet—and then started offering online buying services—such as Auto Trader.
- *Style of resource commitment and decision-making approach.* Batten encouraged people to try new ideas once, and if they worked, he offered more. If they did not, Batten tried to learn from the failures.
- *Attitude toward asset accumulation.* Like a start-up, Batten tried to rent assets—such as satellites—and preferred not to own real estate.
- *Management structure and style.* Batten encouraged a team approach to management because he wanted his board and his people to challenge his thinking and offer new ideas "at least once a year or I don't need you."
- *Approach to rewards.* When Batten sold Landmark, it was clear that his approach to rewards was more like that of a start-up. Its broad group of employee-shareholders did quite nicely after NBC Universal, Blackstone Group, and Bain Capital acquired the Weather Channel in 2008.

The biggest takeaway: CEOs who can run ambidextrous ACs—those that preserve their valuable legacy businesses while inventing new ones—are few and far between. The rest remain vulnerable to their fear of cannibalization when competing with the smart start-ups.

John Kao: Hybrid Organizations

Innovation "advisor, teacher, and speaker" John Kao believes that "incumbents" can enjoy the best of both worlds. They could enjoy the brand, access to distribution and capital, and economies of scale of a big company, while also enjoying the growth and agility of a start-up that springs from a venture's need to experiment and learn with very limited resources[196]

They could do this by building what he calls "hybrid cultures." An old example of a hybrid culture is Lockheed and its World War II "Skunk Works." Trailing Germany in 1943, the United States was frantic to get a competing jet fighter.

Lockheed set up a small unit in a corner of a building to start work on the XP-80 four months before the contract even arrived. Lockheed's Skunk Works became famous as an example of such a hybrid culture.

But Kao gave me a new example I found quite intriguing. In the late 1980s, when Kao was a professor at HBS, he worked with then American Express CEO, Lou Gerstner. According to Kao, Gerstner created two organizational cultures within American Express—the traditional one that kept its legacy business running, and the innovation one that came up with new product ideas to spur more rapid growth.

One of Gerstner's skills as a CEO was his ability to make both sides believe that they were the most important part of the company; as Kao described it, Gerstner believed that each side needed the other. That is, the traditional side needed the innovation part in order to keep American Express's revenues climbing, and the innovation side needed the traditional side's strengths—including its brand, access to distribution and capital, and economies of scale.

In describing the challenge of managing a hybrid culture, Kao cited IDEO's idea that organizations should fail fast so they can succeed more quickly. But that ethos is in direct conflict with the way most incumbent CEOs manage.

Michael Tushman: How Big Companies Can Exploit and Explore

Michael Tushman, HBS's Paul R. Lawrence MBA Class of 1942 Professor of Business Administration, put more rigor into Kao's concept of the hybrid organization—coining the term "ambidextrous organization."

F. Scott Fitzgerald wrote, "The test of a first-rate intelligence is the ability to hold two opposed ideas in the mind at the same time, and still retain the ability to function."

And that's the key to creating an ambidextrous organization—a big company that can make its core business more efficient—what Tushman calls "exploit," while at the same time finding new growth opportunities—"explore."[197]

He ought to know. As Tushman explained, his work with Stanford professor Charles O'Reilly and Bruce Harreld, who retired from IBM and now lectures at HBS, has focused on how incumbent firms deal with the challenge. As Tushman explained, O'Reilly was his collaborator on ambidexterity's "core work," while its "most thorough and systematic implementation was at IBM" with Harreld.

An example of an ambidextrous organization is Ciba-Geigy's crop protection division—a part of Novartis since 1966 when it merged with Sandoz. Ciba-Geigy's managers in Basel, Switzerland, were able to exploit its chemical plant protection business—its products include plant pesticides—by cutting costs while simultaneously *exploring* in its North Carolina R&D lab—thus yielding a bioengineered plant that was insect-resistant.

Cleverly, both outcomes helped to realize Ciba-Geigy's "aspiration" of keeping plants healthy—whether through chemicals or biotechnology. Thanks to this clearly understandable "overarching aspiration," the head of its agribusiness, Wolfgang Samo, was able to engage people in both activities in a way that they could easily understand and use as the basis for action.

For a closer-to-home example, Tushman picked USA Today, a very valuable Gannett property. Back in the 1990s, Tom Curley ran the print version of the paper and was not sure what the impact of the Internet would be, but decided he had to build a Web version.

To that end, he hired different people to create USAToday.com. These included "computer jockeys, aggregators, and Web savvy" people who were housed in a different building from the print part of USA Today.

The heads of the print and Web units both reported to Curley. And he demanded that they both "duke it out" in the battle for resources. Ultimately, the Web part became so successful that it brought in more readers and, over time, more advertisement than the paper version.

But a key to making this work was Curley's incentive system that motivated the two divisions to work together even as they competed for resources. Specifically, the person running USAToday.com's bonus depended on the paper achieving its profit goals—just as the paper head's bonus was linked to USAToday.com meeting its targets.

Getting this approach to work depends on whether the core business has resources—customers, content, distribution channels, and a brand—that can be valuable to the explore part of the business. And if the exploit business offers nothing worth leveraging, the company should spin out the explore business, in Tushman's view

To make the ambidextrous organization work, Tushman argues the exploit and explore divisions must operate with different strategic intent, critical tasks, competencies, structures, controls/rewards, culture, and leadership roles.

How so? The exploit business focuses on cost and profit; spurs efficiency improvement and incremental innovation; is strong at operations; has a formal structure; controls for margin improvement and productivity, values efficiency, quality, and customers; and leads in a top-down manner.

By contrast, the explore unit focuses on innovation and growth; spurs new products and breakthrough innovation; is strong at entrepreneurship; has a loose, adaptive structure; controls for milestones and growth, values risk-taking, speed, and experimentation, and leads in a visionary and involved manner.

In his research, Tushman has found that the idea of an ambidextrous organization regularly fails if the CEO "delegates the tension." Simply put, unless the exploit and explore divisions both report to the CEO, the exploit division will always find a way to use its superior corporate clout to sideline and ultimately neutralize the explore one.

Tushman is optimistic that his idea can spread. In his work at IBM, he has found that by providing a language for discussing the tension, he frees up executives to figure out how to make it work.

And if the idea of the ambidextrous organization catches hold—perhaps many more big companies—like IBM whose market capitalization is $233 billion—will be worth more to investors than ever in their long history.

Klebahn: Focus on Extreme Customers and Composting

Klebahn has two great ideas for what large organizations can learn from start-ups—things he learned from his pre-Stanford career. As he said, he was "doing start-ups in the first half of my career—and running bigger companies in the second half." For example, Klebahn built a company to sell his world-beating snowshoe design and was chief operating officer of clothing retailer Patagonia.[198]

For the past three years he has been teaching the Launchpad class with Dearing. In Klebahn's view, there are two key things that large companies can learn from start-ups:

Ability to Focus

Because of their very limited resources, start-ups operate with the perpetual fear of running out of their limited money, people, and time. Thus, their only path to success is to focus on doing just one thing very well. Ironically, they do that one thing very well by doing it badly at first.

But they learn quickly by giving a minimally viable version of the product to customers, getting feedback, and making ever-better versions, until the market accepts their product. Juntos provides financial services to a potential market of 60 million "unbankable" workers—focusing on Stanford's night janitors.

VC firms could not see why they should invest in a company that targeted these "unbankable" customers. But eventually, the solution that Juntos developed for them opened up opportunities for what the VCs viewed as more bankable groups of customers. Klebahn told me that by February 2012, VCs' changing view made it possible for Juntos to start raising capital from them.

Klebahn sees significant benefits from focusing on what he calls "extreme customers." Since no other competitors are likely to be solving their problems, the odds are high that companies that do focus there could come up with innovative ideas that might be applicable to other groups of customers.

By contrast, large companies take a long time to "perfect" their products before letting customers see them. In practice, this often means that the big company ends up introducing a version that looks perfect to its engineers but leaves customers unwilling to buy.

The implication for big companies is that they should focus on "extreme customers"—without giving up on their core business—and use start-ups' fast learning loops that flow from building quick product prototypes, getting customer feedback, and iterating.

Organizations that serve a lot of customers can innovate by "acting like they're serving just a few with very vivid, unique needs." These unique users have extreme needs that require a radical solution. Usually, believes Klebahn, "the innovations in these extreme cases come back and apply to a mass market segment."

Composting

In big companies, failure is a career killer. When two ambitious executives are vying for a big leap up the ladder, the one that meets her numbers in the core business is likely to get the nod over the rival who tries to start a new initiative and fails to get it off the ground.

By contrast, start-ups view failure as an opportunity to learn. As Klebahn suggested, for a couple of hundred dollars, start-ups think of themselves as "learning $200,000 worth of information." As we saw in Chapter 6, Dearing has dubbed this "composting."

An example of this is that Juntos originally wanted to build a bank to serve those Stanford janitors. And doing that would require Juntos to build a Web site. But Juntos soon discovered that most of the janitors did not own computers; however, they did own cell phones, and text messaging was their preferred medium.

So Juntos offered the janitors a way to text the details of each monthly cash disbursement. When they saw how much of their $600-a-month pay-check was going, say, to their children's cell phone bills, the janitors realized that to reach their goals, they would need to choose what to stop buying.

Mapping out Juntos's initial failure led it to success. In Klebahn's view, start-up success depends on expecting failure and creating a culture of fast learning cycles to compost those failures and use them as nutrients to fuel future success.

As we saw in Chapter 3, an example of such a start-up is Pulse, the news-reading app developer that became very popular on Apple's App Store. Pulse has become quite successful but wants to preserve its culture of producing fast prototypes, so it keeps pushing its developers to their limits.

For example, Klebahn points out that the Pulse founders urge its team to fix technical glitches from the service's public "bug" list—almost assuring that the team will "fail (fast) in the process of pushing a small fix out." That push helps Pulse fight complacency, spur quick failures, and encourage learning that helps it improve.

Klebahn suggests that it is very difficult for large companies to adopt these start-up practices. After all, most large organizations are "execution oriented." They will take small risks to make incremental improvements to products that are likely to help them achieve growth goals. But their primary focus is keeping a steady upward slope in sales, profits, and stock price graphs.

But not all large companies are resistant. Klebahn notes that smart companies such as Procter & Gamble train experts who move around the company helping teams responsible for products that are clearly in need of innovation by teaching those teams to apply design principles.

Since it is so difficult to change corporate cultures, big organizations eager for fast performance improvement are better off with this firefighting approach than waiting—sometimes as long as a decade—to reorient the corporate equivalent of an aircraft carrier.

Errol Arkilic: Clock Speed Separates Start-Up Success from Big Company Failure

The National Science Foundation (NSF) is America's biggest seed-stage investor. And one of NSF's portfolio managers has keen insights on what separates the start-up winners from the pack. The NSF gives $140 million in grants to tech start-ups every year—making it America's biggest angel investor.[199]

Through the Small Business Innovation Research (SBIR) program, the NSF gives grants to start-ups that aspire to "harness the value of novelty," according to Errol Arkilic, program manager in NSF's Division of Industrial Innovation and Partnerships & Office of Integrative Activities.

Arkilic—who holds a PhD from MIT—has been at NSF for over eight years. While there, "he has [worked with] over 250 small business and start-ups" that have received its so-called phase one grant of $150,000 for six months. He has also "managed another 100" that have received $500,000 in phase two funds for up to a year. The NSF also offers 50 cents for every dollar of private capital a later-stage start-up receives over $1 million.

So, why do some start-ups succeed and others struggle? In Arkilic's view, the winners are "learning machines." As he said, start-ups that prevail are "a close-knit group that can close the loop and cycle fast through seven dumb ideas and one good one, make a decision, and implement the idea faster than it takes a big company to make one."

The ones that struggle—like many big companies—want to build what they believe is the "perfect" product before putting it into the hands of potential customers. These start-ups are far more likely to run out of time and money before they can get their first product to market. And even if they do deliver a product, it's likely to be something that nobody wants to buy.

As a part-time teacher, it is not hard for me to imagine that a tenured professor who runs one of these start-ups might have an attitude quite different from that of a poor, but knowledgeable, graduate student. After all, a tenured professor will still have the nice office and the steady paycheck if the start-up fails. An academic's biggest fear is introducing a flawed product too quickly, which gets the unwanted negative attention of other professors, who might conclude that the shoddy prototype does not reflect well on the university's brand.

Moreover, the professor will always believe that the technology is so good that there will always be a way to raise more money to finance its development.

By contrast, the graduate student may be very up-to-date on the technology but has no job security and often is betting her future on the success of the start-up. As a result, that student will feel a tremendous sense of urgency—fearing the financial consequences of running out of money and putting tremendous pressure on the start-up's employees to come up with a winning product before the money runs out.

The academic is in many ways in a situation similar to that of a big company. Both expect to be able to get a regular paycheck along with good benefits regardless of the outcome of their project. And if that project fails, it may be difficult to pin the responsibility on a single individual—if the right memos are written and the strategic sotto voce conversations are held with key executives.

Ultimately, the factor that separates the start-up winners from losers—and big companies—is what Arkilic calls "clock speed." By that, he means how quickly an organization can come up with an idea, build a prototype, get market feedback, and respond. If the feedback is positive, the company invests in the product; if it's negative; the team comes up with a better idea and tries again.

Clock speed varies inversely with a leader's perceived remaining resources. What does that mean? If a leader believes that the company has or can get more than enough money and people to turn the technology into a robust business, then the company's clock speed will be very slow.

Conversely, if the leader fears that the available resources are quickly coming to an end—driven by loss of funding, revenues, or the founder's house—the company's clock speed will be that much faster.

The only way for a large organization to get high clock speed is to create the credible belief that it is soon to run out of cash, people and technology and its continued survival depends on its ability to commercialize a new technology.

IDEO's David Aycan on How Big Companies Can Learn from Start-Ups

David Aycan, an IDEO design director, teaches big companies to act more like start-ups. And in so doing, he provides a powerful way to find good big company entrepreneurship training grounds.[200]

Aycan observes that big companies should empower people to have ownership. He cites Google as an example of a large organization that pairs an executive mentor with an internal entrepreneur who drives the growth. He believes that this combination is ideal for promoting growth initiatives.

But large organizations face another problem when it comes to innovation. Most of them are not used to cross-functional collaboration. This means that an innovation does not transition well from the mind of top management into the parts of the company that must implement the idea.

So, for example, engineering will feel that it is not really important to the idea-generation process and will just try to do its best to interpret what it thinks top management wants. And once engineering develops the idea into a prototype, it will throw it over the transom to marketing—which will be responsible for convincing customers to pay for the product.

However, since none of the functions feels engaged in the innovation process, they lack the strong desire "and cross-functional empathy" required to make the project succeed. This is in sharp contrast to start-up teams that usually work in close proximity to one another—identifying and solving challenges from diverse perspectives.

So what is a big company to do? Aycan believes that big companies need six start-up capabilities:

- *Build prototypes* that seek to draw insight from customer feedback.
- *Explore approaches to market opportunity by building six to twelve different* concepts and get customer feedback on them in parallel instead of spending half a year making one product perfect before letting a customer see it.
- *Push functions together and starve them for resources.* Put all a big company's functional expertise together and give it the start-up discipline of a tight deadline and a low budget. Don't wait a year for the project to get corporate review; instead, require it to get market feedback quickly.
- *Network with customers, suppliers, and partners.* Encourage the project teams to network extensively—as start-ups do—developing contacts among customers, suppliers, and other partners who can help the project succeed.
- *Learn and improve based on market feedback.* Measure the success of the project based on market feedback—for example, how many people are using the product and how it's doing in face-offs against the competition— instead of applying internal metrics.
- *Spur a will to win.* Create a sense of passion among the project's people—trying to emulate the strong sense of ownership that pervades a start-up. To do this, top management must recognize that employees get excited less about increasing shareholder value and more about a mission to make the world a better place and their ability to make a difference in realizing it.

Noam Wasserman: What Start-Ups Do Well and How Big Companies Can Adopt Their Insights

HBS Professor Noam Wasserman believes that big companies can take three approaches to applying start-up insights:

- *Create a "cocoon of start-up-ness."* As Wasserman described, big companies have created so-called "skunk works," which motivate workers to come up with new ideas in a hurry. A variant of this is the very rare big company CEO—think Gerstner at IBM or Jobs at Apple—who can create an ambidextrous organization that both preserves the core while investing in growth businesses, as Kao described.
- *Inject start-up-ness on an exception basis.* Another option is to bring in experts on start-up strategy to a big business with a product that is not growing as fast as management wants. This is the idea that Klebahn pointed out as a popular one at Procter & Gamble.

- *Make innovation part of everyone's job.* A third approach is the one that Google employs—giving all workers 20 percent of their time to devote to products or services that interest them. And as Intuit Founder and Executive Chairman Scott Cook explained to me, this massive decentralization of innovation helps keep Google 60 percent ahead of competitor Yahoo in terms of online advertising effectiveness. Google does this by showing its engineers how to code, test, and measure Google's advertising technology. Within that framework, Google engineers are free to come up with their own ideas. This approach to innovation helped Google stay 60 percent ahead despite Yahoo's Panama initiative—which involved 300 people over twenty months—to catch up.[201]

HUNGRY START-UP STRATEGY APPROACH TO BIG COMPANIES AS START-UP TRAINING GROUNDS

Aspiring entrepreneurs should look for big companies in which to train by following the hungry start-up strategy of big companies as start-up training grounds.

Three Approaches

As Figure 8.1 illustrates, there are three ways that big companies turn themselves into good start-up training grounds by adopting the capabilities that spur start-up success.

FIGURE 8.1 Hungry Start-Up Approaches of Big Companies as Start-Up Training Grounds.

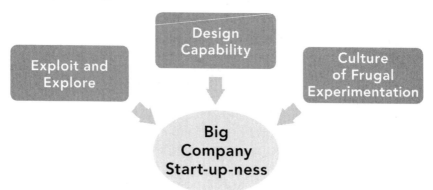

Exploit and Explore

This refers to Tushman's work on the ambidextrous organization. Aspiring entrepreneurs should look for companies such as Landmark Communications under Batten, American Express and IBM under Gerstner, USA Today under Curley, and Ciba-Geigy's agribusiness.

Design Capability

This is the idea described by Klebahn and P&G design guru Claudia Kotchka, in which the CEO of a big company chooses to create an internal design-thinking capability—a process that starts by observing customers performing activities, and ends with a new product that meets their needs based on iterative prototyping. This capability will initially encounter great resistance from most people in the company. But core business units that are not meeting their financial targets will be open to learning design thinking since they are so eager for new ideas that can put out the fire threatening to incinerate their careers. If design thinking can put out the fire and produce a turnaround, then other parts of the organization will be driven by the ambition to find ways to apply the design thinking to their own business.

Culture of Frugal Experimentation

This is an idea best articulated by Cook, who believes that with the right internal mechanisms and methodology, innovation can become part of everyone's job.[202] For example, Intuit created an "idea collaboration portal," that allows employees to come up with new ideas, post them, get feedback from others at Intuit, revise the ideas, and get staffing—all without intervention from managers. Meanwhile, Intuit has adopted a design-thinking methodology—based on testing new business hypotheses by getting feedback on inexpensive prototypes—which it uses to decide whether to invest in a new idea. This approach is also advocated by IDEO and others.

BIG COMPANIES THAT TRAIN START-UP CEOS

As we've discussed, big companies can offer good training grounds for start-up CEOs by applying these three approaches.

Three Case Studies

Here are case studies of three companies that offered excellent training for start-ups, and the CEOs' approaches that made it happen.

Intuit: How Cook Created a Culture of Frugal Experimentation

Cook states Intuit's mission as changing people's financial lives so profoundly that they can't imagine going back to the old way.

Cook, who joined Bain & Co. after earning his Harvard MBA, described his passion for assuring that Intuit is capable of both strengthening its core business and creating innovative new ones. His key finding is that big companies must create a culture of frugal experimentation.[203]

This is a problem that Cook, as of February 2012, had been studying for at least four years. He believes that there is no market category that keeps growing for so long that an incumbent company can avoid eventually perishing unless it hitches its wagon to a new market. As an example, Cook cites Microsoft that "has been unable to invent successful new disruptive businesses—causing its growth to slow down."

Cook finds it strange that large successful companies cannot invent new industries. After all, he reasons, they have the best people, a high profit flow, the largest customer base, and the broadest channels of distribution.

And yet, Cook notes, if you look at enterprise and consumer technology companies, the game-changing innovations almost never come from the big incumbents such as Oracle, SAP, and Microsoft. With the exception of Apple in the past decade, all the big innovations have come from start-ups.

Cook decided to investigate whether there are any large companies that have been able to buck this trend. Cook studied companies like Hewlett Packard, 3M, Procter & Gamble (where he worked), and Toyota. He found that the common thread during the periods of their most successful product and process innovations was the systems they put in place to encourage employees to conduct frugal experiments.

Not all big companies use this approach: Apple and Amazon enjoyed phenomenal success thanks to their exceptionally talented CEOs. However, Cook does not see himself as that kind of leader. Instead, he strives at Intuit to create a company that will be able to continue to create new growth businesses long after he has departed.

Cook told several very interesting stories that illustrate how Intuit has succeeded in inventing new businesses by creating an environment that encourages employees there to come up with new business hypotheses and test them by getting feedback from customers.

One example is a debit card for people without bank accounts. An Intuit finance employee—not a "product person"—noticed that the people who need tax refund checks the most are often ones who don't even have bank accounts.

She came up with the idea of giving those people debit cards and having Intuit accept the tax refunds in its accounts and transfer the funds to the debit card. The idea was born in February, and the employee wanted to test it by April 1 before tax season ran out on April 15th.

Cook criticized the kludgy Web site she developed but she argued that it was better to get something crude that would test her idea than to wait another ten months. She expected 100 takers but got 1,000.

And the surprise was that half the ones that wanted the debit card already had bank accounts. In this way, Intuit discovered that the need for this product was much greater than it expected. One interesting feature of this story is that Cook was not wild about the Web site that the employee had developed but she was able to pursue her idea anyway.

This echoes one of Cook's findings from his studies of Hewlett Packard. His conversation with the author of a 650-page book on HP's history revealed that seven of the eight big new businesses that the giant invented came "from the bottom" and were opposed by CEO David Packard. The pattern Cook has found is that in all these cases, three things were true:

- The company "liberated the inventive power of new people."
- It created a "culture of experimentation."
- It changed the role of the boss from a decider of whether to pursue or cancel innovation projects to an installer of systems that encourage endless cycles of hypothesis generation, testing with customers, and learning from the gap between quantitative expectations and measured market truth.

Cook believes that there is nothing more rewarding to employees than to see their ideas being used by people. To that end, Intuit has created its idea collaboration portal, which lets employees post ideas, and get feedback, coaching, and suggestions, and even sign up others to help implement it.

The beauty of this portal is that all this idea encouragement can happen without a manager getting involved. According to Cook, this portal has turned thirty ideas into "shipping products and features" that boosted Intuit's revenues.

Cook's system sounds eminently doable at big companies around the world—if their executives are willing to adopt it. Here are Cook's eight steps for creating a culture of innovation:

- *Leader's vision.* A culture of experimentation starts with the CEO's vision. In Cook's case, the vision is to change people's financial lives so profoundly that they can't imagine going back to the old way.

- *Strategy-by-experiment.* Rather than trying to curry favor with their bosses, Cook believes it's essential to enable people to make data-based decisions. This means encouraging them to conduct experiments and collect data on customer behavior.
- *Leap-of-faith assumptions.* Citing Ries, Cook encourages people to identify the two or three key assumptions that should be true, but might not be, for the idea to succeed. Then people must find a way to test these assumptions with customers, at a low cost in a very short time frame.
- *Numeric hypothesis.* Next Cook wants people to come up with an estimate of, say, the number of customers who will order the new product.
- *Experimental run.* The employee should then run the experiment to test whether that numeric hypothesis is right or not.
- *Analysis of variance.* Then Cook wants people to analyze the gap between the hypothesis and the actual results, and dig deep to find the reason for that gap.
- *Surprise celebration.* Cook is adamant that start-ups should not try to bury surprises to keep from being embarrassed but rather savor them because surprises expose a market signal that had not yet been detected.
- *Decision.* Finally, executives should make a decision about whether to pursue the idea or try a new one.

The success of this process depends on a blend of confidence in a new idea, coupled with intellectual humility when it comes to testing and refining it. Cook believes that one of his roles is to model this behavior so it will permeate Intuit.

Kotchka's Design Capability: How Procter & Gamble's Design Guru Spurs Growth

Before Kotchka retired from P&G in 2009, former P&G CEO A. G. Lafley charged her with teaching P&G how to practice the fine art of "design." The combination of her knowledge of design thinking and his blessing helped revive P&G."[204]

Kotchka has had a remarkable career. She started off as an accountant at the now-defunct Arthur Andersen. She decided after a few years that she was not cut out for accounting and wanted to do marketing instead.

She was hired by P&G and had a great run there. At one point in her career, P&G's design group reported to Kotchka. That group was thought of within P&G as being responsible for designing product packages. But the design group's leader educated Kotchka—explaining to her that design has a much broader mission—to view products from the perspective of the user.

In 2001, Lafley became CEO—taking over after the less-than-stellar eighteen-month tenure of his predecessor, Durk Jager. P&G needed to return to its roots as a company that put the consumer at the center of its business. And, arguing that P&G could not survive on technology alone, he tasked Kotchka to create a whole new capability at P&G—design.

Why design? Lafley's several years in Japan had impressed him with the effectiveness of intelligent design. And Lafley conducted a study that found that over its long history whenever P&G had strayed from its primary focus on the consumer, it got into trouble. Lafley was convinced that a design capability would help P&G practice his mantra, "Consumer is boss."

While Kotchka humbly admitted to making errors along the way, she introduced a broader process for P&G's people to look for opportunities by observing how consumers behave. Whereas P&G had traditionally watched how consumers used its products, Kotchka taught P&G the importance of watching how consumers performed daily activities—for example, getting ready to go to work.

Ultimately, she helped P&G develop a process based on design thinking. Key steps in the process included building "low-resolution" prototypes of solutions to problems, collecting consumer feedback to them, developing a new version, and repeating these three steps until arriving at a unique solution that worked

One example she gave was P&G's Olay brand; the team believed the product needed new packaging because consumers had so many skin-care choices that it was hard to decide which one best met their specific needs.

But using the design methodology that Kotchka taught them, the Olay group reframed the solution and ultimately introduced Olay for You—a Web site that helped consumers choose the specific product that fit their needs before visiting the retail outlet.

Another example of applying such design thinking is IDEO's work for Bank of America. The bank asked IDEO to help it find ways to encourage people to save more.

IDEO observed that consumers would write checks to pay their bills in an amount that exceeded the dollar value of the invoice. Consumers viewed this as a form of saving because the extra few dollars would be credited to them by the supplier the next month.

Applying this kind of thinking, IDEO helped Bank of America develop a debit card that rounded up a payment and applied the difference to consumers' savings accounts. The result, according to Kotchka, was 12 million new customers and $3.1 billion added to consumers' savings.

I asked Kotchka how she would solve a problem posed by my wife, who told me that she wanted to buy a new perfume but that she was intimidated by all the choices in a department store.

Kotchka said that she would approach this problem by framing a broad problem statement "Help me find a perfume that I love in any easy way." My hunch was that Kotchka might end up with a solution to this problem that would be analogous to the Olay Web site. The only technical problem would be that it's hard to download different perfume smells to your iPhone.

But Kotchka told me an amazing story. During the dot-com era, P&G developed a Web site called Reflect.com. This site let women answer a series of questions online about what kind of perfume they would like.

Based on those answers, P&G would send a perfume sample to the consumer, and 95 percent of the time, the consumer liked it. Although consumer loyalty to the site was very high, P&G ultimately shut it down.

Since retiring from P&G, Kotchka has been working on the challenge of getting other companies to adopt design thinking. She has encountered a range of challenges:

- *Complacency.* Success makes a company very resistant to trying new things.
- *Risk aversion.* Many big companies have what Roger Martin calls a tension between validity and reliability. The punch line is that companies are very reluctant to take any risks that would upset the profit that flows from reliably making a high-quality product that lots of people want to buy.
- *Functional silos.* Kotchka observes that when required to work in cross-functional teams, each group—such as marketing, finance, and manufacturing—looks at problems only from its own functional perspectives. However, she noticed that when those team members take off their functional hats and take responsibility for solving the business problem—as start-up teams do—the results are much better.

For solving that last problem, Kotchka points out that P&G created a program called Clay Street that took different workers out of their usual line jobs to work on a short-term project. During that period of two to ten weeks, the team participants were made to feel "accountable to each other"—not to their functional bosses.

Kotchka encountered all of these problems when she started. But she decided to try to introduce the benefits of design thinking with the P&G teams whose products were in trouble. After working with Kotchka, one general manager stood up and credited the design as a key to turning around her business unit. This helped Kotchka spread her message more widely within P&G.

The result was an unleashing of creativity that boosted P&G top and bottom lines. If more big companies could follow P&G's lead on this, maybe American business would be growing much faster.

AT&T Manages Ambidextrous Organization

Glenn Lurie's leadership of an AT&T Explore division—using Tuchman's term—helped the telecommunications giant win a lucrative deal with Apple's iPhone.

Lurie, president of Emerging Enterprises and Partnerships for AT&T, began his career at a start-up. One of his early jobs was as a salesperson for McCaw Cellular—and he was a regional president of this entrepreneurial firm when AT&T acquired it in 1994 for about $12 billion—forming the core of its wireless business.[205]

For twenty-two years, as of February 2012, Lurie had been with AT&T's wireless business as it changed corporate forms. In the early 2000s, AT&T spun off the wireless unit and then bought it back in 2004. And when Jobs came calling, Lurie was responsible for working with him to figure out how to create a viable business model for the iPhone.

The popularity of the iPhone—and AT&T's exclusive relationship with Apple announced in 2007—resulted, in part, from Lurie's ability to develop a reputation with Jobs and Apple CEO Tim Cook for trustworthiness, flexibility, and speedy decision making.

As a way to build that trust, Jobs needed to be certain that Apple's iPhone plans would not be leaked to the public. Lurie's small team evidently satisfied Jobs that it could be trusted with sacrosanct business details about the iPhone. The result was AT&T's 2007-to-2010 exclusive deal to support the iPhone.

Thanks to the success of that deal, ATT Chairman Randall Stephenson and AT&T Mobility and Consumer Market president and CEO Ralph de La Vega selected Lurie to turn their vision of wireless connectivity for emerging devices into a fast-growing business in the fourth quarter of 2008.

Lurie accepted the challenge, conditional on his ability to run the new emerging devices unit consistent with the principle of high clock speed. More specifically, Lurie wanted to be able to run the unit with flexibility and speed so that it could create value for device manufacturers and consumers, and do so faster and better than competitors.

Lurie asked AT&T to make Emerging Devices a "self-standing group," with dedicated people performing key functions—including pricing, strategy, technology, business development, legal, and accounting—needed to build relationships with the unit's ecosystems.

To that end, Lurie structured Emerging Devices around so-called "verticals." These include subgroups dedicated to developing expertise and deep relationships within industries such as health care, gaming, personal navigation, computing, automotive telematics, and consumer electronics.

Lurie's reasoning was that the needs and key players in each industry are so different that AT&T needs people dedicated to understanding and building relationships in each.

Lurie provided some examples of these partnerships. It works with Sony, Garmin, Amazon, Ford, Nissan, and BMW. As well, AT&T is pursuing growth into new segments, including "consumer connected devices," and when it comes to business users, Lurie says it's "moving beyond machine-to-machine devices."

To staff the emerging devices unit, Lurie has drawn on talent from within AT&T and people with expertise in these verticals. And he binds them together with a strong culture that encourages flexibility and speedy decision making.

While partners such as Garmin were initially skeptical that AT&T could actually deliver on the promise of speed and flexibility, thanks to the actions of AT&T's Emerging Devices people, Garmin's chief technology officer grew convinced.

Lurie's performance is measured based on Emerging Device's ability to bring in new business that's "accretive to AT&T's EBITDA [earnings before interest, taxes, depreciation, and amortization]." Lurie's unit also adds to the top line of AT&T's mobility business, delivers high customers loyalty, and produces "strong margins."

But since Emerging Devices does not cannibalize AT&T's other businesses, its other units are interested to learn about its successes but don't slow down its ability to act.

Lurie confirms that Emerging Devices is getting results in the marketplace. As he said, "AT&T ended 2011 with 41 percent more connected devices on its network than the same time a year earlier. In the fourth quarter it added 1.029 million connected devices to its network, ending 2011 with 13.1 million connected devices on our network—more M2M/emerging devices than any other carrier in the world."

Back in his Boston, Massachusetts, laboratory on March 10, 1876, Alexander Graham Bell asked his colleague over a prototype telephone, "Mr. Watson, come here—I want to see you."

About 136 years later, thanks to Emerging Devices' high clock speed, Lurie—who says, "innovation is part of our culture"—is showing that some of that start-up DNA is still reporting to work at AT&T today.

SUMMARY

If you are thinking that you need to work in a big company before starting your venture, you can follow the principles outlined in this chapter. But if you can't get a job working in one of the companies mentioned in this chapter, you should evaluate the companies that do offer you a job based on the principles developed here.

To assist with that evaluation, consider applying the checklist presented in Chapter 9. Specifically, Table 9.4 can help you test how well a potential big company employer is likely to train you for starting your venture later in your career.

CHAPTER 9

Resources

CHAPTER 9 CONTAINS RESOURCES to help readers interested in learning more about start-up strategy. It contains the following:

- Table 9.1. 162 Start-Up Executives Interviewed
- Start-Up CEO Interview Guide
- Framework for Deciding Whether to Become an Entrepreneur
- Table 9.2. Framework for Deciding Whether to Launch a Start-Up
- Table 9.3. Start-Up Capital Provider Investment Screener
- Table 9.4. Big Company as Start-Up Training Ground Assessment Framework

TABLE 9.1 **Start-Up Executives Interviewed**

Company	Interviewee	Title	Date of Interview
Adapteva	Andreas Olofsson	CEO	November 4, 2011
Adeptol	Prateek Kathpal	CEO	October 3, 2010
AfterSteps	Jess Bloomgarden	CEO	July 6, 2011
AgigA Tech	Ron Sartore	CEO	December 8, 2011
AlgoSec	Yuval Baron	CEO	November 7, 2011
Ammasso	Larry Genovese	CEO	November 20, 2011
Amos Enterprises	Martin Tsang	CEO	January 7, 2012
AnaTango	Michael Saddik	CEO	January 18, 2012
Antenna Software	Jim Hemmer	CEO	November 8, 2011
Applied Network Technology	Dave Paolino	CEO	October 17, 2011
Apptio	Sunny Gupta	CEO	October 3, 2010
Apture	Tristan Harris	CEO	June 13, 2011

continued

TABLE 9.1 *continued*

Company	Interviewee	Title	Date of Interview
Aquantia	Faraj Aalaei	CEO	October 24, 2011
Armor Games	Daniel McNeely	CEO	March 24, 2009
ASSIA	John Cioffi	CEO	November 7, 2011
Avail-TVN	Ramu Potarazu	CEO	November 9, 2011
Avangate	Carl Theobald	CEO	May 24, 2012
Avigilon	Alexander Fernandes	CEO	October 3, 2010
Awareness Technologies	Brad Miller	CEO	November 1, 2011
Axcient	Justin Moore	CEO	September 19, 2011
Balihoo	Shane Vaughn	VP, Marketing	October 3, 2010
Bionée	Ewa Asmar	CEO	August 2, 2011
BlogHer	Lisa Stone	CEO	October 3, 2010
Blurb	Eileen Gittins	CEO	May 24, 2011
Borderless Healthcare	Wei Siang Yu	CEO	January 9, 2012
Bridgeway	Edwin Lee	CEO	January 4, 2012
Bridging the cultural divide through entre-preneurship	Ted Grossman	Founder	June 13, 2011
Broadband Access Systems	Dave Paolino	CEO	October 17, 2011
Bubble Motion	Tom Clayton	CEO	October 11, 2011
Cardlytics	Scott Grimes	CEO	October 3, 2010
Cellfire	Dan Kihanya	VP, Marketing	February 27, 2009
Chattersource	Kristina Anderson	Co-Founder	May 18, 2011
Cirtas	Dan Decasper	CEO	October 3, 2010
ClearStory	Sharmila Mulligan	CEO	April 27, 2012
Cloudera	Kirk Dunn	COO	August 4, 2011
CloudFlare	Matthew Prince	CEO	July 18, 2011
Coolspotters	Aaron LaBerge	CEO	March 2, 2009
Cotendo	Ronni Zehavi	CEO	October 3, 2010
Couchbase	Bob Wiederhold	CEO	January 17, 2012
CoupTessa	David Horn	CEO	November 29, 2011
Coursekit	Joe Cohen	CEO	May 23, 2011
Coverity	Anthony Bettencourt	CEO	December 14, 2011

TABLE 9.1 *continued*

Company	Interviewee	Title	Date of Interview
Critical Software	Goncalo Quadros	CEO	June 3, 2011
Cybershift	Bob Farina	CEO	October 3, 2010
Dash Navigation	Rob Currie	CEO	March 3, 2009
Data Robotics	Tom Buiocchi	CEO	October 3, 2010
Delphix	Jedidiah Yueh	CEO	March 13, 2012
Diagnostics for All	Una Ryan	CEO	July 16, 2011
Doodle	Tilman Eberle	CEO	March 9, 2009
Dyn	Jeremy Hitchcock	CEO	November 13, 2011
Dynamics	Joe Mullen	CEO	May 16, 2011
EchoSign	Jason Lemkin	CEO	December 7, 2011
Egenera	Peter Manca	CEO	October 7, 2011
Egypt Beach Systems	Larry Genovese	CEO	November 20, 2011
Embrace	Jane Chen	CEO	June 16, 2011
Endeca Technologies	Jim Baum	President	October 17, 2011
EnterpriseDB	Ed Boyajian	CEO	December 27, 2011
Euclid Elements	Will Smith	CEO	November 3, 2011
Evernote	Phil Libin	CEO	September 26, 2011
Extra Hop	Jessie Rothstein	CEO	April 12, 2012
Fetchmob	Alisa Boguslavskaya	Co-Founder	June 6, 2011
FireEye	Ashar Aziz	CEO	May 24, 2012
Gameloft	Alexandre de Rochefort	CEO	March 11, 2009
GeckoGo	Pokin Yeung	Co-Founder	February 26, 2009
Good Life Beverages	Dan Rumennik	CEO	June 11, 2012
Grindr	Joel Simkhai	CEO	November 22, 2011
Grockit	Roy Gilbert	CEO	June 7, 2011
GuardTime	Bart Matusow	COO	January 10, 2012
Hearsay Social	Clara Shih	CEO	June 9, 2011
Hong Kong EV Power	Laurence Chan	CEO	January 7, 2012
Huddle	Alastair Mitchell	CEO	February 22, 2012
Hygeia Therapeutics	Yael Schwartz	CEO	October 9, 2011

continued

TABLE 9.1 *continued*

Company	Interviewee	Title	Date of Interview
Imperva	Shlomo Kramer	CEO	June 15, 2012
Incapsula	Marc Gaffan	CEO	November 9, 2011
Innopage	Keith Li	CEO	January 7, 2012
ionGrid	Nick Triantos	CEO	December 9, 2011
iZettle	Jacob de Geer	CEO	October 18, 2011
Jagex	Adam Tuckwell	VP, Marketing	March 13, 2009
Juntos Finanzas	Ben Knelman	CEO	June 1, 2011
Katango	Yoav Shoham	Chairman	July 12, 2011
Kayak.com	Kellie Pelletier	VP, Marketing	March 2, 2009
Kembrel	Stephan Jacob	Co-Founder	June 27, 2011
Levo League	Caroline Ghosn	Co-Founder	July 6, 2011
Locately	Thaddeus Fulford-Jones	Co-Founder	May 19, 2011
LogLogic	Guy Churchward	CEO	February 17, 2012
Loki Studios	Ivan Lee	CEO	June 11, 2011
Lookout	John Hering	CEO	January 25, 2012
Luman Lighting	Freddie Lau	CEO	January 7, 2012
Main Street Hub	Matt Stuart	Co-Founder	June 1, 2011
Makible	Jon Buford	CEO	January 6, 2012
Menu	Devin Kimble	CEO	January 11, 2012
Metra Tech	Scott Swartz	CEO	January 17, 2012
Min.us	John Xie	CEO	May 23, 2011
MocoSpace	Justin Siegel	CEO	September 14, 2011
Modapt	Mark Lederhos	CEO	June 6, 2011
m-Via	Bill Barhydt	CEO	June 21, 2012
Netezza	Jim Baum	President	October 17, 2011
Netvibes	Freddy Mini	CEO	February 25, 2009
Network Engines	Larry Genovese	CEO	November 20, 2011
New Relic	Lew Cirne	CEO	December 14, 2011
Nexenta	Evan Powell	CEO	February 16, 2012
Orbit Baby	Joseph Hei	Co-Founder	June 11, 2011
Outblaze	Yat Siu	CEO	March 1, 2012
Oyster	Elie Seidman	CEO	May 5, 2011
P2 Mobile Technologies	Patrick Lim	CEO	January 7, 2012

TABLE 9.1 *continued*

Company	Interviewee	Title	Date of Interview
Pandora	Tim Westergren	Founder	February 27, 2009
Pano Logic	John Kish	CEO	November 13, 2011
Piazza	Pooja Nath Sankar	CEO	January 20, 2012
Plista	Dominik P. Matyka	CEO	March 12, 2009
Plum	Caroline O'Connor	CEO	June 20, 2011
PoverUP	Charlie Javice	CEO	June 2, 2011
Predictive Biosciences	Peter Klemm	CEO	May 24, 2011
Pulse	Akshay Kothari	CEO	May 26, 2011
Puppet Labs	Luke Kanies	CEO	March 16, 2012
Pure Storage	Scott Dietzen	CEO	August 24, 2011
Pyxis Mobile	Steve Levy	CEO	November 22, 2011
Quantine	Daryl Low	CEO	January 9, 2012
Qype	Andrew Hunter	UK Gen. Mgr.	February 5, 2009
Rebtel	Hjalmar Windbladh	CEO	October 13, 2011
Revision3	Ron Richards	VP, Marketing	February 20, 2009
Second Life	Philip Rosedale	Founder	December 7, 2011
Sentigo	Eran Barak	VP, Marketing	June 8, 2011
Sifteo	Dave Merrill	Co-Founder	June 22, 2011
SIRUM	Adam Kircher	CEO	July 5, 2011
SkyCrepers	Matt Chatham	CEO	May 13, 2011
SoFi	Mike Cagney	CEO	April 2, 2012
Sonatype	Jason van Zyl	CTO	April 23, 2012
SpringLeaf Therapeutics	Frank Bobe	CEO	May 12, 2011
Studio UE	Tony Fernandes	CEO	December 8, 2011
T2 Biosystems	John McDonough	CEO	May 17, 2011
Tagit	Nafi Singh	CEO	January 9, 2012
Taris Biomedical	Sarma Duddu	CEO	May 26, 2011
TECC	Josh Reeves	Co-Founder	June 23, 2011
Terascale	Larry Genovesi	CEO	November 20, 2011
Tintri	Kieran Harty	CEO	February 23, 2012
Tokbox	Ian Small	CEO	February 13, 2012
Trade Show Internet	Seth Burstein	Co-Founder	May 27, 2011

continued

TABLE 9.1 *continued*

Company	Interviewee	Title	Date of Interview
Transpera	Frank Barbieri	CEO	March 4, 2009
Treca	Manuel Rizo-Patron Terrero	CEO	May 4, 2011
TSL Marketing	Kyle Hegarty	VP, Marketing	January 11, 2012
TTAGG	Ryan Frazier	CEO	October 18, 2011
Tutor Vista	Krishna Ghanesh	CEO	June 10, 2009
Type-U	Mike Norwood	CEO	August 4, 2011
UniEats	Liz Wessel	CEO	July 22, 2011
Unwrap	Josh Reeves	Product Manager	June 23, 2011
Value Retail	Scott Malkin	CEO	June 28, 2011
Venuetastic	Helen Belogolova	CEO	August 8, 2011
VivoPath	Walter Lunsmann	CEO	October 31, 2011
WatchDox	Moti Rafalin	CEO	February 15, 2012
WhiteGlove Health	Bob Fabbio	CEO	June 7, 2011
WhiteHat Security	Stephanie Fohn	CEO	December 20, 2011
Worcester Area Thinktank	Lauren Monroe	CEO	October 18, 2011
WorkersNow	Pablo Fuentes	CEO	June 6, 2011
Xeround	Razi Sharir	CEO	June 7, 2012
Xirrus	Dirk Gates	CEO	December 12, 2011
Xsigo	Lloyd Carney	CEO	February 15, 2012
X-trinsic Neurovascular	Chris Sullivan	CEO	October 10, 2011
Yesware	Matthew Bellows	CEO	November 9, 2011
Yoomi	Jim Sheikh	Founder	June 20, 2011
Zazzle	Josh Reeves	Co-Founder	June 23, 2011
Zeicast	Amey Laud	CEO	January 9, 2012

START-UP CEO INTERVIEW GUIDE

I asked company founders the following questions:

- In nontechnical terms, how would you describe what your start-up does?
- Can you provide an example of how a specific customer gets value from your company's product?
- What did you do before you started your company?
- Why did you found your company?
- What is the company's mission? What are its long-term goals? What short-term goals have you set to motivate your team to achieve those goals?
- What market does your company focus on and why did you pick that market?
- Why do you think that market is likely to become large and what are the key trends propelling its growth?
- Have you raised capital from outside? If so, how did you choose the capital providers that eventually invested in your start-up?
- How many people do you employ? How do you select the people you hire? How do you motivate and compensate them? How many people will you hire in the next year and in what functions?
- How does your company gain market share? What are the key features of its product that produces competitively superior customer value? How will your start-up continue to outpace competitors?
- As you contemplate your company's five-year goals, what changes do you anticipate you could encounter—such as upstart competitors, evolving customer needs, and/or new technologies—that would warrant a market response from you? What process do you use to distinguish signal from noise? How do you decide how best to respond?

HUNGRY START-UP STRATEGY APPROACH TO DECIDING WHETHER TO BECOME AN ENTREPRENEUR

While there are no scientifically perfect ways to test your entrepreneurial aptitude, research has been done on successful entrepreneurs.

If you think you regularly display most of the forty-five specific behaviors we'll name shortly, there is a good chance you fit the profile of a successful start-up CEO. If not, it might be worth taking a look at the traits you don't share with these entrepreneurs and trying to figure out how that missing link might impede your progress.

You might also consider taking a course of study in entrepreneurship skills, as entrepreneurship professor Candida Brush of Babson College recommends, who claims that academic research shows that education is correlated with start-up success.

The idea that entrepreneurs are born, heroic figures with unteachable psychological traits has been around for 100 years. Stanford Law School alum Peter Thiel appears to believe in this idea. It certainly helps to reinforce his effort to encourage people to drop out of college to start companies.[205] However, 113,000 papers cited in *Google Scholar* contradict the idea of entrepreneurs as born and not trainable.

More specifically, Brush cites research that shows the probability of start-up survival is 7 percent for a company started by an entrepreneur with no college education or industry expertise; with both education and industry expertise, the odds of start-up survival rise to 77 percent. And the same benefits of education and industry expertise hold true for start-up profitability: Without them there's an 8 percent chance of profits; with them, that number rises to 61 percent.

What exactly do entrepreneurs get out of an education? Brush cites work by Babson professor Patti Greene and her colleagues, which details forty-five "roles and tasks" that entrepreneurs perform. These include creating new products and services, inspiring others to embrace the vision and values of the company, and controlling costs.

Babson is using these forty-five to create a so-called Entrepreneurial Self-Efficacy Scale that aspiring entrepreneurs can use to rank themselves. This scale can help them to identify their strengths and opportunities for improvement. Education can help them improve where they're weak.

Brush estimates that there are about 2,500 programs, like that at Babson, that teach entrepreneurship.

To give you a chance to assess whether you are already comfortable in these forty-five roles and tasks, I have extracted the seventeen that appear to me to be unique to entrepreneurial success. The other twenty-eight seem to apply to running both start-ups and large companies.

If you feel a high degree of comfort with the following seventeen roles and responsibilities, you are probably a strong candidate for running a start-up:

- Working productively under continuous stress, pressure, and conflict
- Creating new products and services
- Targeting new markets and customers
- Creating the vision and values of the organization
- Reacting quickly to unexpected change or failure
- Discovering new ways to improve existing products

- Developing relationships with key people who are connected to capital sources
- Inspiring others to embrace the vision and values of the company
- Reacting quickly to take advantage of business opportunities
- Evaluating the feasibility of a new opportunity
- Developing a working environment that encourages people to try out something new
- Maintaining a positive outlook despite setbacks and negative feedback from naysayers
- Hiring and retaining the right people
- Identifying and building management teams
- Forming partnership or alliance relationship with others
- Setting and meeting business goals
- Calculating and accepting risks[207]

WHICH OF THESE SIX ENTREPRENEURIAL TYPES ARE YOU?

While this list of traits is a helpful way to look at whether you should become an entrepreneur, my interviews have found that there's no one-size-fits-all way to think about what an entrepreneur is. I've concluded that there are six different types of entrepreneurs based on two categories:

- *Pre–start–up work experience.* Some people start companies before or right after graduating from college, others rise near the top of the corporate world before launching their own ventures, and still others become start-up CEOs because investors bring them in to rescue start-ups with the skills that led to their earlier start-up success.
- *Start-up purpose.* People start companies for many reasons but the two most significant ones I found—and they are not mutually exclusive— were to seize a growing market opportunity or to satisfy a hunger for meaning in their work life.[208]

Which of the six entrepreneurial types are you? To help you figure it out, I've outlined a brief definition of each and give an example from my interviews.

College/Market Opportunity

Examples of this type abound; they include most famously college dropouts like Bill Gates and Mark Zuckerberg. But plenty of businesspeople start companies during college and keep on running them after they graduate.

Consider the newsreader app company, Pulse. Kothari, a Stanford master's candidate, wanted an easier way to consume news on his iPad. This idea turned into his company, co-founded in May 2010 with Ankit Gupta, also a Stanford grad student, who handles the software side of the business. Pulse grew from one to 11 million users by the end of 2011.

Kothari is an entrepreneur who saw a market opportunity and used his technical skill to seize it right out of school.

Postcorporate/Market Opportunity

Often it takes significant corporate experience to develop the contacts and learn an industry well enough to identify a market opportunity for an entrepreneur to seize.

After years as a derivatives trader and hedge fund executive, Cagney got a master's from Stanford Business School and saw an opportunity to go after the $1 trillion student loan market based on what he learned about social networking.

As we saw earlier, Cagney co-founded SoFi to tap alumni's wealth and contacts to provide loans to current students at their universities. In 2012, SoFi planned to provide $150 million in loans to both in-school students and recent graduates wishing to consolidate.

Cagney is an entrepreneur who taps his experience and industry knowledge to find and seize a market opportunity.

Rescue/Market Opportunity

Nearly half of start-up CEOs are brought in by investors to save a venture that is struggling to grow. Some of the people who do that have extensive corporate experience that can help them seize the market opportunity they perceive.

Consider networking technology maker, Xsigo CEO Carney. Carney worked for a string of minicomputer and networking companies before 2001 when he joined Juniper Networks as COO. He then became Micromuse's chairman and CEO. And when International Business Machines bought Micromuse in 2006, he became general manager of IBM's Netcool Division.

In 2007, his former engineering colleague from Juniper called Carney and ask him to take over Xsigo's CEO post from the engineer. As of February 2012, Xsigo had almost 260 customers and by July he had closed a deal to sell Xsigo to Oracle.

Carney is an entrepreneur whose large corporate rise gives him the skills to run a growing start-up and to sell to large companies.

College/Meaning

Some people leave college and decide that a start-up is the best way for them to make their working world meaningful. I found that many college meaning-seekers started social ventures.

Javice told me the thing that really kicked her into action was her summer 2008 experience volunteering in a border refugee village in Thailand where she realized that a little money—she bought 50 donuts for $1—could go a long way to helping poor people start businesses that would lift them out of poverty.

Javice is an entrepreneur whose lack of corporate experience is no obstacle to turning a hunger for meaning into a new venture.

Postcorporate/Meaning

Some entrepreneurs leave the corporate world to start companies that they believe will apply their skills to a more meaningful purpose. Consider the case of Cloudera's Hammerbacher.

He walked away from a fortune in Facebook stock—a move he dubbed an egregious act of wealth destruction. But trying to realize Cloudera's mission—to apply the computing power he had built at Facebook to solve more important problems—satisfied Hammerbacher's hunger more than those extra Facebook millions.

Instead of helping to answer what a group of friends "like" the most on Facebook, Cloudera customers would be able to answer questions such as, "What gene do all these cancer patients share?"

Hammerbacher is an entrepreneur who paid a big financial price for his choice of meaningful work. But that choice may pay off financially as well.

Rescue/Meaning

Some experienced executives are drawn to help start-ups founded by others to grow because they believe in that start-up's mission.

A Harvard chemistry professor came up with an inexpensive way to diagnose disease using a specially designed piece of paper. But Dr. George Whitesides did not have the skills or inclination to turn that into a business.

For that, he brought in Una Ryan as CEO. Ryan is impressive. She earned a PhD from Cambridge, authored over 500 original papers and eleven books, and ran biotech companies. Ryan believes in the mission of Diagnostics For All (DFA)—"making affordable point of care diagnostics for the developing world."

Ryan is an entrepreneur who jumps from the large corporate world to a start-up because of her hunger for meaning.

Use this framework as another way to decide whether you could be an entrepreneur.

HUNGRY START-UP STRATEGY APPROACH TO DECIDING WHETHER TO LAUNCH A VENTURE

When a founder decides to launch a new venture, odds are good that passion will blind the founder to thinking about all the risks involved. Start-up success hinges on getting the right answers to two broad sets of questions:

- Why is the venture worth the time of the founder and those who might join the founding team?
- How can the founder turn the vision for the venture into a successful business?

Most start-up CEOs could save themselves a considerable amount of time, money, and heartache if they were willing to invest the time to answer both questions before launching it. This does not mean that many entrepreneurs will take my advice; only that I think they should.

Moreover, if you are an entrepreneur and you have read this far, you may be looking for advice on how to answer these questions. If so, the framework for deciding whether to launch a start-up can help with your decision-making process.

Needless to say, it is impossible to develop completely reliable answers to these questions. The sources of unreliability include:

- The sources on which those answers depend may be imperfect.
- The venture's market may change—making earlier answers irrelevant.
- New technologies may emerge that alter the competitive landscape.
- New business models may become successful that demand a shift in the start-up's focus.
- Key members of the start-up team may be surprisingly unproductive or become less motivated.

Furthermore, as we discussed in Chapter 1, the decision to start a venture is really a series of decisions, each of which builds on the success of the previous decision and how well the start-up implemented those decisions.

The decision to go out on a limb to start a company is exceedingly risky, and the founder should collect as much information frugally and quickly, to address the anticipatable risks. If a founder can answer yes to all the questions in Table 9.2, then pursuing the venture is probably a safe idea.

TABLE 9.2 **Approach to Deciding Whether to Launch a Venture**

Approach/Question	Answer (Yes/No)
Setting Goals	
Does the founder have a compelling reason for starting the venture that will help galvanize employees?	
Can the founder develop and communicate long-term goals for the venture that help bring the mission into focus?	
Has the founder articulated a series of practical short-term milestones that map a realistic path to that goal?	
Picking markets	
Is the founder passionate about the industry?	
Does the founder have considerable knowledge of the industry?	
Is the founder an industry thought leader?	
Are there irresistible trends that could propel the growth of the industry?	
Does the founder have a product concept that will solve a large unmet need to relieve customer pain?	
Raising capital	
Has the founder developed three real options related to the growing capital needs of the venture?	
Is the founder prepared to bootstrap the venture during the first stage—customer discovery?	
Can the founder estimate the resources required in the second phase—to expand market share within the initial market and create a compelling case for angel investment?	
Can the founder estimate the resources required in the third phase—to expand into new markets while improving the product and create a compelling case for VC investment?	
Can the founder conduct adequate due diligence on potential investors?	
Can the founder structure the terms of outside investment to maintain control of the company?	

continued

TABLE 9.2 *continued*

Approach/Question	Answer (Yes/No)

Building the team

Can the founder analyze dispassionately the capabilities needed to grow the venture?

Can the founder find and hire the right co-founders that will fill out the capabilities the venture needs, to grow?

Can the founder articulate a clear set of shared values?

Can the founder build a culture around those values that the founder uses to hire and motivate people?

Can the founder attract and motivate an A-Team of technical, marketing, and other key people?

Does the founder part ways with friends who do not fit the venture's future needs?

Gaining share

Can the founder find customers with unaddressed pain?

Can the founder present those customers with a prototype that relieves that pain?

Can the founder develop hypotheses about how many customers will use the product?

Can the founder test that hypothesis through a frugal experiment, and measure the results?

Can the founder analyze the reasons for the gap between the hypothesis and the actual results?

Can the founder improve the product based on this analysis until the refined version of the product attracts a rapidly growing customer base?

Adapting to change

Can the founder map out the venture's value network?

Can the founder assemble a cross-industry team to analyze changes in the value network?

Can the founder develop specific measures that the venture can track to identify critical industry changes?

Can the founder filter out the signals from the noise?

Can the founder develop and test hypotheses for how the venture should change its business strategy in response to the signals?

Can the founder implement the new business strategy?

HUNGRY START-UP STRATEGY APPROACH TO SCREENING VENTURE INVESTMENTS

Start-up capital providers often sift through as many as 2,000 companies a year to invest in two or three. As discussed in Chapter 7, finding winning investments is an extremely difficult task. However, most successful capital providers have developed a discipline that they use to weed out all but the ones with the best odds for success.

Doing this requires a major investment by start-up capital providers in conducting investigations into the start-up's market and the track record of a start-up's top executives.

Making a guess about the potential size and growth of the start-up's target market involves conducting conversations with a variety of experts who are familiar with the market. These experts could include technology mavens, social trend analysts, experts in start-up business models, and early-adopters and extreme users who might be the initial customers for the start-up's products.

The investigations into the start-up's founder—and team—should include talking with people who have worked with each individual—including former managers, employees, peers, business partners, bankers, other capital providers, and suppliers.

Table 9.3 below provides a framework for scoring each potential investment. The scores on each question are subjective and ought to be done in comparison to other investments. To that end, as a basis of comparison, I have developed a database of the companies interviewed for this book. Start-up CEOs should use this tool to help them prepare for meetings with capital providers. This venture investment ranking tool will help entrepreneurs see how their ventures look through the lens of capital providers. And entrepreneurs should use it to reinforce their start-ups' strengths and to bolster their weaknesses prior to their conversations with capital providers.

HUNGRY START-UP STRATEGY APPROACH TO PICKING A BIG COMPANY AS A START-UP TRAINING GROUND

Aspiring entrepreneurs are not always ready to start companies right after college graduation. And as we saw in Chapter 8, some companies are better suited than others as a start-up training ground.

TABLE 9.3   **Venture Investment Ranking Tool**

Risk Domain/Question	Score (5, best, to 1, worst)
Big Potential Market	
Is the start-up focused on a problem for customers that no companies are solving?	
Can the start-up deliver a competitively superior product that solves this customer problem and generate revenues selling it?	
Will rapidly growing business models, new technologies, or social trends boost market demand for the product?	
Are leading technologists at influential companies trying to solve this problem?	
Great CEO	
Does the founder have superior industry knowledge and a compelling vision for its future?	
Does the founder have a winning track record and the passion to keep winning?	
Is the founder smart, curious, and a doer of frugal, fast experiments?	
Can the founder identify and manage business risk?	
Does the founder have charisma, integrity, and ability to attract, hire, and motivate top talent?	
Total Score	

Table 9.4 provides a framework for assessing whether a big company is a good start-up training ground. To get answers to the questions outlined below, you should conduct independent research. This could include reading articles and cases on the company, talking with current and former employees and executives, and interviewing experts on the companies.

TABLE 9.4 **Big Company as Start-Up Training Ground Assessment Framework**

Approach/Question	Answer (Yes/No)
Exploit and Explore	
Has the CEO managed both "exploit" and "explore" business units directly?	
Can the CEO craft a mission statement that spurs both business units to achieve distinct goals while cooperating?	
Can the CEO hire leaders for exploit and explore business units who are well suited to achieving their diverging missions?	
Can the CEO set different strategic orientations for the exploit and explore business units?	
Can the CEO draw different organization structures for the exploit and explore business units?	
Can the CEO build different capabilities for the exploit and explore business units?	
Can the CEO create performance measurement and incentives that encourage the exploit and explore business units to cooperate to achieve joint success?	
Design Capability	
Is the CEO a strong believer in the value of design thinking as a spur to creating growth businesses?	
Is the CEO willing to hire people internally and get help from outside experts to create a design-thinking capability within the company?	
Is the CEO willing to provide political cover for the leader of the design-thinking capability in the face of organizational resistance?	
As the design-thinking leader accumulates successes, will the CEO promote those successes throughout the organization?	
Will the CEO continue to invest in the design-thinking capability to ensure that it improves and adapts to the company's evolving needs?	
Culture of Frugal Experimentation	
Is the CEO passionate about encouraging people to innovate?	
Is the CEO investigating best practices for how big companies can create disruptive innovation?	
Has the CEO created a process for employees' innovative ideas to be posted, critiqued, and staffed without managerial intervention?	
Has the CEO created a process for deciding whether to fund new businesses based on consumer feedback on inexpensive prototypes of the new ideas?	
Does the CEO celebrate the successes of the process and capture the learning from the failures?	
Does the CEO reward employees who create significant new businesses?	

NOTES

1. Many very valuable companies in the 2000s—such as Twitter and Instagram—attract numerous users but not many paying customers. Their value is related to their growth and their potential to attract advertisers. My successful 1990s start-up investments drew paying customers and the failed ones were unable to attract users or paying customers.
2. From Porter's 1980 book, *Competitive Strategy*, the five forces—rivalry among existing competitors, the bargaining power of buyers, the threat of new entry, the threat of substitute products, and the bargaining power of suppliers. Porter argues, explain why industries vary in their return on equity based on the varying strength of these forces.
3. Peter Cohan, "Head in the Cloud," *Hemispheres*, November 1, 2011, http://www.hemispheresmagazine.com/2011/11/01/head-in-the-cloud/
4. "Head in the Cloud," Ibid.
5. "Head in the Cloud," Ibid.
6. Peter Cohan, "Economic Outlook: U.S. and Key Industries," Peter S. Cohan & Associates, November 5, 2009, p. 11.
7. Peter Cohan interview with James Watt, BrewDog Captain, July 5, 2011.
8. Watt interview, Ibid.
9. Watt interview, Ibid.
10. Watt interview, Ibid.
11. Watt interview, Ibid.
12. Watt interview, Ibid.
13. Watt interview, Ibid.
14. Watt interview, Ibid.
15. Watt interview, Ibid.
16. Watt interview, Ibid.
17. Watt interview, Ibid.
18. Watt interview, Ibid.
19. Watt interview, Ibid.
20. Watt interview, Ibid.
21. Watt interview, Ibid.
22. Watt interview, Ibid.
23. Watt interview, Ibid.
24. Watt interview, Ibid.
25. Watt interview, Ibid.

26. Watt interview, Ibid.

27. Watt interview, Ibid.

28. Watt interview, Ibid.

29. Peter Cohan interview with Dane Spangler, June 24, 2011.

30. Paul Kedrosky, "Right-Sizing the U.S. Venture Capital Industry," The Ewing Marion Kauffman Foundation, http://www.kauffman.org/newsroom/venture-capital-industry-must-shrink-to-be-an-economic-force-kauffman-foundation-study-finds

31. "Entrepreneurial Impact: The Role of MIT," MIT Entrepreneurship Center, accessed June 28, 2011, http://entrepreneurship.mit.edu/article/entrepreneurial-impact-role-mit

32. Peter Cohan interview with Chuck Eesley, June 7, 2011.

33. Peter Cohan, "SoFi's New Take on $1 Trillion Student Loan Market," *Forbes Startup Economy*, April 2, 2012, http://www.forbes.com/sites/petercohan/2012/04/02/sofis-new-take-on-1-trillion-student-loan-market/

34. Peter Cohan, "ExtraHop Keeps Your Applications Running Young," *Forbes Startup Economy*, April 12, 2012, http://www.forbes.com/sites/petercohan/2012/04/12/extrahop-keeps-your-applications-running-young/

35. Peter Cohan, "Tintri's Flash of Storage Lightning Puts EMC In the Dark," *Forbes Startup Economy*, February 23, http://www.forbes.com/sites/petercohan/2012/02/23/tintris-flash-of-storage-lightning-puts-emc-in-the-dark/

36. Peter Cohan, "m-Via To Disrupt Moneygram, Western Union," *Forbes Startup Economy*, June 21, 2012, http://www.forbes.com/sites/petercohan/2012/06/21/m-via-to-disrupt-moneygram-western-union/

37. Peter Cohan, "PoverUp Kick Starts Microfinance One $200 Ice Cream Outing At a Time," *Forbes Startup Economy*, June 2, 2011, http://blogs.forbes.com/petercohan/2011/06/02/poverup-kick-starts-microfinance-one-200-ice-cream-outing-at-a-time/

38. Peter Cohan, "PoverUp Kick Starts Microfinance One $200 Ice Cream Outing At a Time," *Forbes Startup Economy*, July 5, 2011, http://blogs.forbes.com/petercohan/2011/07/05/sirum-gets-surplus-meds-to-the-poor/

39. Peter Cohan, "Embrace Warms Up Premature Babies at the Bottom of the Pyramid," *Forbes Startup Economy*, June 16, 2011, http://blogs.forbes.com/petercohan/2011/06/16/embrace-warms-up-premature-babies-at-the-bottom-of-the-pyramid/

40. Peter Cohan, "HBS MBA Helps Prepare You For Death," *Forbes Startup Economy*, July 6, 2011, http://blogs.forbes.com/petercohan/2011/07/06/hbs-mba-student-helps-prepare-you-for-death/

41. Peter Cohan, "Huddle Wows Diageo, UK Government," *Forbes Startup Economy*, February 22, 2012, http://www.forbes.com/sites/petercohan/2012/02/22/huddle-wows-diageo-uk-government/

42. Peter Cohan, "Stanford MBA's Virtual Square for Student Q&A," *Forbes Startup Economy*, January 20, 2012, http://www.forbes.com/sites/petercohan/2012/01/20/stanford-mbas-virtual-square-for-student-qa/

43. Peter Cohan, "Sifteo Gives New Life To Play Blocks," *Forbes Startup Economy*, June 22, 2011, http://blogs.forbes.com/petercohan/2011/06/22/sifteo-gives-new-life-to-play-blocks/

44. Peter Cohan, "Loki Studios Brings Location To Pokemon," *Forbes Startup Economy*, June 11, 2011, http://blogs.forbes.com/petercohan/2011/06/11/loki-studios-brings-location-to-pokemon/

45. Peter Cohan, "WhiteGlove Health Delivers White Glove to You," *Forbes Startup Economy*, June 7, 2011, http://blogs.forbes.com/petercohan/2011/06/07/whiteglove-delivers-health-care-to-you/

46. Peter Cohan, "Blurb Lets You Publish Your Own Photo Book," *Forbes Startup Economy*, May 24, 2011, http://blogs.forbes.com/petercohan/2011/05/24/blurb-lets-you-publish-your-own-photo-book/

47. Peter Cohan, "The Job Creators: 10 Companies That Are Hiring Now," *Daily Finance*, October 10, 2010, http://srph.it/gBExzo

48. Peter Cohan, "Predictive Biosciences Non-Invasive Cancer Tests," *Forbes Startup Economy*, May 24, 2011, http://blogs.forbes.com/petercohan/2011/05/24/predictive-biosciences-non-invasive-cancer-tests/

49. Peter Cohan, "Locately Will Find Which 50 Percent of Your Advertising Is Wasted," *Forbes Startup Economy*, May 19, 2011, http://blogs.forbes.com/petercohan/2011/05/19/locately-will-find-which-50-of-your-advertising-is-wasted/

50. Martha Amram and Nalin Kulatilaka (1999), "Disciplined Decisions: Aligning Strategy with the Financial Markets," *Harvard Business Review*, January–February 1999, 95–109.

51. Peter Cohan, "Value Leadership: The Seven Principles That Drive Corporate Value in Any Economy," Jossey-Bass Publishers, 2003. Chapter 4 develops the concept of why frugal experimentation is important and how it works.

52. While it may not seem frugal to spend millions of dollars on these experiments, the desire to break their investment into smaller parts is a distinct departure from the way VCs invested in the 1990s. I advised a start-up I worked with then to ask for the most capital it could imagine because VCs wanted invest as much money as they could in each venture as quickly as possible. Because of the feverish nature of the market for initial public offerings, the faster VCs could put the most amount of capital into start-ups, the bigger returns they could generate for their investors.

53. Peter Cohan, "The Job Creators: 10 Companies That Are Hiring Now," *DailyFinance*, October 1, 2010, http://srph.it/cQS9QS

54. "The Job Creators: 10 Companies That Are Hiring Now," Ibid.

55. The idea of remaining a large privately held company can only generate attractive returns for its venture investors if those who put capital into the venture earlier—at a lower valuation—can sell those shares later to another venture investor willing to buy into the venture at a higher price.

56. Peter Cohan, "Adobe Executive's Tutorial on Freemium Pricing," *Forbes Start-up Economy*, December 7, 2011, http://www.forbes.com/sites/petercohan/2011/12/07/adobe-executives-tutorial-on-freemium-pricing/

57. Peter Cohan, "Top Entrepreneurship Prof on Key Start-Up Choices," *Forbes Start-up Economy*, September 20, 2011, http://www.forbes.com/sites/petercohan/2011/09/20/top-entrepreneurship-prof-on-key-start-up-choices/

58. Peter Cohan, "IDEO Helps Big Companies Learn from Start-Ups," *Forbes Start-up Economy*, June 20, 2011, http://www.forbes.com/sites/petercohan/2011/06/20/ideo-helps-big-companies-learn-from-start-ups/

59. Peter Cohan, "HBS's Lion of Entrepreneurship on Five Start-Up Choices," *Forbes Start-up Economy*, June 21, 2011, http://www.forbes.com/sites/petercohan/2011/06/21/hbss-lion-of-entrepreneurship-on-five-start-up-choices/

60. Peter Cohan, "How Harvard's Bill Sahlman Turns Leaders into Entrepreneurs," *Forbes Start-up Economy*, June 17, 2011, http://www.forbes.com/sites/petercohan/2011/06/17/how-harvards-bill-sahlman-turns-leaders-into-entrepreneurs/

61. Author interview with Michael Greeley, General Partner, Flybridge Capital Partners, August 25, 2010.

62. Greeley interview, Ibid.

63. SupplierMarket.com S-1, May 11, 2000, http://ipo.nasdaq.com/edgar_conv_html%5C2000%5C05%5C11%5C08%5C0000927016-00-001737.html

64. Peter Cohan, "PayPal co-Founder's Four Hot Trends for 2017," *Forbes Start-up Economy*, January 31, 2012, http://www.forbes.com/sites/petercohan/2012/01/31/paypal-co-founders-four-hot-trends-for-2017/

65. Peter Cohan, "Plum Rents Clothes As Your Baby Grows," *Forbes Start-up Economy*, June 20, 2011, http://blogs.forbes.com/petercohan/2011/06/20/plum-rents-clothes-as-your-baby-grows/

66. Peter Cohan, "Loki Studios Brings Location to Pokemon," *Forbes Start-up Economy*, June 11, 2011, http://blogs.forbes.com/petercohan/2011/06/11/loki-studios-brings-location-to-pokemon/

67. "The Job Creators: 10 Companies That Are Hiring Now," Ibid.

68. Peter Cohan interview with Fuentes, July 25, 2011.

69. Fuentes interview, Ibid.

70. Peter Cohan interview with T2 Biosystems CEO, Joe McDonough, July 28, 2011

71. McDonough interview, Ibid.

72. McDonough interview, Ibid.

73. Peter Cohan interview with Trade Show Internet CEO, Seth Burstein, August 1, 2011

74. Burstein interview, Ibid.

75. Peter Cohan interview with Oyster COO, Ariel Charytan, August 2, 2011

76. Charytan interview, Ibid.

77. Peter Cohan, email interview with Apture CEO, Tristan Harris, July 22, 2011

78. Harris interview, Ibid.

79. Harris interview, Ibid.

80. Peter Cohan, "Cloudera Finds Insight in a Haystack of Data," *Forbes Start-up Economy*, August 4, 2011, http://blogs.forbes.com/petercohan/2011/08/04/cloudera-finds-insight-in-a-haystack-of-data/

81. "Cloudera Finds Insight in a Haystack of Data," Ibid.

82. Peter Cohan email interview with IDEO's Tom Hulme, July 27, 2011.

83. Hulme interview, Ibid.

84. "Accusoft Pegasus Announces the Acquisition of Adeptol," *PRWeb*, October 10, 2011, http://www.prweb.com/releases/2011/10/prweb8844365.htm

85. Peter Cohan email interview with Adeptol's Sid Joshi, July 27, 2011.

86. Some entrepreneurs have had so much experience dealing with venture investors—or by their nature they think like VCs—that they insist on estimating the size of the market opportunity before they spend time working on their venture.

87. Email from Steve Rothschild, "Re: Chapter 8," January 8, 2012.

88. Many entrepreneurs find this rigorous process very time consuming and tedious. They would prefer to just go with their gut and try selling their product to whichever market they think would buy it. And the hungry start-up approach encourages such frugal experimentation. However, for entrepreneurs seeking to make the most effective use of their limited time and capital, the methodologies outlined here have the potential to lower the risk that those resources will be wasted.

89. Even if start-up CEOs conclude that this is a waste of time, it certainly makes sense for them to understand why specific competitors are growing faster than their start-ups. Insights into why other competitors are growing faster could provide the start-up with excellent ideas that they might be able to replicate if they have the right skills.

90. This is most common for start-ups that sell to large telecommunications firms and take them on as investors.

91. While this refrain from venture capitalists is quite common, the actual practice is less so, according to Proven (formerly Workers'Now) CEO Pablo Fuentes.

92. Peter Cohan, "Why Start-Ups Matter," *Forbes Start-up Economy*, June 27, 2011, http://www.forbes.com/sites/petercohan/2011/06/27/why-start-ups-matter/

93. "HBS's Lion of Entrepreneurship on Five Start-Up Choices," Ibid.

94. Email from Pablo Fuentes, "Re: update and inquiry," October 19, 2011.

95. Peter Cohan, "How Harvard's Bill Sahlman Turns Leaders into Entrepreneurs," *Forbes Start-up Economy*, June 17, 2011, http://www.forbes.com/sites/petercohan/2011/06/17/how-harvards-bill-sahlman-turns-leaders-into-entrepreneurs/

96. Peter Cohan, "Stanford's Fresh Entrepreneurship Factory," *Forbes Start-up Economy*, May 31, 2011, http://www.forbes.com/sites/petercohan/2011/05/31/stanfords-fresh-entrepreneurship-factory/

97. The remaining companies interviewed fall into one of three categories: nonprofit foundations (5%), government grants (2%), and bank lenders (2%).

98. Peter Cohan, "Worcester biotech startups get a boost," *Worcester Telegram & Gazette*, November 8, 2011, http://www.thefreelibrary.com/Worcester+biotech+startups+get+a+boost.-a0271963621

99. "Top Entrepreneurship Prof on Key Start-Up Choices," Ibid.

100. Peter Cohan and Srini Rangan, *Capital Rising* (Palgrave-Macmillan, 2010), p. 178.

101. Peter Cohan, "Min.Us Makes File Sharing a Snap," *Forbes Start-up Economy*,

May 23, 2011, http://blogs.forbes.com/petercohan/2011/05/23/min-us-makes-file-sharing-a-snap/

102. Peter Cohan, "Critical Software Shows Portugal Can Grow," *Forbes Start-up Economy*, June 3, 2011, http://www.forbes.com/sites/petercohan/2011/06/03/critical-software-shows-portugal-can-grow/

103. Peter Cohan, "Trade Show Internet Stops Highway Robbery," *Forbes Start-up Economy*, May 27, 2011, http://www.forbes.com/sites/petercohan/2011/05/27/trade-show-internet-stops-highway-robbery/

104. Peter Cohan, "A Machu Picchu Style Start-Up," *Forbes Start-up Economy*, May 4, 2011, http://www.forbes.com/sites/petercohan/2011/05/04/a-machu-picchu-style-start-up/

105. Peter Cohan, "Wharton Start-Up Chattersource Helps Students Find Housing, Haircuts," *Forbes Start-up Economy*, May 18, 2011, http://www.forbes.com/sites/petercohan/2011/05/18/wharton-start-up-chattersource-helps-students-find-housing-haircuts/

106. Peter Cohan, "Orbit Baby's Safer Car Seat," *Forbes Start-up Economy*, June 6, 2011, http://www.forbes.com/sites/petercohan/2011/06/11/orbit-babys-safer-car-seat/

107. Peter Cohan, "Workers Now: The Blue Collar Set's Linked-In," *Forbes Start-up Economy*, June 6, 2011, http://blogs.forbes.com/petercohan/2011/06/06/workersnow-the-blue-collar-sets-linkedin/

108. Peter Cohan, "Hearsay Social Lets Companies Turn Local Reps into Digital Brand Ambassadors," *Forbes Start-up Economy*, June 9, 2011, http://blogs.forbes.com/petercohan/2011/06/09/hearsay-social-lets-companies-turn-local-reps-into-digital-brand-ambassadors/

109. Email from Ashkay Kothari, "Re: follow up questions about Pulse financing," September 22, 2011.

110. "Pulse Raises a $9 Million Series A from NEA, Greycroft, and Lerer Ventures," *Business Insider*, June 16, 2011, http://www.businessinsider.com/ipad-news-reader-pulse-raises-a-9-million-series-a-from-nea-greycroft-and-lerer-ventures-2011-6#ixzz1XYkMeHp4

111. Kothari email, Ibid.

112. Kothari email, Ibid.

113. Peter Cohan interview with Coursekit founder and CEO, Joseph Cohen, September 14, 2011.

114. Peter Cohan, "PayPal, Facebook Investor, Peter Thiel, Buys Stake in Lore," *Forbes Start-up Economy*, April 25, 2012, http://www.forbes.com/sites/petercohan/2012/04/25/paypal-facebook-investor-peter-thiel-invests-in-lore/

115. Peter Cohan, "Sifteo Gives New Life to Play Blocks," *Forbes Start-up Economy*, June 22, 2011, http://blogs.forbes.com/petercohan/2011/06/22/sifteo-gives-new-life-to-play-blocks/

116. Peter Cohan, "The Job Creators: Business Hungers for Axcient's Back-Up," *Forbes Start-up Economy*, September 19, 2011, http://www.forbes.com/sites/petercohan/2011/09/19/the-job-creators-business-hungers-for-axcients-back-up/

117. Peter Cohan, "Dynamics Wants to Turn Your Card Rewards into Cash," *Forbes Start-up Economy,* May 16, 2011, http://blogs.forbes.com/petercohan/2011/05/16/dynamics-wants-to-turn-your-card-rewards-into-cash/

118. Peter Cohan, "The Job Creators: Evernote Asks Why Seven Billion People Don't Yet Use Its Service," *Forbes Start-up Economy,* June 11, 2011, http://www.forbes.com/sites/petercohan/2011/09/26/the-job-creators-evernote-asks-why-seven-billion-people-dont-yet-use-its-service/

119. Peter Cohan, "The Job Creators: Mocospace's Demand Growth Spells Jobs," *Forbes Start-up Economy,* September 14, 2011, http://www.forbes.com/sites/petercohan/2011/09/14/the-job-creators-mocospaces-demand-growth-spells-jobs/

120. Peter Cohan, "The World's Hotels Are Oyster's Oyster," *Forbes Start-up Economy,* May 5, 2011, http://blogs.forbes.com/petercohan/2011/05/05/the-worlds-hotels-are-oysters-oyster-2/

121. Peter Cohan, "Type-U Wants Better Diabetes Outcomes," *Forbes Start-up Economy,* August 8, 2011, http://www.forbes.com/sites/petercohan/2011/08/04/type-u-wants-better-diabetes-outcomes/

122. Peter Cohan, "HBS MBA Student Helps Prepare You for Death," *Forbes Start-up Economy,* July 6, 2011, http://www.forbes.com/sites/petercohan/2011/07/06/hbs-mba-student-helps-prepare-you-for-death/.

123. Peter Cohan, "Juntos Finanzas Helps Latinos Save, Plan," *Forbes Start-up Economy,* June 1, 2011, http://www.forbes.com/sites/petercohan/2011/06/01/juntos-finanzas-helps-latinos-save-plan/.

124. Peter Cohan, "3-Super-Bowl-Ring Winner's Crepetastic Retail Dream," *Forbes Start-up Economy,* May 13, 2011, http://www.forbes.com/sites/petercohan/2011/05/13/3-super-bowl-ring-winners-creptastic-retail-dream/

125. Peter S. Cohan, "Local Company Will Help Your Aging Skin," *Worcester Telegram & Gazette,* April 11, 2012, http://www.telegram.com/article/20120411/COLUMN70/120419970/0/NEWS07&Template=printart

126. Peter Cohan, "New Relic Up-Ends Tradition," *Forbes Start-up Economy,* December 14, 2011, http://www.forbes.com/sites/petercohan/2011/12/14/new-relic-up-ends-tradition/

127. Peter Cohan, "Angel Investor Proves Doing Good and Profit Co-Exist Nicely," *Forbes Start-up Economy,* December 19, 2011, http://www.forbes.com/sites/petercohan/2011/12/19angel-investor-proves-doing-good-and-profit-co-exist-nicely/

128. "Angel Investor Proves Doing Good and Profit Co-Exist Nicely," Ibid.

129. Noam Wasserman, *The Founder's Dilemmas,* Princeton University Press, 2012.

130. "Top Entrepreneurship Prof on Key Start-Up Choices," Ibid.

131. Peter Cohan, "Stanford's Fresh Entrepreneurship Factory," *Forbes Start-up Economy,* May 31, 2011, http://www.forbes.com/sites/petercohan/2011/05/31/stanfords-fresh-entrepreneurship-factory/

132. Peter Cohan, "IDEO Helps Big Companies Learn From Start-Ups," *Forbes Start-up Economy,* June 20, 2011, http://www.forbes.com/sites/petercohan/2011/06/20/ideo-helps-big-companies-learn-from-start-ups/

133. Peter Cohan, "HBS's Lion of Entrepreneurship on Five Start-Up Choices,"

Forbes Start-up Economy, June 21, 2011, http://www.forbes.com/sites/peter cohan/2011/06/21/hbss-lion-of-entrepreneurship-on-five-start-up-choices/

134. Many entrepreneurs consider it a waste of time to study their competitors' teams. However, based on my investing experience, such study can provide useful insights into competitors' strengths and vulnerabilities, which could be useful for start-ups in creating competitive strategy.

135. Two percent of the start-ups interviewed said they formed their founding teams by hiring friends. If those ventures grow and raise fresh capital, it remains to be seen whether their investors will want to keep the founding team together or replace some or all the team members with leaders who offer the skills the venture needs to grow still further.

136. Peter Cohan, "Embrace Warms Up Premature Babies at the Bottom of the Pyramid," *Forbes Start-up Economy,* June 16, 2011, http://blogs.forbes.com/ petercohan/2011/06/16embrace-warms-up-premature-babies-at-the-bottom-of-the-pyramid/

137. "Jane Chen Co-Founder and CEO, Embrace," *Independent Sector,* accessed April 22, 2012, http://www.independentsector.org/ngen_award_voting#

138. Peter Cohan, "Sonatype's Open Source Boost to Software Productivity," *Forbes Start-up Economy,* April 23, 2012, http://www.forbes.com/sites/petercohan/ 2012/04/23/sonatypes-open-source-boost-to-software-productivity/

139. Peter Cohan, "The Job Creators: Business Hungers for Axcient's Back-Up," *Forbes Start-up Economy,* September 19, 2011, http://www.forbes.com/sites/ petercohan/2011/09/19/the-job-creators-business-hungers-for-axcients-back-up/

140. Peter Cohan, "Silicon Valley's Culture Doctor," *Forbes Start-up Economy,* November 4, 2011, http://www.forbes.com/sites/petercohan/2011/11/04/silicon-valleys-culture-doctor/

141. Peter Cohan, "Hearsay Social Lets Companies Turn Local Reps into Digital Brand Ambassadors," *Forbes Start-up Economy,* June 9, 2011, http://blogs.forbes .com/petercohan/2011/06/09/hearsay-social-lets-companies-turn-local-reps-into-digital-brand-ambassadors/

142. Peter Cohan, "Main Street Hub: Small Businesses Social Media Solution," *Forbes Start-up Economy,* June 1, 2011, http://blogs.forbes.com/petercohan/2011/ 06/01/main-street-hub-small-businesses-social-media-solution/

143. "The World's Hotels Are Oyster's Oyster," Ibid.

144. Peter Cohan, "Grockit Helps Groups Do Great on GMAT," *Forbes Start-up Economy,* June 7, 2011, http://blogs.forbes.com/petercohan/2011/06/07/grockit-helps-groups-do-great-on-gmat/

145. Peter Cohan, "Venuetastic Creates a Market for Happy Hour Venues," *Forbes Start-up Economy,* August 8, 2011, http://www.forbes.com/sites/petercohan/2011/ 08/08/venuetastic-creates-a-market-for-happy-hour-venues/

146. Peter Cohan, "Trade Show Internet Stops Highway Robbery," *Forbes Start-up Economy,* May 27, 2011, http://blogs.forbes.com/petercohan/2011/05/27/trade-show-internet-stops-highway-robbery/

147. Peter Cohan, "Bionée Offers Moms Skin Care and Financial Control," *Forbes Start-up Economy*, August 2, 2011, http://blogs.forbes.com/petercohan/2011/08/02/bionee-offers-moms-skin-care-and-financial-control/

148. Peter Cohan, "Kembrel Wants to Link Designer Labels to College Consumers," *Forbes Start-up Economy*, June 27, 2011, http://blogs.forbes.com/petercohan/2011/06/27/kembrel-wants-to-link-designer-labels-to-college-consumers/

149. Peter Cohan, "UniEats Gives College Students 10% Restaurant Discounts," *Forbes Start-up Economy*, July 22, 2011, http://blogs.forbes.com/petercohan/2011/07/22/unieats-gives-college-students-10-restaurant-discounts/

150. Peter Cohan, "TypeU Wants Better Diabetes Outcomes," *Forbes Start-up Economy*, August 4, 2011, http://blogs.forbes.com/petercohan/2011/08/04/type-u-wants-better-diabetes-outcomes/

151. Peter Cohan, "CEO Replaces Himself to Grow Xirrus Fast From $100 Million," *Forbes Start-up Economy*, June 20, 2012, http://www.forbes.com/sites/petercohan/2012/06/20/ceo-replaces-himself-to-grow-xirrus-from-100-million-to-ipo/

152. Peter Cohan, "Silicon Valley's Culture Doctor," *Forbes Start-up Economy*, November 4, 2011, http://www.forbes.com/sites/petercohan/2011/11/04/silicon-valleys-culture-doctor/

153. "Silicon Valley's Culture Doctor," Ibid.

154. "Top Entrepreneurship Prof on Key Start-Up Choices," Ibid.

155. Peter Cohan, "HBS's Howard Stevenson: How Start-Ups Gain Market Share," *Forbes Start-up Economy*, November 13, 2011, http://www.forbes.com/sites/petercohan/2011/11/13hbss-howard-stevenson-how-start-ups-gain-market-share/

156. Peter Cohan, "Stanford's Fresh Entrepreneurship Factory," *Forbes Start-up Economy*, May 31, 2011, http://www.forbes.com/sites/petercohan/2011/05/31/stanfords-fresh-entrepreneurship-factory/

157. Peter Cohan, "IDEO Helps Big Companies Learn From Start-Ups," *Forbes Start-up Economy*, June 20, 2011, http://www.forbes.com/sites/petercohan/2011/06/20/ideo-helps-big-companies-learn-from-start-ups/

158. Peter Cohan, "HBS's Joe Lassiter Loves High Growth," *Forbes Start-up Economy*, June 23, 2011, http://www.forbes.com/sites/petercohan/2011/06/23/hbss-joe-lassiter-loves-high-growth/

159. Peter Cohan, "ASSIA Create Billions in Value for DSL Providers," *Forbes Start-up Economy*, November 7, 2011, http://www.forbes.com/sites/petercohan/2011/11/07/assia-creates-billions-in-value-for-dsl-providers/

160. Peter Cohan, "iZettle Lets Europe's Moms and Pops Take Chip Cards," *Forbes Start-up Economy*, October 19, 2011, http://www.forbes.com/sites/petercohan/2011/10/19/izettle-lets-europes-mom-and-pops-take-chip-cards/

161. Peter Cohan, "Xsigo Aims A Dagger At Cisco's Heart," *Forbes Start-up Economy*, February 15, 2012, http://www.forbes.com/sites/petercohan/2012/02/15/xsigo-aims-a-dagger-at-ciscos-heart/

162. "Bionée Offers Moms Skin Care and Financial Control," Ibid.

163. Peter Cohan, "Growth Matters: Kayak.com Travels with $200 million in

Capital," *DailyFinance*, March 2, 2009, http://www.dailyfinance.com/2009/03/02/growth-matters-kayak-com-travels-with-200-million-in-capital/

164. "Kayak Software Form S-1," September 20, 2011, http://www.sec.gov/Archives/edgar/data/1312928/000119312511252291/d117777ds1a.htm

165. Peter Cohan, "The Job Creators: 10 Companies That Are Hiring Now," *DailyFinance*, October 3, 2010, http://www.dailyfinance.com/2010/10/03/the-job-creators-10-companies-that-are-hiring-now/?icid=sphere_copyright/

166. Peter Cohan, "Growth Matters: Coolspotters Lets You Buy What Celebs Wear," *BloggingStocks*, March 2, 2009, http://www.bloggingstocks.com/2009/03/02/growth-matters-coolspotters-lets-you-buy-what-celebs-wear/

167. Peter Cohan, "Malkin's Outlet Shopping Empire," *Forbes Start-up Economy*, June 28, 2011, http://blogs.forbes.com/petercohan/2011/06/28/malkins-outlet-shopping-empire/

168. Peter Cohan, "Eric Ries: How Lean Start-Ups Adapt to Change," *Forbes Start-up Economy*, November 23, 2011, http://www.forbes.com/sites/petercohan/2011/11/23/eric-ries-how-lean-start-ups-adapt-to-change/

169. "HBS's Lion of Entrepreneurship on Five Start-Up Choices," Ibid.

170. Peter Cohan, "Harvard's Lion of Entrepreneurship Packs Up His Office," *Forbes Start-up Economy*, June 15, 2011, http://www.forbes.com/sites/petercohan/2011/06/15/harvards-lion-of-entrepreneurship-packs-up-his-office/

171. Peter Cohan, "Stanford's Fresh Entrepreneurship Factory," *Forbes Start-up Economy*, May 31, 2011, http://www.forbes.com/sites/petercohan/2011/05/31/stanfords-fresh-entrepreneurship-factory/

172. "Top Entrepreneurship Prof on Key Start-Up Choices," Ibid.

173. Porter is largely silent on the topic of how companies resist adapting to change. These comments derive from Peter Cohan, "The Technology Leaders: How America's Most Profitable High-Tech Companies Innovate Their Way to Success," Jossey-Bass Publishers, 1997.

174. Peter Cohan, "Riding the Value Cycle," *Business Strategy Review*, Summer 2008, http://papers.ssrn.com/sol3/papers.cfm?abstract_id=1127450

175. This term is particularly relevant to business customers for whom a new technology's economic value can be calculated with considerable precision. For example, if a new machine can save a company 10% of a particular raw material it uses in its manufacturing process, then the company's WTP for the machine would be the amount of money it saves by not having to buy as much of that raw material.

176. I introduced the concept of boundaryless product development in *The Technology Leaders*. Here I am extending that concept from developing products to adapting a company's growth strategy to changing customer needs, technologies, and upstart competitors.

177. The companies I interviewed used other approaches—but less frequently. For example, 5% of the companies were in the medical device field and those map out their future on the basis of their ability to satisfy specific regulatory

milestones; 3% are social enterprises and they staked their survival on a hybrid legal structure that enabled them to serve both a social mission and to raise capital by selling a for-profit product; and one company was able to persuade competitors to meet annually with the start-up to monitor key industry developments.

178. Peter Cohan, "Yesware boosts sales productivity, financial forecasts," *Forbes Start-up Economy*, November 9, 2011, http://www.forbes.com/sites/petercohan/2011/11/09/yesware-boosts-sales-productivity-financial-forecasts/

179. Peter Cohan, "Antenna Software Brings Rust Belt Into Mobile World," *Forbes Start-up Economy*, November 8, 2011, http://www.forbes.com/sites/petercohan/2011/11/08/antenna-software-brings-rust-belt-into-mobile-world/

180. "Vaultus sells to N.J. firm Antenna Software," *Mass High Tech*, April 5, 2010, http://www.masshightech.com/stories/2010/04/05/daily46-Vaultus-sells-to-NJ-firm-Antenna-Software.html

181. Peter Cohan, "Pyxis Mobile Lets Business Build its Own Apps," *Forbes Start-up Economy*, November 22, 2011, http://www.forbes.com/sites/petercohan/2011/11/22/pyxis-mobile-lets-business-build-its-own-apps/

182. "iZettle Lets Europe's Moms and Pops Take Chip Cards," Ibid.

183. Bobbie Johnson, "iZettle launches across Nordics — next stop U.K.," GigaOM, February 26, 2012, http://gigaom.com/2012/02/26/izettle-launches-across-nordics-next-stop-u-k/

184. Peter Cohan interview with Pat McIntyre, CEO of ET Water Systems, September 15, 2010.

185. McIntyre interview, Ibid.

186. Peter Cohan, "AlgoSec Accelerates Enterprise Security," *Forbes Start-up Economy*, November 7, 2011, http://www.forbes.com/sites/petercohan/2011/11/07/algosec-accelerates-enterprise-security/

187. Peter Cohan, "Cloudflare Makes the Web Faster, Safer," *Forbes Start-up Economy*, July 18, 2011, http://www.forbes.com/sites/petercohan/2011/07/18/cloudflare-makes-the-web-faster-safer/

188. Peter Cohan, "5 Tests a VC Uses To Turn You Down in 3 Minutes," *Forbes Start-up Economy*, February 9, 2012, http://www.forbes.com/sites/petercohan/2012/02/09/5-tests-a-vc-uses-to-turn-you-down-in-3-minutes/2/

189. Peter Cohan, "Angel Investor Proves Doing Good and Profit Co-Exist Nicely," *Forbes Start-up Economy*, December 19, 2011, http://www.forbes.com/sites/petercohan/2011/12/19/angel-investor-proves-doing-good-and-profit-co-exist-nicely/

190. Peter Cohan, "Oxford Historian Creates Silicon Valley's Future," *Forbes Start-up Economy*, December 30, 2011, http://www.forbes.com/sites/petercohan/2011/12/30/oxford-historian-creates-silicon-valleys-future/

191. Peter Cohan, "Five Tips for Aspiring Venture Investors," *Forbes Start-up Economy*, February 24, 2012, http://www.forbes.com/sites/petercohan/2012/02/24/five-tips-for-aspiring-venture-investors/

192. Peter Cohan, "Stanford Investor Loves the Underdog," *Forbes Start-up Economy*,

December 19, 2011, http://www.forbes.com/sites/petercohan/2011/12/19/stanford-investor-loves-the-underdog/

193. Peter Cohan, "PayPal Co-Founder's Four Hot Trends for 2017," *Forbes Start-up Economy*, January 31, 2012, http://www.forbes.com/sites/petercohan/2012/01/31/paypal-co-founders-four-hot-trends-for-2017/

194. HBS Professor Noam Wasserman mentioned this idea in a February 2012 conversation with me.

195. Peter Cohan, "HBS's Howard Stevenson: What Big Companies Can Learn from Start-Ups," *Forbes Start-up Economy*, February 13, 2012, http://www.forbes.com/sites/petercohan/2012/02/13/hbss-howard-stevenson-what-big-companies-can-learn-from-start-ups/

196. Peter Cohan, "Can Big Companies Learn from Start-Ups?," *Forbes Start-up Economy*, February 6, 2012, http://www.forbes.com/sites/petercohan/2012/02/06/can-big-companies-learn-from-start-ups/

197. Peter Cohan, "How Big Companies Can Exploit and Explore," *Forbes Start-up Economy*, February 27, 2012, http://www.forbes.com/sites/petercohan/2012/02/27/how-big-companies-can-exploit-and-explore/

198. Peter Cohan, "Stanford Prof's Two Things Big Companies Can Learn from Start-Ups," *Forbes Start-up Economy*, February 19, 2012, http://www.forbes.com/sites/petercohan/2012/02/19/stanford-profs-two-things-big-companies-can-learn-from-start-ups/

199. Peter Cohan, "America's Biggest Seed-Stage Investor on Start-Up Success," *Forbes Start-up Economy*, February 9, 2012, http://www.forbes.com/sites/petercohan/2012/02/09/americas-biggest-seed-stage-investor-on-start-up-success/

200. Peter Cohan, "IDEO: How Big Companies Can Learn From Start-Ups," *Forbes Start-up Economy*, February 22, 2012, http://www.forbes.com/sites/petercohan/2012/02/22/ideo-how-big-companies-can-learn-from-start-ups/

201. Peter Cohan, "HBS Profs on 3 Big Co. Lessons from Start-Ups, and 3 So-Whats" *Forbes Start-up Economy*, March 2, 2012, http://www.forbes.com/sites/petercohan/2012/03/02hbs-profs-on-3-big-co-lessons-from-start-ups-and-3-so-whats/

202. The term frugal experimentation derives from a chapter in my book, *Value Leadership* (Wiley, 2003), based on the idea that one of the seven key values of companies I dubbed "value leaders" is that growth matters and to grow, companies must experiment frugally.

203. Peter Cohan, "Can Scott Cook Revive Corporate America?" *Forbes Start-up Economy*, February 29, 2012, http://www.forbes.com/sites/petercohan/2012/02/29/can-scott-cook-revive-corporate-america/

204. Peter Cohan, "How Procter & Gamble's Design Guru Spurs Growth," *Forbes Start-up Economy*, March 2, 2012, http://www.forbes.com/sites/petercohan/2012/03/02/how-procter-gambles-design-guru-spurs-growth/2/

205. Peter Cohan, "Faster Clock Speed Turns AT&T Into Emerging Devices Leader," *Forbes Start-up Economy*, February 23, 2012, http://www.forbes.com/sites/petercohan/2012/02/23/faster-clock-speed-turns-att-into-emerging-device-leader/

206. Peter Cohan, "Memo to Peter Thiel: Start-Up CEOs Are Not Heroes," *Forbes Start-up Economy*, June 27, 2011, http://www.forbes.com/sites/petercohan/2011/06/27/memo-to-peter-thiel-start-up-ceos-are-not-heroes/

207. Chao C. Chen, Patricia Gene Greene, and Ann Crick, "Does Entrepreneurial Self-Efficacy Distinguish Entrepreneurs from Managers?" *Journal of Business Venturing*, Volume 13, Issue 4, July 1998, pp. 295–316.

208. Peter Cohan, "Which of These Six Entrepreneurial Types Are You?" *Forbes Start-up Economy*, June 6, 2012, http://www.forbes.com/sites/petercohan/2012/06/06/which-of-these-six-entrepreneurial-types-are-you/

ACKNOWLEDGMENTS

Many people helped conceive, research, write, and revise this book.

In August 2010, my Babson College colleague, Dwight Gertz, made the comment about client reactions to Porter's work that got me thinking about creating this book. My editor Neal Maillet's enthusiasm for the idea, and his efforts to engage his colleagues at Berrett-Koehler, helped turn the book into a reality. And managing director Jeevan Sivasubramaniam's marvelous orchestration of Berrett-Koehler's many talented collaborators helped turn the rough manuscript into a more polished final book.

In researching this book, help from entrepreneurs, start-up experts, and capital providers proved invaluable. While the entrepreneurs I interviewed are listed in Chapter 9, several of them stand out, not only for their insightful and thought-provoking comments but also, in some cases, their willingness to comment on drafts of certain chapters.

These include BrewDog's captain, James Watt; Proven's CEO, Pablo Fuentes; Ariel Charytan, COO of Oyster.com; Axcient's CEO, Justin Moore; Evernote CEO, Phil Libin; and ASSIA CEO, John Cioffi.

Start-up experts HBS's Howard Stevenson, Bill Sahlman, and Noam Wasserman offered their intriguing insights, as did Babson College's Les Charm and Srini Rangan. And Stanford's Hasso Plattner Design School *Launchpad* co-leaders, Perry Klebahn and Michael Dearing, both played critical roles in shaping my thinking and introducing me to start-ups that follow the principles they teach.

Several capital providers shared fascinating insights into their backgrounds and investment approach. Elad Gil (Twitter), Peter Bell (Highland Capital), Asheem Chandna (Greylock), Max Levchin (PayPal and Yelp), and Ping Li (Accel) were particularly helpful. I am deeply grateful to Intuit founder and executive chairman Scott Cook, and Procter & Gamble (P&G) alumna Claudia Kotchka, who gave me great insight into how big companies try to apply the best of what start-ups have to offer.

Many people helped arrange introductions and coordinate my interviews. These include Stanford's Debbe Stern, HBS's Jim Aisner, Babson

College's Mike Chmura, Aaron Endre, Mikala Vidal, Clinton Karr, and Vitor Souza.

Finally, I'd like to thank my column editors—*Forbes*'s Eric Savitz, *Entrepreneur*'s Diana Ransom, *Inc.*'s Nicole Carter, and the *Worcester Telegram & Gazette*'s Aaron Nicodemus—for their sharp questions and inspiration.

INDEX

ABOUT THE AUTHOR

PETER S. COHAN is president of Peter S. Cohan & Associates (http://peter cohan.com), a management consulting and venture capital firm he started in 1994. His management consulting unit has conducted over 150 projects for companies—helping them identify, evaluate, and profit from business opportunities created by changing technology—as well as the governments of Singapore, Japan,. and Portugal.

His VC business has invested in six companies—three of which failed and three of which were sold for over $2 billion. These include Andromedia, an Internet software company, which Macromedia purchased in 1999 for $440 million; SupplierMarket.com, an online marketplace for industrial supplies, which Ariba purchased in 2000 for $930 million; and Lexar Media, a digital media company that was sold in 2006 to Micron Technology for $690 million.

Cohan teaches strategy to MBA and undergraduate students at Babson College (since 1992, *U.S. News & World Report* has ranked its undergraduate entrepreneurship program number one in the United States), including courses such as Strategic Problem Solving, Strategic Decision Making, and Competitive Environment and Strategy. Cohan also created and led its Hong Kong/Singapore Start-Up Strategy Offshore elective for twenty-five Babson MBAs.

Cohan has authored eleven books, including Hungry Start-Up Strategy (forthcoming November 2012); Export Now (Wiley, 2011) co-authored by Frank Lavin—selected as one of the top small business books of 2011; and *Capital Rising* (Palgrave-Macmillan, 2010) with Srini Rangan. He has contributed to six management compendiums. He has published in *Business Strategy Review* and writes for five blogs: Forbes Startup Economy, Inc.'s The Hungry Start-Up, Entrepreneur, Wharton Blog Network, and the *Worcester Telegram & Gazette*'s Wall and Main.

Cohan has spoken at Stanford University's Forum for American/Chinese Exchange (FACES) and taught in its Industry Thought Leaders program, in Columbia University's Senior Executive Program, at the University of Hong Kong, and he was a visiting professor at Bareclona's EADA. He has also conducted management development programs in the United States and Asia sponsored by IBM, Intel, Hewlett Packard, Oracle, Fidelity Investments, and Procter & Gamble.

He is a frequent commentator on developments in economics, technology, and finance. He has been a guest on ABC's Good Morning America, CBS's Evening News and Early Show, CNN, CNBC, Current TV, PBS's Wall Street Week, and New England Cable News (NECN). He has been quoted in *The New York Times, The Wall Street Journal, The Washington Post, Barron's, Time, BusinessWeek, Fortune,* and *Newsweek International.*

Cohan holds an MBA from Wharton, did graduate work in computer science at MIT, and earned a BS in electrical engineering from Swarthmore College. He began his career at Index Systems, a management consulting firm founded by several MIT professors. While there he worked with James A. Champy, co-author (with former MIT professor Michael Hammer) of Reengineering the Corporation (HarperBusiness, 1993). Following business school, Cohan worked at the Monitor Company, a strategy consulting firm co-founded by HBS professor Michael E. Porter.

Free Instructor's Guide Available!

A Nine-Part Module on
Hungry Start-Up Strategy: Creating New Ventures with Limited Resources and Unlimited Vision

Those trying to start their own companies or learn from upstart ventures face a significant obstacle: Strategy theory is not designed to help them. The work of standard-setting strategist Michael E. Porter focuses on the key strategy questions that big organizations face, while start-ups must grapple with a broader set of strategic questions and need different answers.

The *Hungry Start-Up Strategy* module provides frameworks and cases to help students think about how to address choices that can determine the ultimate survival of a start-up, including how entrepreneurs should

- Set goals;
- Pick markets;
- Raise capital;
- Build their team;
- Gain market share; and
- Adapt to change.

Module Objectives

- To help students understand the key choices they must make in order to start and run a new venture successfully
- To provide students with the skills necessary to experience and apply hungry start-up strategy principles in their work—whether for a start-up or a large enterprise
- To give students a perspective on how venture capitalists view start-up investments
- To highlight ways to bring start-upness into the large enterprise

To review and download this free instructor's guide, go to www.petercohan.com or to www.bkconnection.com/hungrystartupguide

Berrett–Koehler
Publishers

Berrett-Koehler is an independent publisher dedicated to an ambitious mission: *Creating a World That Works for All*.

We believe that to truly create a better world, action is needed at all levels— individual, organizational, and societal. At the individual level, our publications help people align their lives with their values and with their aspirations for a better world. At the organizational level, our publications promote progressive leadership and management practices, socially responsible approaches to business, and humane and effective organizations. At the societal level, our publications advance social and economic justice, shared prosperity, sustainability, and new solutions to national and global issues.

A major theme of our publications is "Opening Up New Space." Berrett-Koehler titles challenge conventional thinking, introduce new ideas, and foster positive change. Their common quest is changing the underlying beliefs, mindsets, institutions, and structures that keep generating the same cycles of problems, no matter who our leaders are or what improvement programs we adopt.

We strive to practice what we preach—to operate our publishing company in line with the ideas in our books. At the core of our approach is stewardship, which we define as a deep sense of responsibility to administer the company for the benefit of all of our "stakeholder" groups: authors, customers, employees, investors, service providers, and the communities and environment around us.

We are grateful to the thousands of readers, authors, and other friends of the company who consider themselves to be part of the "BK Community." We hope that you, too, will join us in our mission.

A BK Business Book

This book is part of our BK Business series. BK Business titles pioneer new and progressive leadership and management practices in all types of public, private, and nonprofit organizations. They promote socially responsible approaches to business, innovative organizational change methods, and more humane and effective organizations.

 **Berrett–Koehler**
Publishers

A community dedicated to creating
a world that works for all

Visit Our Website: www.bkconnection.com

Read book excerpts, see author videos and Internet movies, read our authors' blogs, join discussion groups, download book apps, find out about the BK Affiliate Network, browse subject-area libraries of books, get special discounts, and more!

Subscribe to Our Free E-Newsletter, the *BK Communiqué*

Be the first to hear about new publications, special discount offers, exclusive articles, news about bestsellers, and more! Get on the list for our free e-newsletter by going to **www.bkconnection.com**.

Get Quantity Discounts

Berrett-Koehler books are available at quantity discounts for orders of ten or more copies. Please call us toll-free at (800) 929-2929 or email us at **bkp .orders@aidcvt.com**.

Join the BK Community

BKcommunity.com is a virtual meeting place where people from around the world can engage with kindred spirits to create a world that works for all. BKcommunity.com members may create their own profiles, blog, start and participate in forums and discussion groups, post photos and videos, answer surveys, announce and register for upcoming events, and chat with others online in real time. Please join the conversation!

FSC
www.fsc.org

MIX
Paper from
responsible sources
FSC® C012752

Certified

Corporation
bcorporation.net